INDIAN POLITICAL SYSTEM

INDIAN POLITICAL SYSTEM

Mohammad Abbas Khan

ANMOL PUBLICATIONS PVT. LTD.
NEW DELHI - 110 002 (INDIA)

ANMOL PUBLICATIONS PVT. LTD.
4374/4B, Ansari Road, Daryaganj
New Delhi - 110 002
Ph.: 23261597, 23278000
Visit us at: www.anmolpublications.com

Indian Political Sysem

First Published, 2006

ISBN 81-261-2563-2

PRINTED IN INDIA

Published by J.L. Kumar for Anmol Publications Pvt. Ltd., New Delhi - 110 002 and Printed at **Arora** Offset Press, Delhi.

Contents

Preface

India is having a parliamentary democratic system. It's a quasi-federal state. It has the features of a unitary state also. While all the powers including national security, external affairs, etc., are vested with the union, the states enjoy all other powers.

However, several aspects of our political system very often appear to be not suitable for our people. Our multi-party political system results in several sorts of exploitation and rifts in our society. For preserving its integrity and unity, India needs retain only the national parties. It is better to ban those political parties, which contest the elections on regional, religious and casteist grounds.

To make this system a success, the common people should be made aware of this very system, their leaders and the exploitation to which they are subjected. Therefore this work presents a thorough study of Indian Constitution and polity. In short, this book gives an elaborate picture of Indian political system for the benefit of scholars, students and general readers.

—Editor

1

Nature of Polity

(Theories of Political Culture; Culture and Politics in Third World Countries)

Salient Features

Though some of the them evoked by the concept of political culture were not unknown to classical political thought, the term political culture appears to have been first used in the late eighteenth century by Herder (Barnard, 1969) and its elaboration and development as a concept of modern political science dates from the 1950s (especially Almond, 1956). Substantive empirical, research organized around the concept began to appear in the 1960s (for example, Almond and Verba, 1963: Pye and Verba, 1965). These early applications of the concept were linked to questionable theories of 'political development', but more recent studies have demonstrated that the value of the concept of political culture in no way depends upon its incorporation in a particular type of developmental, structure-functionalist or system analysis.

There have been numerous definitions of political culture, but they can be classified into two broad categories : (1) those which confine the scope of political culture to the subjective orientation of nations, social groups or individuals to politics; and (2) those which broaden the concept to include patterns of political behaviour., Most political scientists have favoured the more restrictive category. Representative definitions in this first group include those which see political culture as 'the system of empirical beliefs, expressive symbols, and values which defines the situation in which political action takes place' (Verba, 1965), or as 'the subjective perception of history and politics, the fundamental beliefs and values, the foci of identification and loyalty, and the political knowledge and expectations which are the product of the specific historical experience of nations and groups' (Brown, 1977).

Scholars who prefer the second, and broader, type of definition of the concept have suggested that in characterizing political culture in subjective or psychological terms, 'political scientists have parted company with the great majority of anthropologists' (Tucker, 1973), although that view has recently been questioned (Brown, 1984). There is a minority of political scientists employing the concept who prefer the more anthropological approach, whereby political culture can be defined as 'the attitudinal and behavioural matrix within which the political system is located' (White, 1979).

Those who favour a `subjective' definition argue that quite enough has already been brought under the umbrella of political culture and that to broaden its scope further reduces its analytical usefulness. Specifically, it makes it difficult, if not impossible, to examine what part the particular perceptions, beliefs and values to be found in different societies may play in explanation of political conduct if no clear conceptual distinction is made between behaviour and subjective beliefs.

Accepting that this criticism has some force, a prominent proponent of the 'anthropological' approach has questioned whether the scholarly value of the concept of political culture actually depends upon its 'explanatory potency' and suggests that its central importance lies rather in the fact that 'it assists us to take our bearings in the study of the political life of a society .... to describe and analyse and order many significant data, and to raise fruitful questions for thought and research-without explaining anything' (Tucker, 1973).

The study of the political cultures and subcultures of societies ruled by authoritarian governments brings out acutely the definitional dilemma. On the one hand, political behaviour (for instance, voting behaviour in communist systems) may - as a result of coercion or more subtle pressures - bear only a tenuous relationship to citizens' real beliefs and values. Thus, a more restrictive definition may, in principle, permit useful investigation of lack of congruence between the 'dominant' (as distinct from 'official') political culture and the political system. On the other hand, it is precisely in authoritarian regimes that it is hardest to get reliable quantified data on fundamental political beliefs and values, political knowledge and expectations, and so on, because of the difficulties not only of conducting surveys on such politically sensitive themes but also of getting honest answers from respondents. Behaviour, including deviant behaviour, may be more readily observable.

Yet, whereas early political culture studies concentrated on the First World and the Third World (where the frequent failure of transplanted Western-style political institutions to work in anything like the manner expected by the constitution-writers was a stimulus to the study of political culture), more recently increasing attention has been paid to the Second, or Communist, world (Brown and Gray, 1977; White, 1979; Almond and Verba, 1980). The special interest of these societies lies in the fact that unusually elaborate and conscious efforts have been made by the political powerholders to effect a radical transformation of political culture. Recent evidence indicates a much more limited success in this endeavour than might have been predicted, given Communist leaders' substantially tighter control over most of the major agencies of political socialization than that wielded by their counterparts in more pluralistic political systems. This, in turn, is now leading political scientists to examine more carefully the transmission and evocation of political beliefs and values, and to treat with equal seriousness both the psychological and historical dimensions of the study of political culture.

Various Dimensions

The study of people's orientations to polities is the study of a country's political culture. The concept of political culture is essentially psychological; it refers to what people think refer to actual political behaviour. Indeed behaviour may conflict with prevailing attitudes. For example, the amount of popular participation in democracies is distinctly limited despite a participant political culture. Political culture is comparatively a new concept and has been popularised by writers like Ulam and Almond.

It varies from nation to nation, political culture is a combination of attitudes, beliefs, emotions and values of a society with particular reference to political issues. It can be measured in terms of public opinions, surveys, public statements and writings. It is multi-facet in the sense what it consists of several analytically distinct factors, though inter-connected with each other. It doesn't coincide with political system and extends beyond its boundaries. According to L.W. Pye, "The attitudes, sentiments conditions that inform and govern political behaviour in any society are not just rundom congeries but represent coherent pattern which fit together and are mutually reinforcing, that in any particular community there is a limited and distinct political culture which gives meaning, predictability and form to political process."

A.R. Ball while defining political culture has said that "A political culture is imposed of the attitudes, beliefs, emotions and values of society that relute to political system and political issues." G.A. Almond and Powell in their famous volume 'Comparative politics : A Development approach" have said "political culture is pattern of individual attitudes, as orientations towards polities among the members of a political system." Thus when emotional and attitudinal environment become a permanent feature of a political system serving thus as an important means of devoting the character of the latter and of distinguishing if from other political systems, we çall it political culture. It its growth political authority plays a big role political culture is distinctly different from political ideology.

Political culture is not static, it changes as a result of response to new ideas, the impact of new leaders, population changes and many other culture but it has two distinct cultures namely those of the elites and the masses. The higher is the congruence between these two cultures, the greater is the homogeneity of the political culture that ensures the stability of the system. Homogenity of political culture also depends on the extent to which there has been a fusion between its: traditional and modern beliefs and attitudes, political culture and culture are quite opposed to each other - political culture can be both diverse as well as homogeneous but in both the cases it is the product of many inter-related factors. It is influenced by historical, geographical and socioeconomic factors and these are its very foundations.

In political culture traditions play a very big role. No new political culture can violate or all of à sudden change its traditions or historical background. It is because traditions have their value in society and these are liked by vast majority. Geography also considerably helps in fashioning political culture. England's political culture didn't remain disturbed in the past simply because of geographical isolation. On the other hand, after World War II West Germans are said to have accepted the particular structure of the federal republic party because of their Geographical position between the two big powers.

Geographical boundaries also play their own part in so far as political culture is concerned. Those nations which are surrounded by such geographical boundaries which can be violated possess a different political culture than those nations which have safe and inviolable boundaries. Political culture is very much— influenced by socio-economic system. An urban industrialised society is always none complex one but has rapid communication system. The people are literate and they are very much participants in decision making process. They are also ready to accept changes. On the other hand, rural societies resist changes and people are largely conservative. Therefore, countries with two different types of societies are sure to have two different types of political cultures.

Economic systems and the extent to which the people are ready to accept economic changes also influence the political culture. Karl Marx has established deep relationship of economic system with political system. An industrial society will always have a complex class as well as political structure and a distinct political culture than what is to be found in a non-industrialised society. The political culture which is quote different from culture, has its own foundation and these combined together develop a homogenous political culture.

Division and Various Dimensions of Political Culture : According to Almond and Powell political culture has three dimensions namely congnitive orientations, affective orientations and evaluative orientations. These have also been called individual orientations. By cognitive orientation they mean recognition of political objects and views. It means knowledge of political system by the people. By effective orientation they mean their feeling about acceptance or rejection of particular political culture and objects. From evaluation orientation they mean application of judgements and opinions of political objectives and events. But all these are inter-dependent.

Then another dimension is what is called emotional attitudes. These are based on and have links with the past history. It is difficult to have emotional detachments, sometimes are so strong that these retard the process of innovative changes and at times innovative changes do not appear new and are gladly accepted.

Still another dimension is that of political beliefs. These

Constitute an important part of political culture. Bear and Ulam say that, "The ideas that do not appear at first glance to have relevance to politics may be intimately connected within through the belief system of the political culture." Sidney happening in the world of politics but also what people believe about happenings. He has also said that such a belief can be empirical i.e. what is actual state of political life. There can be belief about goals and values that ought to be pursued in political life and these can also have emotional dimensions.

Lastly then comes political values dimension. These values are an important part of every political culture but those are not uniform. These differ from culture to culture and at times even in the same culture. These considerably change. When the values change with that political culture changes and vice versa is equally true.

Typology of Political Culture : Almond and Vebra have divided culture under three categories namely parochial political culture, subject political culture and participant political culture. From parochinal culture, they mean the system in which the people have by and large no awareness of national political system. The people are politically not conscious and their expectations from their political bosses are very low. Then is subject political culture. In this system the people are considerably familiar with political roles and they have sufficient knowledge about methods of influencing political decision makers. Lastly is political participant culture in which the people are aware of structure and processes of political system. They have orientation towards the system as a whole.

Aspects of Political Culture : Political Culture has different aspects of study. One aspect is how the people view theii national political system. Then another is whether the people feel proud of that or they just tolerate that. Then another is what is the attitude of the people towards public servants i.e. about their integrity and sense of duty. Then another is whether the people just tolerate or appreciate the view point of their bosses on major issues etc.

Symbols and Political Culture : Symbols like national anthem and national flag express the idealised elements of political institutions. These are not necessarily related to political knowledge of the people. Totalitarian regimes lay much stress on political symbols to give reality to abstractions. Everywhere national flag is required to be respected and any disrespect is considered a punishable offence. In political culture myths play a big role. It is however, essential that myths and symbols, in order to have effectiveness, should be directly relevant to the existing political system. These become more important for national unity in nations which have passed through political upheavals.

Thus political culture has its own dimensions. But what need be remembered is that it is not static but always goes on changing. It is influenced by new political ideas, industrialisation, changes in the economic system, changes in values and attitudes. Even large scale influx of immigrants, war and revolution can change political culture.

Ideology and Political Culture : Ideologies have always changed political culture provided an ideology is rational and has acceptability with the masses. We know that political culture of the societies changed when such ideologies as capitalism, socialism, Communism, Fascism were propagated and accepted by the people. A.R. Ball is of the view that the dividing line between political culture and political ideology is very thin one. But inspite of this close relationship, there is very sharp distinction between the two.

One such point of distinction is that whereas ideology is action oriented and those who appreciate and follow it launch a vigorous campaign for its propagation and spread, political culture is not action oriented but it consists of beliefs, values and emotions. Then one finds that whereas ideology is proclaimed by someone who have considerably pondered over it before proclamation, political culture is not a proclamation but an evolution.

Next point of difference between the two is that ideology

is rigid whereas political culture is flexible. It is constantly changing. Ideology is coherent and consistent whereas political culture is implicit and multiple. Last but least point of difference between the two is that one ideology can be distinguished from the other whereas differences in political cultures cannot be easily identified.

Choice of Democracy

One of the important characteristic of democratic government is that it provides politically, culturally, a proper balance between governmental power and governmental representatives. In this culture it is expected that all decisions should be taken after taking into consideration known wishes and aspiration of the people. For knowing these wishes there should be formal and informal channels of communication. In it the institutional framework within which governmental decisions are taken vary from polity to polity. A good constitution in a democracy is no guarantee for ensuring that underlying their various arrangements provided in the Constitution there is also an appropriate political culture. According to Almond and Verba the most appropriate political culture for a democratic system of government is the civic culture and to the extent the country's political culture deviates from the ideal mix to that extent it lacks an effective and stable democratic government.

Behind the idea of political culture is the assumption that societies require for their stability some consensus on values and norms.

Critical Assessment : Concept of political culture though comparatively new one is of great significance. It has helped in the study of comparative different political systems and in studying the degree of congruence that exists between political culture and political structures. It is because of this that focus has shifted from the study of individuals to that of the society. It is the study of political culture which makes us clear as to why different societies during the course of their political development move in different directions.

But difficulty with this concept is that it is difficult to measure political culture. The hindrances are illiteracy, lack of political maturity, wrong information etc. Popularity or acceptability of political culture cannot be measured in terms of attendance at public meetings, with the help of even questionnaires or sampling techniques. For proper and scientific study of political culture of society therefore, several methods combined will have to be used which is not an easy affair.

Position in Developing Countries

If the political cultures of the first world have a strong participant element, and those of the second world a strong subject element can the third world be seen in terms of parochial political cultures? Parochial cultures, it will be recalled, are those where citizens are not oriented towards national government; they do not see themselves as contributing to, or being affected by, central decisions. Undoubtedly the state is weaker in the developing than the developed world; it penetrates less deeply into society and so provides only a weak focus of public attention. But is the parochial cultural a cause of state-weakness, as advocates of the cultural approach claim? Our answer is yes, to an extent. Certainly the post-independence generation of third world leaders invested considerable effort in attempting to nationalise the political culture. Primary education stressed allegiance to the nation rather than the ethnic group, the mass media reported national events and memories of the independence struggle were frequently invoked. But just as communist party states have failed to create the new man, so too have attempts to transform third world political cultures had only limited success.

In consequence efforts at nation-building in the developing world have taken on a ritual quality in recent years. Primary school children may be given the national flag to wave when the Education Minister comes to visit but real nation-building is not achieved so easily. In addition to the inherent difficulty of reshaping a culture, third world governments face the additional problems of weak mass media and a consequent inability to reach the mass of the population except through traditional leaders. Indeed central government are often forced by resource limits to administer localities through traditional leaders, thus in practice contradicting their own efforts at nation-building. Thus after the modern ceremony at the school, the Education Minister will go into conference with traditional local leaders. Nation-building without state-building is inevitably a hollow exercise.

The concept of a parochial culture implies a 'top-down' perspective on politics. People may only be dimly aware of the national government but they are often well aware of the intricacies of local and ethnic politics through which resources are in fact distributed. For example the Hausa-Fulani emirates in Northern Nigeria, based on the unquestioned authority of the emir (the traditional religious ruler known as 'the shadow of God'), are resilient regional systems which have survived successive changes of regime at national level.

Even to describe these cultures as sub-cultures is often to understate their significance. Many third world countries are best considered as plural or poly-cultural societies rather than as countries with a weak national culture and distinct subcultures. In India, for example, where state institutions are relatively well-established, the enormous variety of religions and the complexities of the caste system are fundamental to an understanding of the country's politics. From a 'bottom - up' perspective, third world cultures are better described as local than parochial.

The distinction between tradition and modernity has been central to the analysis of political culture in developing countries. Many authors have argued that tradition, not parochialism, or even localism, is the essential quality of third world cultures. Traditional relationships are modelled on the idea of kinship. They are based on the personal qualities of the participants and embrace a wide range of activities. In politics this means that politicians and civil servants have obligations to kin, friends and supporters which conflict with a 'modern' interpretation of their role. The idea of a bureaucrat applying rules in an impersonal way, or of politicians seeking fairly to balance the claims of competing interests, is alien to this traditional perspective. Hence Western observers often describe as 'corrupt' activities which in the developing countries themselves are viewed as straightforward fulfilments of social obligations.

There is no doubt that this distinction between tradition and modernity is analytically useful. For example disputes between centre and periphery are often sharpened by an overlaid tension between modern and traditional cultures. But is modernization of the political culture a prerequisite of economic development and the growth of a strong, independent state? In the 1960s, many Western political scientists were convinced that this was the case. They suggested that political actors needed to adopt an essentially western approach their tasks if economic and political development were to proceed.

Now-a-days such imperialistic thinking is less fashionable. As the Japanese economic miracle abundantly shows, the traditional and the modern can coexist and even coalesce. It is apparent too that traditional loyalties, such as those to an ethnic group, can provide an effective mode of political mobilisation as well as giving people a support network as they move from the countryside into the cities. So today most political scientists would argue that at least some elements of traditional culture provide a potential resource for, rather than a barrier to economic and social development.

2

Nation Supreme

(State Sovereignty: Marxist and Pluralistic Theories; Globalisation and the State)

State's Sovereignty

Meaning of Sovereignty : The term "Sovereignty" has been derived from the Latin word "Superanus" which means supreme or paramount. Although the term "Sovereignty" is modern yet the idea of "Sovereignty" goes back to Aristotle who spoke of the "supreme power of the state".

Throughout the Middle Ages the Roman jurists and the civilians kept this idea in their mind and frequently employed the terms "Summa" potestas and "Plenitudo potestatis" to designate the supreme power of the state. The terms "Sovereign" and "Sovereignty" were first used by the French jurists in the fifteenth century and later they found their way into English, Italian and German political literature.

The use of the term "Sovereignty" in Political Science dates back to the publication of Bodin's "The Republic" in 1576. "The word sovereign", says J.S.Roucel and others,. "entered the vocabulary of political theory from the feudal order, wherein it designated a relationship between persons. The term sovereign had been applicable to any feudal overlord with authority over subjects in his own dominions".

Different Aspects : There are two aspects of sovereignty: internal sovereignty and external sovereignty. Internal Sovereignty means some persons, assembly of group of persons in every independent state have the final legal authority to command and enforce obedience.

This sovereignty exercises its absolute authority over all individuals or associations of the individuals within the state. Professor Harold Laski has very aptly marked in this connection: "It issues orders to all men and all associations within that area; it receives orders from none of them. Its will is subject to no legal limitation of any kind. What it proposes is right by mere announcement of intention."

We mean, by External Sovereignty, that the State is subject to no other authority and is independent of any compulsion on the part of other States. Every independent state reserves the authority to renounce trade treaties and to enter into military agreements. Each estate is independent of other states. Every independent State is at liberty to determine its foreign policy and to join any bloc of power it likes. Any other state does not reserve any right to interfere with the external matter of an independent state. Thus, by external sovereignty we mean that every state is independent of other states.

In other words, External Sovereignty means national freedom. Professor Laski has very correctly observed in this regard, "The modern state is a sovereign state. It is, therefore independent in the face of other communities. It may infuse its will towards them with a substance which need not be affected by the will of any external power". This statement of Professor Laski makes it very clear that the State possesses both external and internal sovereignty.

Definitions of Sovereignty : There are various definitions to the concept of sovereignty. According to Grotius

"Sovereignty is the sovereign political power vested in him whose acts are not subject to any other and whose will cannot be over-ridden."

"Sovereignty is the supreme power of the State over citizens and subjects unrestrained by law": Bodin viewed this.

Sovereignty is "the supreme, irresistible, absolute, uncontrolled authority in which the 'jurist summi imperi' reside" Blackstone opined it.

The sovereignty is "legally supreme over an individual or group", says Laski, he possesses "supreme coercive power".

After closely studying and carefully examining the definitions of sovereignty, given above, "we arrive at the conclusion that sovereignty is the supreme political power of the state. It has two aspects: internal and external. Sovereignty is an unlimited power and it is not subject to any other authority."

Salient Features

According to Dr. Garner, following are the characteristics or attributes of Sovereignty:

(1) Permanence.

(2) Exclusiveness.

(3) All-Comprehensiveness.

(4) Inalienability.

(5) Unity.

(6) Imprescriptibility.

(7) Indivisibility.

(8) Absoluteness or illimitability.

(9) Originality.

(1) *Permanence :* Permanence is the chief characteristics of sovereignty. Sovereignty lasts as long as an independent state lasts. The death of the king, the overthrow of the government and the abduction of power does not lead to the destruction of sovereignty.

We should keep in mind the basic fact that the king or the ruler exercises sovereign power on behalf of the state and, therefore, sovereignty lasts as long as the state lasts. This is the reason why people in England used to say "The King is dead, long live the King". Dr. Garner has beautifully summed up this idea in the following manner:

"Sovereignty does not cease with the death or temporary dispossession of a particular hearer or the reorganisation of the state but shifts immediately to a new bearer, as the centre of gravity shifts from one part of physical body to another when it undergoes external change".

(2) *Exclusiveness* : By exclusiveness we mean that there can be two sovereigns, in one independent state and if the two sovereigns exist in a state, the unity of that state will be destroyed. There cannot exist another sovereign state within the existing sovereign state.

(3) *All Comprehensiveness* : The state is all comprehensive and the sovereign power is universally applicable. Every individual and every association of individual is subject to the sovereignty of the state. No association or group of individuals, however, rich or powerful it may be, can resist or disobey the sovereign authority. Sovereignty makes no exception and grants no exemption to anyone. It grants exemptions only in the case of foreign embassies and diplomatic representatives of foreign countries on the reciprocal basis. This does not in any way restrict the sovereignty of the state in the legal sense. The state can abolish and withdraw the diplomatic privileges granted to foreigners.

(4) *Inalienability* : Inalienability is another characteristic of sovereignty. Sovereignty is inalienable. By inalienability we mean that the State cannot part with its sovereignty, in other words, we can say that the sovereign does not

remain the sovereign or the sovereign state, if he or the state transfers his or its sovereignty to any other person or any other state. Sovereignty is the life and soul of the state and it cannot be alienated without destroying the state itself. Lieber has very aptly remarked in this connection: "Sovereignty can no more be alienated than a tree can alienate its right to sprout or a man can transfer his life or personality to another without self-destruction.

(5) *Unity* : Unity is the very spirit of Sovereignty. The sovereign state is united just as we are united.

(6) *Imprescriptibility* : By Imperscriptibility, we mean that if the sovereign does not exercise his sovereignty for a certain period of time, it does not lead to the destruction of sovereignty. It lasts as long as the state lasts.

(7) *Indivisibility* : Indivisibility is the life-blood of sovereignty. Sovereignty cannot be divided state. American statesman Calhoun has declared, "Sovereignty is an entire thing; to divide it is to destroy it. It is the supreme power in a state and we might just well speak of half square or half a triangle as half a sovereignty". Gettell, has also very aptly remarked in this regard, "If sovereignty is not absolute, no state exists if sovereignty is divided, more than one state exists".

(8) *Absoluteness* : Sovereignty is absolute and unlimited. The sovereign is entitled to do whatsoever he likes. Sovereignty is subject to none.

(9) *Originality* : By originality we mean that the sovereign wields power by virtue of his own right and not by virtue of anybody's mercy.

Various Categories

Following are the different kinds of sovereignty:

(1) *Nominal and Real Sovereignty* : In ancient times many

states had monarchies and their rulers were monarchs. They wielded absolute power and their senates and parliaments were quite powerless. At that time they exercised real sovereignty. Therefore, they are regarded as real sovereigns. For example, Kings were sovereigns and hence they were all powerful in England before fifteenth century, in U.S.S.R. before eighteenth and nineteenth centuries and in France before 1789. The state of affairs changed in England after the Glorious Revolution in 1688. Now the king is like a rubber stamp. The British king has a right to encourage, warn and advise his Ministers or seek any information about the administration. Except these ordinary powers, all other powers of the British king are wielded by his Ministers. Lowell has summed up the position of the British sovereign in these words: "According to the early history of the constitution, the ministers were the counsellors of the king. It was for them to advise and for him to decide. Now the systems are almost reversed. The king is consulted but the ministers decide".

(2) *Legal Sovereignty* : Legal sovereignty, is that authority of the state which has the legal power to issue final commands. It is the authority of the State of whose directions the law of the State attributes final legal force. In every independent and ordered state there are some laws which must be obeyed by the people and there must be a power to issue and enforce these laws. The power which has the legal authority to issue and enforce these laws is legal sovereignty. In England, the King-in-Parliament is sovereign. According to Dicey, "The British Parliament is so omnipotent legally speaking ....that it can adjudge an infant of full age, it may attain a man of treason after death; it may legitimise an illegitimate child or if it sees fit, make a man a judge in his own case". The authority of the legal sovereign is absolute and law is simply the will of the sovereign. Since the authority of the sovereign is unrestrained, he

reserves the legal right to do whatever he desires. It is the legal sovereign who grants and enforce all the rights enjoyed by the citizens and, therefore, there cannot be any right against him. The legal sovereign is, thus, always definite and determinate. Only the legal sovereign has the power to declare in legal terms the will of the state. The authority of the sovereign is absolute and supreme. This authority may reside either in the monarch or in an absolute monarchy or it may reside in the body of persons.

(3) *Political Sovereignty* : Dicey believes that "behind the sovereign which the lawyer recognises, there is another sovereignty to whom the legal sovereign must bow. Such sovereign to whom the legal sovereignty must bow is called political sovereign. In every ordered state the legal sovereignty has to pay due attention to the political sovereign. In modern representative government we might define it roughly as the power of the people". In other words by political sovereign in the representative democracies, we mean the whole mass of the people or the electorate or the public opinion. But at the same time it cannot be emphatically asserted that political sovereignty can definitely be identified with the whole mass of the peoples, the electorate or the public opinion and in all other influences in the state which mould and shape the public opinion. In the words of Professor R.N. Gilchrist, "Political sovereign manifests itself by voting, by the press, by speeches, and in many other ways not easy to describe or define. It is, however, not organised and it can become effective only when organised. But the organisation of political sovereignty lead to legal sovereignty. The two are aspects of the one sovereignty of the state". As a matter of fact, legal and political sovereignty are the two aspects of the one sovereignty of the state. But at the same time both the aspects stands poles apart. Legal sovereign is a law-making

authority in legal terms, whereas political sovereignty is behind the legal sovereign. The legal sovereign can express his will in legal terms. But the political sovereign cannot do so. Legal sovereign is determinate, definite and visible whereas political sovereign is not determinate and clear. It is recognised. Legal sovereignty is vested in the electorate, public opinion and other influences of the state which mould or shape the public opinion. Legal sovereign is recognised by lawyers while political sovereign is not. Legal sovereign cannot go against the will of the political sovereign whereas political sovereign, though not legally powerful, controls over the legal sovereign. The concept of legal sovereign is clear whereas the concept of political sovereign is vague Legal sovereign is elected by the political sovereign whereas political sovereign is the electorate or the people. These are the points of difference between the legal sovereign and the political sovereign.

(4) *Popular Sovereignty :* Popular sovereignty roughly means the power of the masses as contrasted with the power of the individual ruler of the class. It implies manhood, suffrage, with each individual having only one vote and the control of the legislature by the representatives of the people. In popular sovereignty public is regarded as supreme. In the ancient times many writers on Political Science used popular sovereignty as a weapon to refute absolutism of the monarchs.

According to Dr. Garner, "Sovereignty of the people, therefore, can mean nothing more than the power of the majority of the electorate, in a country where a system of approximate universal suffrage prevails, acting through legally established channels to express their will and make it prevail."

(5) *De Facto and De Jure Sovereignty :* Sometimes a distinction is made between the De Facto (actual) sovereignty and

De lure (legal) sovereignty. A de jure sovereign is the legal sovereign whereas a de facto sovereign is a sovereign which is actually obeyed. In the words of Lord Bryce, de facto sovereign "is the person or a body of persons who can make his or their will prevail whether with the law or against the law; he or they, is the de ruler, the person to whom obedience is actually paid". Thus, it is quite clear, that de jute is the legal sovereignty founded on law whereas de facto is the actual sovereign. The de facto sovereign may not be a legal sovereign or he may be a usurping king, a dictator, a priest or a prophet, in either case sovereignty rests upon physical power or spiritual influence rather than legal right. History abounds in example of de facto sovereignties. For example, Oliver Cromwell became de facto sovereign after he had dismissed the Long Parliament. Napolean became the de facto sovereign after he had overthrown the Directory. Likewise, Franco became the defacto sovereign after he had dislodged the legal sovereign in Spain. On October 28, 1922, Mussolini's Black Shirts starched on Rome. At that time, Parliament was the legal sovereign. Mussolini became the Prime Minister in the legal manner. He ruled parliament and ruled the country through parliament. Parliament remained the legal sovereign but he was the actual or de facto sovereign Hitler also did same in Germany. He too became the de facto sovereign. He controlled the legal sovereign and became the de facto sovereign. Similarly, Stalin remained the actual sovereign in U.S.S.R. for about three decades. After the Second World War and before the Eygptian Revolution King Farouk was the legal sovereign. General Naguib's 'Coup de'etat' in Egypt and the abdication of King Farouk is another example of de facto sovereignty. Nazib was expelled and Nasser succeeded him as de facto sovereign. After the death of Nasser, Mr. Sadat succeeded him. After his assassination, Hosni Mobarak became the President of Egypt. Similarly, Ayub became the de facto sovereign after he had staged the military coup in Pakistan. When Ayub was overthrown Yahya Khan rose to power with the help of the army and became the de facto sovereign. After his defeat in 1971 sovereignty fell in the hands of an Indian.

State Sovereignty Theory by Marxists : In 1847, a Congress of all associations was held in London and the outcome of that was the formation of 'International Communist League'. It was here that both Engles and Marx were assigned the formidable task of preparing a manifesto which subsequently became 'Bible' of Communist world. The authors of the Manifesto believed and preached that capitalism was bound to end and on its debris working classes were bound to come to power. The theory of class struggle and exploitation of the poor by the rich was also enunciated here. In addition to this the Manifesto said that ultimate aim was withering away of the state. Marx, however, suggested immediate reforms namely state ownership of banking, taking over of landed property, abolition of right of inheritance and so on, so that the lot of the people could be improved. The Manifesto also preached public education for all children.

In the end it said, "The Communists consider it superfluous to conceal their opinions and their intentions. They openly declare that their aims can only be achieved by the violent overthrow of the whole contemporary social order". The Manifesto also made it clear that in such a change the workers are to lose nothing but their chains. "Let the governing classes tremble before communist revolution. The proletarians have nothing to lose in it but their chains. They have the whole world to gain." The Manifesto also gave a call to all the workers of the world to unite and come together for fighting for their own cause.

In Germany, Marx brought out 'Demands of the Communist

Party in Germany' which subsequently became the basis for revolution in that country. In his 'Wage, Labour and Capital' Marx successfully analysed the system of capitalist exploitation.

Publication of Das Kapital : The outcome of his deep study, knowledge and analytical approach to political, economic and social conditions was 'Das Kapital' which gave him immortal fame and made him an international personality. This publication made the world think of him, his ideas and philosophy. The world was obliged to give serious thought to the philosophy of a man who had been turned out from country to country and place to place. The person who himself was poverty-sticken cattle forward and was studied as the champion of the cause of toiling masses of the world.

Karl Marx was deadly against capitalism which he felt was a theft. In his view capitalism was based on injustice and exploitation of the poor by the rich. It was a system, which he felt ought to be condemned. It created class barriers and divided society into hostile groups. It divided the loyalties of state and on the whole could not be justified on any ground. He, however, believed that modern capitalist system was sowing the seeds of its own degeneration. He foresaw that in near future, the modern capitalist state will wither away and that in its place a new state will emerge. It will have majority of proletariats or the working classes, which incidentally will also be ruling classes.

He felt that democracy of the capitalist order was not real democracy but that it was an artificial arrangement. In this system the capitalists who are in minority mould democratic institutions to suit their convenience, thus defeating democracy in the real sense of the term. But in the new society there will be real democracy because the majority consisting of working classes shall rule the society. It shall be true and real democracy and shall be used for collective interests.

Communist Manifesto says that "In place of old bourgeois society with its classes and class antagonism, we shall have an association in which free development of each is the condition for the free development of all". It further says "The Proletarian movement is the conscious movement of immense majority in the interests of the immense majority".

Marx on Class Conflict : Marx repudiates the old idea that state exists for the sake of good life or that it is a natural organisation. On the other hand, he believes that state is an agency for exploiting the poor. He also believes that history is a witness that the state has always stood by the side of rich or capitalists or those who are economically well off. For him, no one can repudiate this very fact that those who are economically strong have always controlled the society as well as legal, social and political institutions. In fact these systems have been so set up that these suit the convenience of the rich. Though the state appears above all class conflicts and claims to be natural yet in actual practice it does not play such a rule. It is class organisation which reflects ideas of dominant class in society.

Communists believe that history is an evidence that the state has always stood by the side of those who are in power. It is the constant endeavour of the state to see that the laws of the state are enacted in a way that the proletariats do not rebel against the bourgeoisie. They further say that the agencies like schools, colleges and the church are also primarily meant and used by the state for exploiting the workers. These agencies teach workers and train them for subordination and submission.

These try to convince them that their poverty is because of God's will. It is an expression of class antagonism. According to Lenin: "Where, when and to what extent the state arises depends directly on when, where, and to what extent the class antagonism of a given society cannot be objectively reconciled. But conversely, the existence of the state proves that class antagonisms are irreconcilable."

Marx on Proletariat Revolution : According to Marxian Philosophy, present differences are irreconcilable and if at all these can be reconciled that can only be revolutionary means and methods. This proletariat revolution is likely to be two-fold. Firstly it will try to destroy capitalist by order and secondly change old institutions into new ones. Marx, however, says that "Between Capitalism and Communism lies the period of the revolutionary transformation of the one into the other. There corresponds to this also a political transition period of the proletariats." He believes that in the existing order majority is exploited by minority, but in the changed set-up majority will expropriate the minority or the bourgeoisie.

Marx is, however, of the view that the change-over from bourgeoisie to proletariat society cannot be sudden. It will be at least in two stages. In the first stage, the means of production will not remain in the hands of a single individual but will go under the control of the society as a whole. At this stage every individual will be obliged to perform some socially essential functions.

This period will, however, entail heavy responsibilities on the workers. It is during this period that the proletariats will have to work with care and defend themselves from all aggressions even from within the society. Those who are in authority at present shall try to foil every attempt for bringing a change in the existing social order. They will keep their own centralised agencies to check every change and also to maintain normal conditions. It will be a very critical period and the workers will have to work with patience.

The second stage shall be final one on which dictatorship of the proletariats will be established. Marx is of the opinion that it will be stage on which a new idea will have to be inculcated. The very psychology of the masses will have to be changed and a new order will have to be established.

In the words of Lenin 'Under the dictatorship of the proletariats we will have to re-educate millions of peasants and petty proprietors, hundreds of thousands of office workers and bourgeoisie and others, to re-educated in a protracted struggle under the controlling auspices of dictatorship of the proletariats. He has further said that such a change is not likely to came at the first stroke, as if by magic, or at the behest of the Virgin Mary, or by a slogan, resolution, or decree, it can be done only in the course of a long and difficult mass struggle against the mass of petty bourgeoisie influences.

Marx on Character of the State : Karl Marx believes that the state has nothing to do with the representation of the people but only is an agency for expressing the will of the ruling classes. He is of the view that the State maintains armies, prisons and similar other institutions simply to protect and safeguard the rights, interests and privileges of ruling classes. Privileged classes of the past maintain their privileges only through these arms of oppression and with the solid backing of the state. The present society and state can be changed and dislodged only with the use of force and not by peaceful means.

Marx on Democracy : According to Marx since the modern capitalist system is in the hands of a few capitalists therefore, they have devised such means and methods that power does not easily, shift from their hands. Democracy is one such device which helps the capitalists in retaining its power and authority. The working classes, therefore, should win the battle of democracy if they can. Peaceful means and methods which democracy preaches are useful but these should be carefully watched. The capitalists should not be given an opportunity to misuse democratic institutions.

Marx's Concept of Classless Society : Marx believes that when the proletariats will capture power from the capitalists and the means of production will come under their control, a new system of production will emerge. The new society will hand over means of production to the community as a whole and not to any individual. He believes that in the last phase of the revolution capitalists are bound to be thrown out of power and the proletariats shall then capture authority. It is then alone that a classless society will emerge and existing class distinctions will disappear.

According to Karl Marx, class distinctions exist because means of production are in the hands of only one class and that dominant class exploits other classes. When the proletariates will capture power, the means of production will come in the hands of working classes and then there shall be none to be exploited. All shall work for the common welfare or in the interest of the community at large. It is at this stage that classes society will emerge. In the words of Engles "But in doing this it abolishes itself as a proletariat, abolishes all class distinction and class antagonism abolishes also the state as state".

The Analysis : Karl Marx's theory of state has however been put to severe criticism on various grounds namely:

1. *It is Fundamentally Wrong :* Marxian theory of state is against the established classical theory of state. For him state is a wheel of oppression and its authority is used against the weak classes. He believes that state represents the will of the economically strong classes. But it is not always correct. The state has not always represented economically better classes. The Rajas and Badshahs in the past were neither economically the most 'powerful' nor did they always represent the economically powerful classes. They generally represented all the classes in the society at least in theory. Even in modern times, the state is meant for the welfare of all irrespective of any class distinction. In fact the modern Parliament have representatives from all classes of society who look after the welfare of all rather than the welfare of the few. Marxian theory is, however, correct when applied to 19th century when laissez faire theory was in operation. But after abandoning that policy the states have now become welfare states and not instruments of exploitation.

2. *Disputes can be Peacefully Settled* : Marx's whole philosophy is based on the ground that it is impossible to reconcile differences between the working classes and capitalists. But today it is not so. There are various methods of reconciling, the disputes more particularly industrial ones to which Marx frequently refers. Labour Tribunals, Trade Unions etc. now represent the labourers and on their behalf settle disputes mostly to the satisfaction of both the disputing parties.
3. *No Guarantee against Future* : Then another point of criticism is about his views about exploitation. Marx feels that the capitalists, who are now in power, exploit the working classes, but he has failed to give a logical arguments to convince that when proletariats will come to power they will not exploit the capitalists. Logically if power comes in the hands of the working classes that also is bound to be misused. They will most likely use that in the spirit of revenge. Marx has suggested no mechanism for checking exploitation of the capitalists by the proletariats.
4. *He has Under-estimated Peaceful Methods* : Marx believes that the only way to bring about a change is through violent revolution. But he forgets that there are peaceful methods also for bringing about changes. Gandhiji brought change in Indian political and social life without any bloody revolution in the Marxian sense of the term but only by non-violent means and methods. In the words of Ebenstein "If Marx had accorded the political factor its due weight, if he had fully grasped the importance of the Reform Act in England and of the Jacksonian revolution in the United States, he might have realised that socialism, too, might be accomplished without violence in countries that possessed democratic traditions strong enough to absorb far reaching social and economic changes without resorting to civil war. A recognition of the cultural and political factors in the

equation of social change would have amounted, however, to a virtual abandonment of the central position of Marx; that history is the history of class wars and that ruling classes defend their position to the bitter end."

Marxian theory of state is not so sound as prima facie it may appear. His stress on armed revolution is rather too much and cannot be justified especially today when nations are thinking more in terms of peaceful co-operation rather than on war. Who can deny that force brings with it hatred and counter-revolutionary forces which bring instability in the society. Settlement of disputes by force is bound to retard political and social progress. It is beyond all doubts that an armed and violent revolution is less durable than the changes brought about by peaceful means and methods on the one hand and persuasion of the other.

(i) *Role of Religion Ignored* : According to Marxian philosophy religion is the 'opium of the people'. He has outrightly condemned religion and even gone to the extent of saying that 'Man created God.' But all his philosophy is against practical life. Religion has its own role to play and is very much deep-rooted in mankind. Beyond all doubts it develops our spiritual feelings which are the basis of modern life. Without such feelings whole world will be dominated by opportunists.

(ii) *Stress on Economic Factor* : According to Marxian philosophy economic factor is the only one which motivates people or in other words in modern drama of world, each one is a mere actor and economic factor is pulling his wires. But again it is not correct. Each one is not merely an actor but also a great wire-puller. In the universe he determines many things, including his own economic conditions and also political and social systems.

(iii) *Politics Made Hand Maid :* Then another flaw of Marxian political philosophy is that his society is built only on economic basis. He has made politics as the hand-maid of economics but in actual life economics is the hand-maid of politics and it is the latter which determines the former. Those who enjoy political authority also decide economic life of the people.

(iv) *State not Withering away :* In actual practice, many Marxian prophecies have not come true. Marx believed that 'state will wither away'. But it has not come true. With the passage of time the state has changed its character. Modern state, instead of withering away, is becoming increasingly powerful and strong. Today we cannot imagine a society without a state. The state is being assigned more and more duties and responsibilities. Instead of remaining merely a police state it is now becoming a welfare state.

(v) *Undue Stress on Revolution :* Then another failing of Marxian philosophy is that according to him revolution is the only method for bringing about social changes. But in actual practice even great changes have come by 'non-violence' and by change of mind of the people. India got independence and brought political changes by 'non-violence'. So was the case with Ashoka who successfully adhered to the idea that change of mind only could bring successfully and lasting revolution. Not only this but we find that even the communists are now trying to seize power by democratic means. The Communists in Bengal and Kerala have captured power by appealing to the electorates and through ballot boxes.

(vi) *Possibility of Continuing Struggle :* Then Marx is of the opinion that with the establishment of classless society there will be no struggle. But again it is not according to human imagination. A party coming to power after constant use of violence will at once abandon violence is something which can only be done by a magic wand.

Practical experience shows that one struggle leads to another. In this struggle there will be no place for reasoning but the focus will always be on capturing power and authority.

(vii) *Marx-a Utopian :* Then in his philosophy Marx has failed to devise means by which it could be ensured that the working classes would not take revenge on the capitalists for their long oppression after coming to power. He has also in no way ensured that after being once overthrown, the capitalist, classes will not try to recapture power. He has no means to ensure that establishing a classless society will be end of revolutions and struggles. In fact he made struggle a permanent phenomenon.

Marxian philosophy, in so far as the concept 'Classless Society', Materialistic Interpretation of History' etc. are concerned is utopian in nature and character. Though Marx condemned Fourier and Owen for being utopian, yet he himself is no exception to that.

(viii) *Two Fatal Ambiguities :* According to Dunnings, "But the theories of Marx which at the first sight seem to be so compact and well provocative of dissensions, have two fatal ambiguities. The first is that he nowhere describes the general outlines of society which is to spring from the old ....Marx moreover expressed the most contradictory statement as to the methods to be pursued. His doctrine of capitalistic development would naturally minimize the importance of active organisation and propaganda as a means of consolidating the proletarian forces for final cataclyism".

(ix) *A Continuous Struggle :* If Marxian theory is accepted then in actual practice that will mean a continuous struggle. If once the working classes throw away the capitalists from power, then the later will try to outthrow the former and a never ending struggle will start. In this way it will be a society of struggle. In such a society there can be no peace, prosperity and development as well as advancement.

But in spite of all these defects, Marxian philosophy today appeals not only to thousands but millions of people living not only in one corner of the world but around the globe. His philosophy has engulfed one-third of the world which has accepted his ideas both as a creed as well as a way of life. His philosophy is now the only ray of hope for millions of the toilers being exploited by the capitalists.

Conclusion : Socialist philosophy, as expounded by Marx and subsequently modified and improved by Lenin and Stalin, opened a new era in world political philosophy. The writing of these great men were followed in practice and changed the very outlook and philosophy of life. The workers and labourers who were hitherto being exploited tried to get their due place in society. Evils of capitalism and the system under which the capitalist was keeping the worker under his control came to light. The role which the state was to play and the sphere of its activities came under searching enquiry.

The workers were encouraged to organise themselves and get themselves ready for the struggle with the capitalists in which they were to lose nothing but their chains but on the other hand they were to gain everything. The idea that capitalism was sowing the seeds of its own destruction and that with the passage of time the state shall wither away came to the front. In fact, in the writings of these great philosophers, thinkers and politicians whole concept of capitalist-labourer struggle was given a scientific outlook and thus scientifically arranged. It was made appealing and convincing both to mind and brain. The chief exponent of this school of thought was Karl Marx who laid down the basic principles of his philosophy but credit goes to his followers who did not make it static or outdated. On the other hand, they tried and tried successfully to make Marxian philosophy dynamic. They gave every justification for his prophesies not coming true to the expectations of its founder.

Sovereignty: Pluralistic Theory

Meaning of Pluralism : Pluralism is a powerful protest against the monistic theory of sovereignly which endows the state with supreme and unlimited power. Harold Laski, J.N. Figgis, Ernest Barker, G.D.H. Cole, A.D.Lindsay, Duguit, MacIver and others are the exponents of Pluralism. According to Pluralists, sovereignty resides not with the state but it resides with many other institutions. There exist many social, political, cultural and economic institutions in society and many of these institutions are prior to the State. For example, Family and Church are prior to the State. According to Pluralists, the State is not the only supreme institution. On the contrary, like other institution, the State is also one of the institutions of society. There the State does not reserve the authority to exercise sovereignty according to his will. Sovereignty is not his private property.

The Pluralistic state is, therefore, "simply a state in which there exists no single source of authority". According to pluralists "sovereignty is not indivisible and exclusive". On the contrary "it is a multiplicity in its essence and manifestation, it is divisible in two parts and should be divided"; A.D.Lindsay has very aptly remarked in this connection "if we look at the facts it is clear enough that the theory of sovereign state has broken down". Professor Laski is of the opinion that "it is impossible to make the legal theory of sovereignty valid for political philosophy". He believed that "it would be lasting benefit to political science if the whole concept of sovereign was surrendered". Krabbe is of the opinion that the "notion of sovereignty must be expunged from political theory". While Barker says, "We see the State less as an association of individuals in a common life; we see it more as an association of individuals, already united in various groups for a'further and more embracing common purpose".

These associations have an inner life which is atleast as autonomous as that of the state. Thus, the pluralists ardently advocate the autonomy and freedom of profession, political, religious, economic, social and educational associations. Gettell has beautifully summed up the idea of pluralism in these words. "The pluralists deny that the state is a unique organisation, they hold that other associations are equally important and natural. They argue that such associations for their purpose are as sovereign as the state is for its purpose.

They emphasise the inability of the state to enforce its will in practice against the opposition of certain groups within it. They insist on the equal rights of all groups that command the allegiance of their members and that perform valuable functions in society. Hence, sovereignty is possessed by many association. It is not indivisible unit, the state is not supreme or unlimited".

3

Political Theories

Introduction : Political Science is, mainly, the science of state. In the study of Political Science, the most important question, which arises, is that how and when the State originated. It is very difficult to answer this question. It is not only difficult but rather impossible to point out any exact date when the State might have come into existence. According to Dr. Garner, "the circumstances under which primitive men first saw the light of political consciousness and came to associate themselves together under some form of political organisation, are facts that are veiled largely, if not wholly, in the mists of obscurity." According to Gettell, "the exact origin of political life cannot be historically determined." Prof. Gilchrist writes, "where history fails, we resort to speculation."

On the basis of speculation, various political thinkers have originated different theories of the origin of the State. Plato believed that State originated because of necessity of division of labour. Aristotle said that the state originated because of social instincts of man. Karl Marx called the State a means for the exploitation of the poor by the rich. Following are the important theories regarding the origin of the State

1. Social Contract Theory
2. Historical or Evolutionary Theory of origin of the State
3. Marxist Theory of the State
4. Some other theories of origin of the State

Social Contract Theory

Statement of the Theory (Meaning of Contract). The Social Contract Theory dominated the European political thought in the eighteenth century, and played a very important part in the development of the modern political theory and practice of all the speculative theories, the Social Contract Theory is most important. It is one of the oldest theories. This theory came into being as a result of reaction against the theory of Divine Origin. According to this theory, the state was not created by God. On the contrary, under the compulsion of circumstances, people contracted with the rulers and as a result the State was organised. This theory offers an explanation for the origin of the state and shows the relationship between those who govern and those who are governed. It is a mechanical theory which starts with the assumption that prior to the organisation of the state, man lived in "a state of nature".

It deals with two fundamental assumptions—first "a state of nature", second a contract. The contract, according to Prof. Gilchrist, again may mean either (a) the social or political contract which marks the origin of civil society or (b) agreement between rulers and subjects. In sixteenth and seventeenth century this theory gained enduring popularity. Richard Hooker, Hugo Grotius, Milton, etc. also supported this theory, but the Social Contract Theory reached its culmination in the hands of Hobbes, Locke and Rousseau.

State of Nature : Hobbes, Locke and Rousseau are the chief exponents of the Contract Theory. All of these three exponents establish their thesis from the beginning of human habitation. But their ideas and opinions are quite distinct. According to Hobbes, in the State of Nature man's condition was deplorable. It was the state of wild savagery in which the guiding principle was "might is right". At this stage man led a lonesome and animal life. According to Locke, in the very beginning human life was very peaceful and man led a very natural life. The pious laws of nature gave him the right to life, the right to property and the right to freedom. But at that time, there was no government to regulate these rights nor was there a judge to interpret these rights properly. Everybody started interpreting these rights in his own way. This led to the rise of conflicts. In the opinion of Rousseau man led an ideal life in the pre-political age and enjoyed heavenly bliss. But later on the increase in the population and the tradition of keeping property led to the rise of conflict and being fed up with this state man entered into a contract, Hobbes, Locke and Rousseau believed that when man could not bear the natural state, he entered into a contract.

Social and Political Contract : Hobbes and Rousseau have described only one contract, whereas Locke has described two contracts. According to Hobbes, man entered into a social contract and put the natural state to end. It was this contract which led to the creation of society. And the ruler was also the outcome of the same contract. Since the ruler did not take part in the contact. According to Hobbes, people surrendered all their powers to the king. In this way Hobbes is an exponent of absolute monarchy. But Locke is of the opinion that human beings entered into two contracts-Social and Political. The first contract led to the creation of society and the second to the formation of the government. John Locke believed that people did not transfer all of their rights to the king. The king was given only the right to life, the right to property and the right to security. So the king is only the trustee. The people reserve the right to dethrone the king if he fails to safeguard the security of the people. In this way, he supported limited or constitutional monarchy.

According to Rousseau, people transferred all of their rights to society and put the natural order to an end. Rousseau regarded the real or true will of society as the general will. He considered general will sovereign. It is this general will that forms the government. Government is the agent of general will. In this way, Rousseau regarded government as an institution functioning under the general will of the people. He was the exponent of direct democracy and popular sovereignty.

Critical Assessment : The Social Contract Theory dominated the European political thought in eighteenth century. But in nineteenth century it was severely criticised. Even before the publication to Rousseau's Social Contract, Hume the English philosopher, declared the contract as the basis of relations between the government and the governed was incompatible with the facts of history.

(i) *This Theory is Unhistorical :* History does not make any such example available as can prove that the state is the outcome of any such contract A few exponents of this theory cite the example of Mayflower Compact, Providence Agreement. But this agreement does not throw light on the political and pre-political activities of primitive men. The travellers who went to America from England were quite aware of the characteristics of the state. The Mayflower Agreement did not, however, result in the formation of the state. Therefore, this theory is unhistorical and proves to be a bad history.

(ii) *This Theory is Illogical :* This theory does not prove sound on the touchstone of logic. According to Locke in the state of nature, nature gave man the right to life, right to law, right to property and right to freedom. Similarly, Rousseau also believed that people possessed in their primitive stage, a few rights and enjoyed personal liberty to a certain extent. But all this depended on their institutions. All these arguments are illogical because it is the state that gives rights to its people and assures their guarantee.

(iii) *Gives a Wrong Picture of the Progress of Mankind :* The exponents of the Social Contract Theory argue that people entered into a contract in order to protect themselves from aggression and safeguard their interests. But history presents before us a different version. According to an eminent author, the family was the unity, property was held in common, custom formed law and each man was born into his status in society. In this it is quite clear that man advanced from a primitive stage and took to contract and not the vice-versa.

(iv) *A Contract cannot be Binding on the Succeeding Generation :* In a contract there always enter two parties. A contract cannot be entered into by one party alone. Therefore, Hobbes's notion of a single party contract is decidedly wrong. Despite this when those who had entered into a contract die, the contract does not remain binding on their posterity. Thomas Paine has also criticised the conception of the contract because it is entirely binding and in consequence a dead weight on the wheel of progress.

(v) *This Theory is Legally Invalid :* This theory tells us that the state is the outcome of the contract. But the fact is that state was formed first and the contract was conceived much later. The contract is not possible in the absence of the state.

(vi) *This Theory is Artificial :* This theory tell us that the state is like a machine, manufactured by man. But the reality is that the state and the practical institutions under it are the result of evolution. Aristotle has very aptly remarked that the state is a natural institution.

(vii) *This Theory had a Bad Philosophy :* This theory tells us that our relations with the State are optional. For example, Locke has asserted that the people reserve the right to dethrone the king if he fails to perform his duties. And if people can go against the bindings of the contract, the state will meet its end and anarchy will prevail. Dr. Garner also believes that "membership in the state and the obligations of allegiance and obedience cannot be interpreted in the terminology of legal contract. These relations rest upon unity and the general interests and necessities of society".

(viii) *This Theory is Dangerous* : In the opinion of Bluntschli, the Social Contract Theory is a dangerous theory. He believes in examples which prove that kings entered into contracts with certain classes of people and administered and enforced their own laws. "The Social Contract Theory", says Bluntschli," is highly dangerous, since it makes the state and its institutions a product of individual caprice."

(ix) *This Theory is far form Reality* : The exponents of Social Contract Theory did not aim to trace the origin and development of the state. Only to serve their own ends, they conceived this theory and, therefore, this theory is far away from reality.

Contract Theory

(i) Despite the above mentioned short coming and limitations of the Social Contract Theory, we cannot overlook its merits. Though this theory does not dominate these days, yet it had a very great hold in the past. The emergency of this theory gave a very severe blow to the Theory of Divine Origin and the Theory of Divine Right. Contrary to the spirit of the Divine Origin Theory, the Social Contract Theory lays emphasis on the fact that the state is the outcome of a contract and it is not God's creation. Therefore, the king is not entitled to rule over people at the cost of God's name.

(ii) Though Hobbes' theory was undemocratic yet it was he who first of all propounded the theory of legal sovereignty which was presented before the world later on by Austin. Though we fail to accept this theory in practice yet we discuss it, throw a flash of light on it and accept it as principle.

(iii) In spite of the inadequacies of the Social Contract Theory, we cannot ignore or overlook its contribution in the development of democracy. John Locke has very emphatically asserted that the consent of the people forms the basis of democracy. He regarded the government as a kind of trust. The people, according to him, reserve the right to dethrone the king if he fails to performs his duties. This statement of Locke enabled the people to restrain the despotic activities of the king.

(iv) This ideology of John Locke influenced a very great deal the makers of American constitution. They realised the fact that people established the government for protecting their lives and safeguarding their freedom and property. Therefore, it is the sole aim of the government to protect its people. Thinking these rights legal, the makers of American Constitution included the fundamental right in the Constitution of U.S.A.

(v) John Locke regarded the separation between the Executive and the Legislative as essential. Montesquieu carried it further and propounded a new theory of separation of powers. It was the first attempt to restrain the despotic activities of the cruel rulers.

(vi) Locke's distinction between the State and the Government will never be forgotten.

(vii) Rousseau was a great worshipper of democracy. He preferred direct democracy to indirect democracy. The reflection of Rousseau's ideas is clearly visible everywhere. The state which happens to have indirect democracy or the representative democracy also tends to follow some of the canons of direct democracy. Panchayati Raj System in India is the glaring example. Switzerland has translated Rousseau's idea into action by adopting the process of Referendum, Initiative and passing laws directly by the people in certain states.

Evolutionary Theory

The origin of social institutions is shrouded in obscurity. Theories concerning their origin are, at best, approximations to what might have taken place in the past. This is certainly true of theories concerning the origin and evolution of the state. Inspite of a number of important theories of state origin, no single discussion seems to be adequate. In fact, modern sociologists have made it clear that social phenomena cannot be explained by reference to any single factor. As one of the multifarious agencies of social control, the state, in history, has passed through different states of development. It is the product of steady evolutionary process in which more than one factor participated. The generally accepted theory of state origin, known as the evolutionary theory, is thus based on a pluralistic explanation of political phenomena.

Today, however, writers like Lowie do not subscribe to the theory of linear evolution of the state. According to them, all societies posses some system of government for regulating the relations of individuals and safeguarding the interests of the group. Slowly and imperceptibly, the state developed from a simple to a complex type. In recent days, however, archaeology, philology and anthropology have contributed much to our knowledge regarding the origin of the state.

The most important forces contributing to the origin of the state are:

(i) Natural and Social Instinct;
(ii) Kinship;
(iii) Religion;
(iv) Economic activities;
(v) Force;
(vi) Political Awareness

(i) *Natural and Social Instinct* : Man is a social animal by nature. Nature impels and necessity compels him to live in the society.. According to Aristotle, "State originated in the bare needs of life and continues in existence for the sake of good life." In order to regulate the social life, some rules and regulations were framed for the individuals. At some later stage these rules and regulations took the form of laws. Slowly and gradually society became politically organised and it led to the evolution of the state. In this way the social nature of man helped in the evolution of the state.

(ii) *Kinship—As MacIver Says :* "Kinship creates society and society at length creates the state. The role of kinship is important in the evolution of the state. The primary social unit is the family. The primitive family took various forms, ranging from a condition approaching promiscuity to restricted groups within which intermarriage was forbidden." The members of a family are tied together by blood-relationship, and kin is a product of "the recognition of consanguinity." As the sexual impulse leads the young adolescent outside the known family circle, it culminates in the formation of a new family. The extension of the thread of blood-relationship extends and subdivides the kin further and further. The feeling of unity and solidarity which is essential to political life is strengthened by such ties of kinship. Still, kinship everywhere provided the nucleus around which successive organisations had developed.

(iii) *Religion :* As a force in state-formation, religion played a vital role in history. Primitive men were at the mercy of the unexplainable natural phenomena like flood, lightning, thunder etc. In course of time, they came to worship these forces, imagining the hands of unseen agents behind them. This primitive form religion, called animism, was accompanied by fetishism, a superstitious belief in the effectiveness of material objects, and, later took the form of nature worship, often developing into a beautiful mythology. Also, the cult of worship of the deceased ancestors was general feature of the primitive communities. Such religious forms ranging from animism to ancestorworship provided the sanction for law and government and ensured the unity and obligation of the group.

Throughout history the priestly class has exerted powerful influence in government and politics on the strength of the supernatural sanctions of religion. In the primitive ages there was hardly any distinction between religion and politics. Common religious beliefs held men together and taught them reverence and obedience. The wide prevalence of the theory of divine right of kings which has recently been abandoned amply proves the vital role of religion in the formation and continuance of the state.

(iv) *Economic Activities* : The economic activities of primitive people contributed greatly to the origin of the state. The activities by which men secured food and shelter and subsequently came to possess property and wealth facilitated the emergence of the state. Co-operation is the essence of every form of economic life. It demands conformity to certain recognized rules. The emergence of the idea of private property and the social distinctions based on wealth, necessitated the adoption of new rules to cope with the changing situation. According to Maclver, the interaction of the forces of sex and property is highly significant in the building of the social structure. "The problem of the family, its permanence against the waning and variability of the initial sex-impulse, is solved by its association with the unswerving desire for the control of property." Again, exchange of commodities gave rise to occupation diversification. Wealth came to be unequally distributed and class-distinctions arose. For the regulation and protection of property rights and the settlement of property disputes new laws were created. Thus the economic activities of early people led to the rise of government.

(v) *Force* : The role of force in state-building has been stressed by a number of eminent writers. For instance, Marx viewed the state as a creation of the dominant economic class that uses it as a means of exploiting the masses. The origin and evolution of the state were similarly made possible by the interaction of antagonistic forces.

Inspite of exaggerated references to the role of force by some sociologists, historically speaking, struggle and warfare proved an important element in state formation. Early political organisations were rather simple, as those had to interfere little with the activities of the individuals. But with the expansion of the group and the consequent weakening of the tie of kinship, the application of force was necessary for the maintenance of peace and order. Also for the purpose of defence or aggression, the members of a group had to work concertedly under the authority of a recognised leader.

(vi) *Political Awareness* : The evolution of the state has greatly been helped by political consciousness. Consciousness of common ends has always been present in human beings. It might at first have started in vague awareness of the efficacy of political organisation, to maintain peace and order. Thus customary laws began to take roots almost imperceptibly. When Aristotle characterised man as a political animal, he merely pointed out this spontaneous acquiescence of men in the imperative codes of social co-ordination. Later, however, in the process of development instinctive desire was more and more replaced by conscious purpose. The primitive forces of kinship, religion, need for food, and defence, became the tool, of active minds willing something coherent and organised and usually imposing their wills on individuals in the group and on other groups.

Conclusion : The evolutionary theory, it is said, highlights the evolution and not the origin of the state. The purpose of this theory is to systematise the diverse forces and factors that contributed to the origin and evolution of the states in general. The operation of all the factors might not have been uniform or necessary in particular cases of state-building. Still some or all of these forces worked together slowly and imperceptibly facilitating the evolution of the state throughout human history.

As the state is a moving phenomenon that knows no finality, the political scientist can at best hazard a guesswork. The evolutionary theory does something more than that. It clearly shows that the state is neither the gift of God nor the deliberate work of man. The beginning is of the state lost in the shadowy past in which social institutions were unconsciously arising, and its development has followed the general laws of evolutionary growth.

Liberal-welfare and Socialist Theory of the State : The history of the idea c.' welfare state is very old. Among the modern political thinkers, Laski was the first who turned the attention of the world from the idea of police state to a welfare state. The idea of welfare state started developing in different countries at different times.

The modern state has evolved into a welfare state. The liberal welfare theory of the functions of the state is most popular and is in vogue these days. Every modern and civilised state takes pride in branding itself as a welfare state. The welfare theory of the state activity enlarges the scope of the state. The Welfare State besides performing the police functions, also performs millions of other public utility functions. The welfare theory considers the state as a 'means' for welfare of the individual. The intellectual, social, political, physical, moral and cultural development of the individual and the community is the responsibility of the liberal welfare state. The welfare state provides sufficient opportunities and freedom for the development of the personality of the individual.

History of Political Liberalism : The term liberalism was first used by a Spanish political party, the "Liberates" in the early 19th century. About 1830 it was used by British political leaders and economists. The great leader of British liberalism was Prime Minister William E. Gladstone. His Liberal party stood for extending the right to vote, for free trade, for resistance to religious domination of government and other social institution, and for improving the conditions of labourers and of the middle classes. Liberalism's leading economic philosopher was John Stuart Mill: Politically, the movement was influenced by the 17th century philosopher John Locke.

On the continent of Europe, liberal ideas led to the revolutions that in 1848 swept through Hungary, Italy, Germany, France, and other countries.

Thomas Jefferson was thought to be the greatest early American liberal, although he was not called by that term in his lifetime. As a political term liberalism did not become common in United States politics until 1872, when the short-lived Liberal Republican Party was formed. Since 1872, the usual tendency in the United States has been for liberals to stay in the major parties, calling themselves Liberal Democrats or Liberal Republicans. However, in 1912, 1924, and (to a lesser extent) 1948 liberals united to form temporary Progressive Parties.

Since 1896 most United States liberals have been Democrats, although there have been notable exceptions such as the La Follettes and George W. Norris. Liberals were especially active and prominent in Franklin D. Roosevelt's 'New Deal'. In the 1940's a group called Americans for Democratic Action became the voice of many United States Liberals.

There is no national political party in the United States with the name Liberal, but there is a group in New York City with that name, which is usually allied with the Democratic party there. The once great Liberal Party in England declined in importance in the 20th century. But liberal parties are strong in Canada, Australia, and some Latin American countries.

The Meaning of Liberalism : It is not easy to define Liberalism because it does not represent any coherent body of doctrine. It is rather a historical tendency embracing diverse and even contradictory currents of thought that manifested in certain countries at a given epoch. Liberalism in this wide sense should not be confused with the programme or creed of a particular party which adopts the liberal designation but may or not represent the essential philosophy of Liberalism.

It is difficult to state what exactly constitute the essential principles of Liberalism. In the first place, the representative political thinkers of the liberal school themselves do not agreed about it. Secondly, circumstances under which the Liberal State emerged in different countries have been so various that they have necessitated a corresponding change in liberal outlook in those countries. Lastly, the liberal state has been susceptible to changing economic patterns in the same country requiring a restatement of the Liberal ideology.

Laski has presented us in "The Rise of European Liberalism" with a coherent analysis of the philosophy of the European Liberal movement in its proper social perspective. This analysis is all the more valuable as it has made a sustained attempt to utilize the Marxian method of social research in tracing the economic foundation of Liberalism. He shows considerable sympathy in his treatment of the various aspects of the Liberal Philosophy. It appears that Laski's own political outlook was far more in harmony with the fundamental spirit of Liberalism than he himself cared to admit.

Even when he declared himself to be a convert to Marxian socialism, he did not abandon or even mitigate his enthusiasm for some of the most fundamental assumptions of liberalism. Liberalism had in fact become an ingrained habit with Laski's political behaviour and it was simply impossible for him to effect a complete break with the liberal tradition of his country in which he was brought up. Liberalism is a habit of mind no less than a political creed or doctrine. Laski may reject some or most of the doctrinal aspects of liberalism but as a mental attitude Liberalism never deserts him. Even when he is talking pure socialism, a liberal under-current of thought can Basil, be discerned.

Middle Class Philosophy : Liberalism was primarily the philosophy of the victorious middle class in Europe that came into power and prominence after the eclipse of the feudal classes. But the vitality of the Liberal doctrines depended less on their logic than on their agreement with the interests of the class that mainly produced them. Liberalism has found its adherents and spokesmen with equal case, in persons professing such varied creeds as Christians and atheists, monarchists and republicans, aristocrats and democrats, idealists and utilitarians, rationalists and empiricists, or even individualists and collectivists. But even these strains have not been able to destroy the inner unity of the Liberal doctrine. This inner unity is derived from the fact that it always remains the ideological instrument of a particular class in social evolution. That class is the Capitalist class. The Capitalists first utilized the body of liberal ideas in their ideological offensive against the landowners.

A new opposition arose between the Capitalists and the wage-earners, with the result that liberalism tended to become more and more a defence mechanism of the Capitalist class against Proletarian attacks. Liberalism no longer remained an ideology of progress and radical change. It was now transformed into an ideology of conservative decadence and reaction. The consistency of the Liberal doctrines should be sought in the social purpose which they serve and not in the philosophical assumptions which they make.

Tradition of Liberalism : If we examine the various historical forces and intellectual trends that have shaped the evolution of the Liberal doctrines in the period between the Reformation and the Russian Revolution, we realize that the number and character of such influence is bewildering. Laski believes that liberal ideas were propounded and developed sometimes by political thinkers, who were not even conscious of what they were doing. Liberalism school of political philosophy did not evolve in a direct and straight forward manner. The doctrines of liberalism lack clarity and precision because they have been derived from several sources with little internal affinity. People who were otherwise indifferent and even antagonistic to the objectives of liberalism, have contributed, without being conscious of it, to the theory and practice of the liberal state. The liberal tradition has been enriched by such important men as Machiavelli, Calvin, Luther, Copernicus, Henry VIII and Thomas More in the sixteenth century and by Hobbes, Jurieu, Louis XIV, Richelieu, Pascal and Baçon in the seventeenth century. Besides this, the liberal outlook that period was also generated by constantly changing social environment in Western Europe during that period.

The rise of a new social class to political power has always synchronized in history with radical adjustments in the social philosophy of the people of that period. The advent of the middle class to the position of political supremacy was no exception to this rule. It signified a violent break from the intellectual conceptions of the feudal past. Theology and ethics, jurisprudence and politics, arts and science were reconstituted on a new basis. The entire outlook of the age was so changed as to become receptive to new norms of social behaviour and new forms of social organisation.

Failure of Feudalism : The breakdown of the medieval society was not achieved by peaceful means. The liberal capitalistic state was born in the midst of violent struggles and factional fights which culminated in the liquidation of the feudal state system in a large part of Western Europe. The destructive role of liberalism in this period is as important as the constructive role which it assumed subsequently.

In the sixteenth century, the liberal state was only slowly emerging. The commercial and industrial classes first allied themselves with the cause of monarchical absolutism in order to secure national freedom from papal control on the external side. Absolute monarchy was favoured on the internal side because by crashing the feudal particularist state it provided better facilities of trade for them. Machiavelli was the first political thinker of some repute through whom the hopes the desires of the rising middle class of Europe found a concrete expression. The secular outlook of Machiavelli ultimately became an important element of the creed of Liberalism.

Machiavelli's conception of human nature as that of the English philosopher Hobbes was also strikingly modern. His view that human beings are fundamentally egoistic, long remained the acknowledged creed of individualistic Liberalism. His conception of a supreme law-giver gave rise to the later liberal theories of sovereignty. His interest in stable government led him to favour absolute monarchy for the moment, but he was not a monarchist by conviction. Once the causes of perpetual anarchy were removed, the popular and republican form of government was the desirable ideal. This appreciation of popular government coupled with this condemnation of nobility and aristocracy, entitles Machiavelli to be counted as one of the founder-philosophers of liberalism. Liberal state was destined to become a nation-state in course of time. Thus the contribution of the Italian philosopher in building up the liberal tradition was not insignificant.

The Reformation and Liberalism : Liberalism derived indirect support from the Reformation as well. Max Weber believes that the Protestant doctrines facilitated the triumph of the Liberal ideals to a very great extent.

But the alliance between Liberalism and Protestanism was accidental rather than consciously designed. It is true that the social philosophy of Luther and other leaders of the Reformation was essentially conservative. But their protestant mood in the realm of theology could not but have repercussions in other fields of intellectual inquiry. By questioning the Catholic tradition of revering the papal authority, it produced a violent earthquake in mass psychology. Protestantism brought about immense changes not only in theological doctrines but also effected far-reaching changes in the distribution of wealth by transferring ecclesiastical property to lay hands. It also facilitated the growth of the secular state by opposing papal interference in national affairs. Protestantism aided the emancipation of the individual by creating rationalist temper although it was only a by-product of the Reformation and could in no case be called its essence. There were even trends like Calvinism which were definitely hostile to everything Liberalism has stood for.

Bodin, Hobbes, Locke and Rousseau's Thinking of Liberalism : Jean Bodin and Hobbes played important roles in developing the Liberal theory. Their theories of sovereignty were pleas for the supremacy of the liberal state in social affairs. They dismiss the claim of the church to dispute its sovereignty. But Bodin unlike Hobbes could not completely eradicate the influence of the medieval doctrine of natural law. 'He maintained that even the sovereign was bound by the moral conventions of his generation, a view rejected by Hobbes completely.

Another distinctive feature of Bodin's philosophy as that of Hobbes or Locke was his conscientious respect for bourgeois property which the sovereign should consider as inviolable. In Bodin's time the struggle between eccelesiastical and civil power was finally decided in favour of the latter and against the former. In the sphere of theory, it implied the victory of the secular over the theocratic ideal. But the secular state that emerges at the end of the sixteenth and seventeenth centuries is still a paternalistic state and has yet to travel a long way before it can properly be called a Liberal state. In the seventeenth and eighteenth centuries the liberal state was further consolidated. The battle for liberal ideas assumed a violent struggle in the civil war of England and the French Revolution of 1789, Hobbes, Locke and Rousseau were the main advocates of the Liberal theory of state during this most interesting age in the history of western political thought. Utilitarianism is essentially an English school of thinking. It played a notable part in England in the nineteenth century, particularly in the earlier half, in effecting reforms of a far-reaching character.

Definitions of Liberal-welfare State : The Welfare State is not a matter of 'charity' but of 'right'. It is necessary that there must be consciousness of the idea of welfare among the masses. The initiative of the people must not be killed if it is to be a genuine welfare state. It has been defined thus:

Hobman : "Welfare State is a compromise between communism on one side and unbridled individualism on the other."

Abraham : A Welfare State is "a community where state power is deliberately used to modify the normal play of economic forces so as to obtain a more equal distribution of income for citizen, a basic minimum irrespective of the market value of his work and his property."

G.D.H. Cole : "The Welfare State is a society in which an assured minimum standard of living and opportunity becomes the possession of every citizen".

T.W.Kent : A Welfare State is a "State that provides for its citizens a wide range of social services".

A.Schlesinger : "The Welfare State is a system wherein government agrees to underwrite certain level of employment, income, education, medical, social security and housing for all its citizens."

Venkatagay : "Welfare State is a state which does not confine itself to the discharging of mere police functions, but takes a wider view of its obligations and undertakes all activities which are considered necessary and desirable to remove social evils and promote the welfare of population."

The above definitions indicate that the welfare state has to perform multifarious functions for the well-being of the community. In fact the welfare state has a reference to such schemes as social insurance old age pension, free education, medical aid, poor relief and a number of other welfare activities.

Non-liberal Theory

New Various political and philosophical concepts begin with the word 'neo'. This is often used to give an idea or theory respectability by tracing its roots back historically. Sometimes the word 'neo' is added to discredit a concept by linking it to a theory which is now consensually disapproved of by the scholars.

Liberalism : Liberalism can mean either a particular party creed in a particular time period, especially the late 19th century (the hey-day of Liberalism), or a general social and political attitude and orientation. Historically Liberalism was a middle-class or bourgeois movement for freedom from remaining feudal and monarchical control, and was associated, inter alia, with freedoms both legalistic, such as the economic theory of laissz-faire, and individual. From this position of supporting basic civil liberties or human rights, liberalism has developed a modern political creed in which the independence of the ordinary citizen labour, is taken as vital.

Modern liberal parties, and they exist in most democratic states, although not necessarily under that title, tend to argue that traditionally-organized class politics, with an apparently insoluble conflict between capitalism and some form of socialism or Marxism, is misplaced, and that a greater concentration on the talents, capacities and needs is possible and desirable. Liberalism is one of the best reasons for doubting the suitability of the standard i.e. right model of politics because it contains both the commitment to equality by the left and to approval of individual human effort and freedom by the right. In this sense it is often seen as being in the middle of the political spectrum. But most Liberals would argue that, far from being 'centre' or 'moderate', they are in fact radical, wishing to change much in society. Their opposition to class politics is illustrated by the example of recent British general elections, in which the Liberal Party/Liberal Democrats have gained almost exactly the same percentage from all social classes. A similar patterns tends to be found in most other Western countries.

Neo-liberalism : "Neo-liberalism" simply means new liberalism. The label is appropriate to John Stuart Mill, and to others who were persuaded that laissez faire did not promote the survival of the fittest but only ensured the exploitation of the many by the few.

"Neo-liberalism" is especially appropriate in the American context where the much abused label of "liberal" has come to mean ideological support for government programs that seek to encourage a greater equality of opportunity for all citizens.

Thus contemporary liberals or, more properly, neo-liberals favor an expanded role of government in the affairs of citizens. But government's involvement in the economy, education, race relations, and in all the areas affected today by government, is justified by neo-liberalism according to the same logic that originally inspired classical liberalism: inequality is an acceptable characteristic of social relationship only in so far as all citizens have an equal opportunity to show how unequal they are. Certainly the historical record of government's relationship to the larger society confirms the apparent inevitability of the increasing role of government as the society undergoes modernization.

Following table shows the steady increase of United States government spending at the national level, even as the country's economic productivity grows by leaps and bounds. This partial measure of government's increasing involvement in a developing economy also makes clear the importance of a political variable that is neglected by the whole economic concerns of classical liberalism and laissez faire capitalism war. It is the government's necessary mobilization of all the society's principal resources for waging war that most dramatically accelerates the government's involvement in the economy.

Military and Total Expenditures by the Federal Government of the United States, as a Percentage of Gross Nation Product, 1799-1967.

Year	*Military expenditures*	*% Total expenditures*
1799	0.8	1.4
1819	1.2	2.4
1839	0.9	1.6
1859	0.7	1.5
1879	0.5	3.2
1899	1.3	3.4
1909	0.8	2.3
1919	11.8	16.7
1929	0.7	3.0

Contd...

Year	*Military expenditures*	*% Total expenditures*
1939	1.2	9.8
1949	4.6	15.3
1959	9.0	16.6
1967 (est.)	8.3	15.5

The Working of Government : Whether because of war, economic crisis, or compassion for a suffering humanity, government gets bragger as society grows more complicated. The ideology of neo-liberalism generally approves of this trend, not because it is inevitable, but because it is understood to be consistent with the basic purpose of liberalism, both old and new. That purpose is to secure for all citizens and equal opportunity for self-development. What has changed during the three centuries since John Locke is our understanding of the means necessary to realizing that end.In an age when "liberalism" has come to mean "one person one vote" instead of political domination by a property-owning elite, it has fallen to government to ensure that equal access to policy makers is a working reality as well as a natural right. And in an age of giant business corporations, the free market is no longer a guarantee of economic efficiency or the "wealth of nations."

The "invisible hand" of Adam Smith may have been operative in an economy with many essentially equal competitors, but it has little relevance to an economic system in which the decisions of a few conglomerates, and of government, affect the income, employment opportunities, and price level of consumer expenditures of virtually every citizens. Pressures inevitably are brought to bear on policy makers to develop and augment the role of government, not only as a regulatory authority, but as an agency of social welfare. Thus government comes to assume more and more of those welfare functions that were earlier performed by family, the tribe the peasant village, and religious institutions.

4

Modern Democracy

Definition : The word 'Democracy' is the most emotionally provocative word in our political vocabulary. From the times of Paricles to the present day, it has enchanted the human race and has been popular, fascinating and key political ideal. Yet, the term `democracy' is enmeshed in terminological chaos and has defied human ingenuity to provide it an exact or precise meaning or connotation. Bernard Erick calls `democracy' the most promiseuous world in the world of public affairs. In the present day world, democracy is the most popular political concept. In recent times the idea of democracy has expanded steadily.

Freedom is the basis and essence of a healthy society. And, the state in which this free society is realised, is usually termed as a 'Democratic' state. Therefore the importance of democracy lies in providing `a political and social framework of society based on principles of freedom', or 'the body for a would be free spirit'. The importance of democracy is also obvious from the fact that it is accepted as the 'key political ideal' of the present times and the 'major ideal' of the present century. Indeed the twentieth century is a century of democracy conceived in Greece, developed through the puritan movement in England in the 17th century. Gaining universal appeal through the American war of independence and the French Revolution in the eighteenth century, democracy has ultimately established itself as an ideal to be cherished and a goal to be achieved by humanity. It has become a most inspiring rallying flag. The importance of democracy, therefore lies in the fact that it is universally acceptable and because everywhere, everybody today has started to believe or pretend to believe in democracy, claims to be a democrat.

Nature and Meaning

The term 'democracy' enchants people. It has become "a word of praise". It is "welcomed, worshipped". It is politically fashionable to speak of it and sing about its charms. Yet, democracy has always been an ambiguous word. It is a term which is apparently easy to understand but actually very difficult to define and explain clearly and comprehensively. The terms 'democracy' and 'democratic' has been used so often and so differently to explain political ideals, economic and social forces, ethical principles or forms of Govt. that it has become impossible to give it a precise or definite meaning.

R.H. Soltau in his work, An Introduction to Politics, say : "The terms 'democracy' and 'democratic' have been used so often and so differently that they are like coins on which all inscriptions and designs have become effaced, with the result that they can be made to apply to anything one wishes to defend or to attack according to one's preferences." "Democracy", observes Laski, "has a context in every sphere of life; and in each of these spheres it raises its special problems which do not admit of satisfactory or universal generalisation". After discussing at length the case of democracy as a form of Govt. we may now pass on to the study of democratic theory as espoused by the classical liberals and the maxian socialists.

Democracy : A Classical Approach : Democracy is very old form of Govt. and so its theory dates back to the days of the Greeks who identified it with 'people's power', or a system in which rulers are accountable to the people for what they do therein. Such a view saw its reaffirmation in modern times when Abraham Lincoln in his Gettysberg oration of 1863 called it "a govt. of the people, by the people, and for the people".

Great liberals like John Locke and Edmund Burke developed the same theme in the direction of a `limited govt.' bound by the laws of the land. Later on, the utilisations like Bentham and J.S.Mill justified the case of democratic Govt. in the name of their formula of the greatest good of the greatest number and John. S. Mill did the same on the force of his moral or ethnical agreement. This trend continued in the present century and saw its powerful reiteration at the bands of Dicey, Bryce and Laski. Apart from this, the idealistic argument of democracy prevailed side by side that had its brilliant manifestation at the hands of Rousseau, Green and Lindsay. All such affirmations constitute the classical theory of democracy.

The classical theory of democracy as espoused by the liberals and the idealists of the modern age has these salient features:

(1) Power is vested in the people and its exercise is given to them or to their chosen representatives accountable to them for their acts of commission and omission. All decisions must be based on the consent of the people, whether express or implied, which in practical terms means the will of the majority. Thus it stands on the premise that 'people are always right' or the 'decision of the majority is always correct'. Bryce defined democracy as "government in which the will of the majority of qualified citizens rules, taking the qualified citizens to constitute the great bulk of the inhabitants, say, roughly, at least three fourth so that the physical force of the citizens coincides with their voting power".

(2) The people have certain natural and inalienable rights which the govt. cannot abrogate or diminish. The doctrine of 'natural rights', as it came to be known, emerged as the most powerful instrument at the hands of the democrats who struggled for the rights of the people against arbitrary power of the kings. Reacting

against the arbitrary powers of the kind, John Milton asserted that "all men are naturally born free and from this principle he derived "the liberty and right of free born men to be governed as seems them best."

(3) The doctrine of "natural rights' lost its significance with the growth of the idea of positive liberalism that sought to reinterpret the relationship between individual liberty and state activity. Thus. Bentham offerered his principle of utility that sought to give a new interpretation to the justification of democracy. The doctrine of natural rights was rejected, rather replaced by the doctrine of the happiness of man measured in terms of material pleasures. He gave the formula of 'one person, one vote'. It implied that although all persons are not naturally the same in intelligence, energy, thrift, inventiveness and perseverance, yet all normal men-just as they have equal rights to life, freedom and access to the courts of law have equal rights to a voice in govt. because they have equal stakes in the justice and efficiency of governmental action. Democracy means govt. by those who have the greatest concern for and the greatest awareness of the interest and right of the people generally. The natural self interest of human beings is the best security against political action that is oppressive or tolerant of oppression.

(4) The classical theory of democracy has a peculiar dimension when we examine the view of the idealists like Rousseau and Green. To Rousseau democracy alone ensures prevalence of the general will. In every community there is a section of really selfless and enlightened people who think in terms of public interest and it is the inherent force of their selfless argument that ultimately prevails in any matter under discussion before a body of the people. Through the process of cancellation, good would set aside the bad, all contradictions would be resolved and in the end only

'dominant good' would emerge. This good, which would be what was left at the will of all becomes integrated, would be in effect the same as the general will. Influenced by the idealistic interpretations of Rousseau, Green says that 'will, not force is the basis of the state'.

(5) Above all, democracy has no substitute in terms of excellence from a practical point of view. Every form of govt. has its merits and demerits. But in case of Democracy where merits outweigh its demerits. Hence, it is the substituteless form of govt. The liberals keep in view the case of democracy as developed in the west based on the principle of universal adult franchise, free and fair periodic elections, multi-party systems, basic rights of the people, freedom of dissent, tolerance of opposition and the like. Bryce goes to the last extent of posing a question that if democracy "has not brought all the blessings that were expected. It has in some countries destroyed, in others materially diminished."

The classical or traditional doctrine of democracy has been in part a theory of certain original rights of man—a view that government is made in virtue of those rights and must conform to them. The men have a natural right to participate equally in political power, just as they have a natural right to be free from enslavement or to appeal on equal terms to judicial tribunals for protection of their lives and property against assaults, trespass or encroachment of any kind. What is known as 'democratic method' is that institutional arrangements for arriving at political decisions which realises the common good by making the people itself decide issues through the election of individuals who are to assemble in order to carry out its will.... There exists a Common Good, the obvious beacon light of policy, which is always simple to define and which every normal person can be made to see by means of rational argument...

Thus every member of the community, conscious of that goal, knowing his or her mind, discerning what is good and what is bad, takes part, actively and responsibly, in furthering the former and fighting the latter and all the members taken together control their public atyairs.

The classical theory of democracy has been criticised on many counts. First, it is thoroughly normative. It is loaded with high ideals and bombastic proposition like 'general will', 'people's rule', 'people's power', 'common good', and the like that cannot be subjected to an empirical verification. All these terms are quite elusive. Second, it attaches no importance to the role of numerous interest groups and organisations that play their part in the struggle for power, or which compete among themselves and that all constitutes the stuff of a democratic system in practice. The utilitarians talk about 'greatest happiness of the greatest number' without taking into consideration the powerful role of groups, factions and elites that ever strive to protect and promote their specific interests. Third, the Socialists and the Marxists have their own version of democracy that stretches the system of political democracy into social and economic spheres. To the Marxists, it is all like a defence of the discredited bourgeois system. All these points shall be discussed in the following sections.

Advantages : The classical theory of democracy has its own salient merits which are thus summed up by Schumpeter:

1. Though the classical doctrine of collective action may not be supported by the results of an empirical analysis, it is powerfully supported by its association with religious beliefs. The very meaning of a term like 'equality' may be in doubt, there is hardly any rational warrant for exalting it into a postulate, so long as we move in the sphere of empirical analysis. Christianity harbours a strong equalitarian element. Any celebrated word like 'equality' or 'freedom' may become a flag, a symbol of all a man holds dear, of everything that he loves about his nation whether rationally contingent to it or not.
2. It is a fact that the forms and phrases of classical

democracy are for many nations associated with events and developments in their history which are enthusiastically approved by large majorities. Any opposition to an established regime is likely to use these forms and phrases whatever its meanings and social roots may be. Under these circumstances a democratic revolution has meant the advent of freedom and decency, and the democratic creed meant a gospel of reason and betterment. To be sure, this advantage was bound to be lost and the gulf between the doctrine and the practice of democracy was bound to be discovered. But the glamour of the dawn was slow to fade.

3. It must not be forgotten that there are patterns in which the classical doctrine will actually fit facts with a sufficient degree of approximation. It provides an effective mechanism for talking and implementing decisions whether is a small and primitive society of Switzerland or a big and industrialised society of the United States. This is the case with many small and primitive societies which, as a matter of fact, served, as a prototype to the authors of that doctrine of classical theory. It may be the case with those societies also that are not primitive, provided they are not too differentiated and do not harbour any serious problems.
4. Of course, the politicians appreciate a phraseology that flatters the masses and offers an excellent opportunity not only for evading responsibility but also for crushing opponents in the name of the people.

The intrinsic merits of the democratic system cannot be denied. At the same time, some other points should be taken into account that have been stressed by the empirical theorists like role of numerous groups, factions, elites, leadership etc. so as to present a theory of democracy approximating the world of reality. However, before passing over to the study of empirical theory of democracy, this point must be stressed with amount of force that the new interpretation is a revision, not a rejection, of the classical theory of democracy. The spirit of liberalism informs both. As Macpherson says: "What the addition of democracy to the liberal state did was simply to provide constitutional channels for popular pressures, pressures to which governments would have had to yield in about the same measures anyway, merely to maintain public order and avoid revolution.

By admitting the mass of people into the competitive party system, the liberal state did not abandon its fundamental nature; it simply opened the competitive political system to all the individuals who had been created by the competitive market society. The liberal state fulfilled its own logic. In so doing, it nether destroyed nor weakened itself-, it strengthened both itself and the market society. It liberalised democracy, while democratising liberalism.

Democracy : A Contemporary Approach : The traditional theories of democracy were chiefly concerned with democracy as a form of government and they focussed on ethical justification of democracy. The contemporary theories, especially the elitist and pluralist theories, deal with the question whether and in what form the democratic principle is capable of realization in the face of recent sociological findings.

The Elitist Theories : The elitist theories were originally developed in the field of sociology to explain the behaviour of men in a social setting. Their implications in the field of politics posed a challenge to democratic theory, which was in turn revised by several thinkers. Broadly speaking, the elitist theories hold that every society consists of two categories of men: (a) the elite or the minority within a social collectivity, which exercises a preponderant influence within that collectivity; and (b) the masses or the majority which are subjected to the influence of the elite. Vilfredo Pareto (The Mind and Society. 1915-1919) and Gaetano Mosca (The Ruling Class, 1939) pointed out that there may exist, in any society, a minority of population which takes the major decisions in society. The dominant minority may or may not hold political offices but its decisions are of such wide scope and affect all aspects of the society, that they may be termed political decisions.

Mosca considered the capacity for organization as the outstanding quality of the elite while Pareto regarded intelligence and talent as their chief assets. Robert Michels, another notable elite theorist, propounded his 'iron law of oligarchy', which added a new dimension to this theory. According to Michels, the majority of human beings are apathetic, indolent and slavish and are permanently incapable of self-government. Leaders take advantage of these qualities to perpetuate themselves in power. They employ all kinds of methods-oratory, persuasion, and playing upon sentiments in order to fool them. Thus, whatever form of government is adopted, in practice it is inevitably reduced to oligarchy, that is, the rule of the chosen few. James Burnham's theory of the 'managerial revolution' and C.Wright Mills' theory of the 'power elite' are some other important versions of the elite theory.

Western and Indian Views

The elite theory had empirically demonstrated that democracy as the government of the people is incapable of realization. The champions of democracy found it difficult to repudiate the arguments advanced by the elitist theories. They therefore, sought to accommodate the elite theory in the framework of democratic theory which led to its revision. The elitist democratic theory of 'democratic elitism', was developed by several writers.

Schumpeter View : Joseph A. Schumpeter in his 'Capitalism, Socialism and Democracy' (1942) pointed out that the forms of government should be distinguished by their institutions, and especially by their methods of appointing and dismissing the supreme makers of law and policy. Accordingly, the democratic method is that institutional arrangement for arriving at political decisions in which individuals acquire the power to decide by means of a competitive struggle for the people's votes'. This implies that (a) in a democracy, political decisions are taken by the 'leadership', not by the people themselves; and (b) there is free competition among the leaders for wining people's votes. In other words, democracy is not a government of the people, nor is it a means to give effect to the will of the people; rulers comprise a different set of individuals than the common people.

The role of the people is reduced to choosing their rulers from the competing elites. The redeeming feature of democracy is that, unlike other forms of government, it does not allow political leadership to wield absolute power. It must draw up policies with an eye on gaining a larger support of the electorate than its opponents can obtain. In any case, the initiative remains in the hands of the leadership while the people simply respond to it according to their choice. The leaders trade in votes and the better combination of policies will fetch more votes by appealing to wider section of the political market.

Aron's View : Raymond Aron, in his 'Social Structure and the Ruling Class' (1950), advanced another version of the democratic theory which combines it with the elite theory. Liberal democracy, according to Aron, is characterized by a general system of checks and balances and plurality of elites. He points out that the erstwhile Soviet type society is distinguished by a 'unified citie' belonging to the Communist Party while the Western type society, that is, liberal democracy, is characterized by a divided elite, which makes it a pluralistic society. With the plurality of the elite, government becomes a business of compromise. Those in power arc well aware of their precarious position. They are not sensitive to public opinion but are also conscious of the opposition with which they have to change seats in due course. According to this theory, the initiative still remains in the hands of the elite; the masses are left to play the relatively passive role of choosing the ruling elite and to pressurize them in their functioning.

Sartori View : Giovanni Sartori, in his Democratic Theory, developed his views on democracy which are similar to those of Schumpeter in all essentials like Schumpeter, he regards democracy as a procedure in which leader's compete elections for authority to govern. Sartori argues that the role of the elite does not suggest any imperfection of democracy. On the other hand, it is the core of the democratic system. For Sartori any notion of sell-governing people is a delusion. Government is necessarily the business of competent leaders; the people exercise their right to govern only at elections when they select their leaders.

The real danger to democracy emanates not from the existence of leadership but from the absence of leadership which would result in the masses being exploited by anti-democratic counter-elites. Sartori even envisages the role of leadership in educating public opinion which is otherwise not enlightened enough.

Mannheim View : Karl Mannheim, who had initially related elite theories with Fascism and with anti-intellectualist doctrines, later championed a reconciliation between the elite theory and the democratic theory. In his 'Ideology and Utopia: An Introduction to the Sociology of Knowledge', Mannheim argued that society did not cease to be democratic by entrusting the actual shaping of policy to the elites. The people cannot directly participate in government but they can make their aspirations felt at certain intervals, and this is sufficient for democracy: 'In a democracy the governed can always act to remove their leaders or force them to take decisions in the interests of the many'. Mannheim insists on selection by merit and shortening of distance between the elite and the masses in order to ensure compatibility between elite rule and democratic government.

New Approach

The Pluralist theories of democracy fall into two categories: (a) the elitist democratic theories which regard the plurality of elites as the foundation of modern liberal democracy, such as those advocated by Raymond Aron and Karl Mannheim; and

(b) the group theories which interpret democracy as a process of bargaining among relatively autonomous groups; the existence and functioning of these groups in a democracy lends a pluralistic character to the polity.

In the U.S.A., A.F. Bentley (The Process of Government) and David Truman (The Governmental Process) in the early twentieth century interpreted democracy as a political game played by a great variety of groups. According to this interpretation, the government is the focal point for public pressure and its task is to make policies which reflect the highest common group demand. Thus, democratic society is seen as a pluralist, differentiated society where the management of public affairs is shared by a number of groups having differentiated society where the management of public affairs is shared by a number of groups having different values, sources and methods of influence. Robert Dahi in his 'Modern Political Analysis', has developed a model of the democratic process which he describes as polyarchy. This corresponds to the models developed by Bentley, Truman and Latham variously known as pluralism or the group theory. The term pluralism is used here in the sociological sense, that is, to describe the pluralistic nature of democratic society not in the philosophical sense as a political ideal, associated with the pluralistic theory of sovereignty. The pluralist theory of democracy, on the other hand, introduces pluralism for a scientific explanation of the political process.

The gist of pluralistic democracy may be given as follows: The policy-making process, however centralized it may appear in form, is, in reality, a highly decentralized process of bargaining among relatively autonomous groups. In other words, public policy is not a product of the will of the elite or the chosen few, as the elitist theories of democracy hold; on the contrary, it is an outcome of the interaction of all groups who make claims upon or express interest in that particular issue. The extent to which different groups will get their way, is a function of the strength of the groups and the intensity of their participation.

In fact, the pluralist theory calls for a revision of the democratic theory itself as well as of the elitist theories; policy-making is actually done neither by the representatives of a coherent majority, not by an autonomous and unresponsive elite, but is a product of the interaction among the groups. This theory goes to the extent of claiming that since public policy is largely an outcome of the bargaining among groups interested in a given policy issue, the form of government becomes almost insignificant. In other words, whether you adopt the democratic form of government or any other form, the result is not likely to vary significantly. In any case, public policy will reflect the interests of more organized and vocal groups in society. For instance, the interests of producers are likely to dominate over those of the consumers because the former are usually more organized, vocal and influential than the latter.

Critical Evaluation : The elitist and pluralist theories of democracy have added an empirical dimension to democratic theory, by incorporating the results of sociological theory and research. In a nutshell, (a) the elitist theories concede that policy-making in a democracy is the function of the elite while the people's role is confined to approval and rejection of particular policies made or advocated by the competing elite; and (b) the pluralist theories view policy-making in a democracy as a decentralized process characterized by the bargaining between competing autonomous groups. The pluralist theories are more optimistic than elitist theories because they repudiate the authoritarian basis of policy-making in a democracy as suggested by elitist theories. In any case, both theories arrive at conclusions which are far removed from the essence of democratic theory.

The traditional or classical theory of democracy was erected on a moral foundation; it saw democracy as a developmental process, as a matter of the improvement of mankind. The elitist-pluralist theory, or the empirical theory, on the other hand, treats democracy as a mechanism whose essential function is to maintain equilibrium. C.B.Macpherson

(Democratic Theory: Essays in Retrieval) has eloquently criticized the elitist pluralist theory of democracy. Under this theory, according to him, democracy is reduced from a humanist aspiration to a market equilibrium system. And although the new orthodox theory claims scientific neutrality, its value judgement is clear enough: whatever works, is right-that is, whatever enables the existing class-stratified society to operate without intolerable friction is best.

The classical theory had throughout treated democracy as the cry of the oppressed, their claims for recognition as equal human beings-a means by which all men could enjoy and develop their human capacities. The exponents of the elitist pluralist theory have reduced democracy to a means by which men can register their wants as political consumer in the political market. This theory identifies democracy with a static political system which takes the dominant groups in society for granted, whether they are elite groups or strong interest groups. With the acceptance of this principle of domination, the principle of equality is relegated to the background, or even considered redundant.

Men no doubt differ in their physical and intellectual capacities and other natural gifts. But the social inequalities in the present-day society do not always correspond to natural inequalities. In most cases the phenomenon of domination in society is closely related to economic disparities. The elitist-pluralist theory of democracy tries to justify the phenomenon on grounds of certain outstanding inborn qualities of persons, or on grounds of better organization of certain interests. In fact, it tends to maintain the status quo. However, if the economic structure of the society is transformed so that rewards are directly related to the quality and amount of work done, instead of the privileged position and manipulative power of certain persons, the existing system of domination will disappear and the principle of equality based on reason will reign supreme-which is the essence of democracy.

5

Dream of Gandhi

Gandhiji condemned the present state being based on violence and wanted to have an ideal state in which society will be based on non-violence and in which there will be maximum independence for the individuals. According to him, it will be a state based on village autonomy and each village enjoying maximum possible autonomy. The villages will be combined together to form a sort of loose federation based on moral strength. There will be no need and necessity for the police or military forces. Instead of centralization there will be decentralization and the way of living will be very simple.

The people shall practise self-discipline and control and everybody will be most willing to perform his duties by persuasion. The policemen and all executive officers will act as the servants of the people and national arms will very rarely be used. In jails there will be reformative houses and the criminals there will come out as reformed citizens. According to him, it will be an ideal society or Rama Rajya in which, he says. "Justice is prompt, perfect, cheap, there is freedom of worship and speech and of the press, all this is because of the reign of self-imposed law of moral restraint, such a state must be based on truth and non-violence and must consist of prosperous lofty and self contained villages and village communities."

Gandhian Democracy

Gandhiji favoured democratic system in his ideal society. He believed that it was the only compromise formula in which individual freedom was attained and at the same time the authority of the state was not altogether dispensed with. For him, in a democracy, if properly followed, there can be no difficulty in adjusting individual freedom with state authority. He, however, had a different notion about democracy. "The nearest approach to the purest anarchy would be democracy based on nonviolence-in such a state everyone is his own ruler.

He rules himself in such a manner that he is never a hindrance to his neighbour. In the ideal state, therefore, there is no political power because there is no state." He in fact, wanted to have a stateless society where the individual will be an end and his self-realization the sole object. He believed that in a stateless society there will be proper adjustment' between law, freedom and social restraint on the basis of dharma. He felt that dislocation came only because state wanted to use violent means which were not acceptable to the people and this dislocation could be properly adjusted by means of dharma which could bound all in a harmonious social order. Not only this but he felt that evil of the present political order was that the people care more for rights than duties. In his ideal stateless society the people should not demand rights but perform their duties. Their only right is proper performance of duties.

Decentralisation of Economic and Political Power : In his ideal society, Gandhiji believed that there should be both economic as well as political decentralization. By political decentralization he meant that the state authority should be reduced to the minimum, and maximum authority should be given to the village community. In other words he meant Panchayat Raj. For him, the best Government was one which governed the least. In the economic field by decentralization he meant abolition of large-scale industry and their replacement by cottage industry He felt that many of our international tensions and problems could be solved if this very basic principle of economic decentralization was adopted in which one felt satisfied with what one produced. He, therefore, pleaded Swadeshi or the use of' Khadi as the first step.

He felt that it was only through the system of cottage industries that spiritual values would be properly understood and appreciated. In his own words, "Decentralization of political and economic power provides for the working of democracy based upon individual freedom and initiative and for the individual being allowed to participate in the government of his country. It would also regulate automatically both the production and distribution of the commodities necessary to human life; and both the production and the consumption of these would be in the same locality rather than having production concentrated in particular areas only, thus necessitating regulations for the distribution of products and wealth Decentralization would also bring about the regulation of the use of machinery."

Promoting Ancestral Professions : Gandhiji's ideal state had also another significant feature. In his ideal state each one will stick to his ancestral profession unless there were very sound reasons for changing that. But he very clearly made the people understand that all professions will be equally respected and there will be no superiority or inferiority of profession. All will be given more or less equal wages for the professions which were performed by the individuals. It will not be on caste system but due to love for work which will become a part of life of the family. Thus in his system there will be equal wages for work and no unhealthy competition for changing from one profession to another. He believed that if the system was followed, generations will be benefitted because these will have at their command the accumulated knowledge of previous generations. Through specialised knowledge both the individual and the community, will be benefited.

Minimum Possession of Wealth : In his ideal society Gandhiji said everyone will keep only what was required by him for his day-to-day life. No one will keep unnecessarily accumulated wealth or surplus goods. He felt that the rich should have only what was their minimum basic necessity and rest of the wealth they should distribute among the poor and deserving. He, however, pleaded that it was not at all justified to use force for getting surplus wealth from the rich but the effective method was that of persuasion. The consciousness and sense of justice of the rich should be aroused and they should themselves feel that they had no justification in keeping surplus wealth with them. In other words the rich should act as trustees of the surplus wealth which they had with them. For him, if such an attitude was adopted there would be no heart-burning and classless society would be established without use of any violence or force.

In his own words, "The rich man would be left in possession of his wealth of which he would use what he reasonably required for his personal needs, for the remainder he would act as a trustee, using it for the benefit of society. But if the rich do not become the guardians of the poor what is to be done? The only right and infallible solution to this problem lies in non-violence, non-co-operation and civil disobedience." Gandhiji also believes that in an ideal society everyone should work at least to the extent to which he eats. For him, intellectual labour was no substitute for manual labour and as such even those engaged in intellectual activities should perform manual labour. He also felt that if everyone did some manual labour there will be no wastage of man-power and the world will be far happier than what it is today. He has gone to the extent of saying that this will help in eliminating class distinctions and there will be no distinction between the rich and the poor. There will be dignity of labour and national production everywhere will go up.

Idea of Trusteeship : Gandhi ji believed that everyone who owns a capital should feel that he is a trustee of the capital, which belongs to the society as a whole. The people should realise that they should possess only that much of capital and property which is needed by them. No one should use capital disregard of collective social interests. For him difference between the minimum and maximum wages should be reasonable. Gandhiji, therefore, said that character of production will be determined by social necessity. He said that everyone should have balanced diet, a good house to live, facility for education and adequate medical relief. Every one should believe that everything belonged to God. There was no idea in appropriating money from capitalists to the workers, if the former behaved properly and in collective social interest. He was opposed to class antagonism, but instead promoted class collaboration and co-ordination.

An Assessment : Gandhiji's ideas have been much criticised on the ground that these are not progressive. The critics have gone to the extent of saying that his plea for cottage industries is most outdated. If that is accepted, the nations shall not be in a position to take advantage of modern scientific discoveries. They have also pleaded that his plea for Varna Vyavastha is also not based on scientific principles because everyone should be allowed to practice a profession of his choice and should not be compelled to adopt his ancestral profession. It is also said that the rich who have accumulated wealth after squeezing the blood of the poor and also exploiting vast majority of the population cannot give up their wealth simply by persuasion. They criticised him by saying that history is a witness that the rich have never agreed by persuasion but have always given concession after they have been forced to do so. The critics also feel that Gandhiji's overstressing on manual labour is not desirable. Atleast those who are engaged in scientific, cultural or intellectual activities should have been exempted.

But the critics have not done much justification to Gandhian philosophy. No doubt there is some valid justification in the points of criticism advanced by these critics but virtually Gandhiji pleaded what had already been said by many others.

His ideas about decentralization of state authority had long before been preached by the Pluralists or Syndicalists. Similarly we find that Gandhiji fully well realised the appetite of man for utilisation of modern scientific discoveries and thus allowed them to be used till a time when the man had fully established himself and was ready to work in a stateless society of his ideas. His plea for Panchayat Raj or village federation is more or less on the ideas propagated by Laski, Cole and Huxley. Similarly the use of *Swadeshi* or that of national self-sufficiency is appreciated and followed by many nations of the world. Equally there is justification for his Plea for Varna *Vyavastha* under the condition that all shall have equal status in the society with almost equal payment and no superiority or inferiority complex. If his ideas about Manual labour are properly appreciated and followed there are valid reasons to believe that proper utilisation of man-power can enrich the universe much more than what it is today.

The intellectual workers can do manual labour as a hobby and thus can contribute in national production. No doubt the rich cannot normally be persuaded to act as trustees of surplus wealth but that is always better than force. Force can be used as the last method but not as the first weapon for achieving the object.

Therefore, it is safe to conclude that Gandhian ideas are practicable though, it requires patience and practice to follow them in our actual life. Once the basis are allowed and established there will be little difficulty in building the superstructure of a society which will really be casteless and classless.

Religious Philosophy

Gandhiji was one of those political thinkers who believed that religion and politics must go hand in hand. For him, both could not be separated from each other and in healthy politics it was essential that religion must be introduced in it. Similarly he also had faith in the existence of God and for him for a fearless and bold life it was essential that God should be feared. For him, God was truth and love.

Gandhiji used to say that religion is as good a part of politics as diplomacy or any other similar institution. For him, those who believed that religion should be separated from politics, were miserably mistaken. He said that most of the politician come forward pleading that they are not religious whereas actually they have faith in some kind of religion. On the other hand, I come forward saying that I have complete faith in religion and I do not conceal my deep faith that religion was essential for promoting morality and he used to say, "Most religious man I have met are politicians in disguise. I however, wear the guise of a politician but I am at heart a religious man". It was wrong to believe that the life of a man can be divided and one aspect separated from the other. In his own words, "The whole gamut of man's activities constitutes an indivisible whole; you cannot divide social, economic, political and purely religious work into water-tight compartments. I do not know religion apart from human activities. It provides a moral basis to all activities which they would otherwise lack reducing life to a maze of sound and fury signifying nothing." In this opinion without religion politics will be a dirty, underhand and a shameful game. Religion alone can bring morality in politics. It is though good means that good results can be achieved and religion is a step forward for good means. He said that while achieving ends means should not be ignored.

Concept of Universal Religion : Gandhiji, however, had a different conception about religion. For him, his religion was neither that of the Hindus nor of the Muslims nor any other communal religion but on the other hand he meant a universal religion which sought truth and pleaded for help to the helpless. It was a religion which was based on social justice and promoted brotherhood, truth and happiness. It should be a religion which should stand for equality of all religions and should be broad-based enough to adjust itself to all good qualities of all religions and thus should not be narrow in outlook but above all narrow conceptions. He said, "Let me explain what I meant by religion. It is not the Hindu religion which I certainly prize above all other religions, but it is the religion which transcedents Hinduism, which changes one's very nature, which binds upon indissolubly to the truth within and which ever purifies. It is a permanent element in human nature which counts no cost too great in order to find full expressions." At another place he himself said, "My religion is based on truth and non-violence is the means of realising Him."

Gandhiji on God : Gandhiji had full faith in the existence of God and pleaded that people should have faith in Him. It is through love for God that people can become fearless and instead of hatred they begin to love mankind. He, however, believed that God was something mysterious. It is something which we can only feel but cannot know. It is conscience, truth and love. God and truth are one and the same thing. *In* his own words, "God is ethics and morality. God is fearless. God is source of life ana light and yet he is above and beyond all these. God is conscience. He is even the Atheism of the Atheist. He transcendents speech and reason. He is a personal God to those who need his touch. He is the purest essence. He simply is to those who have faith." He used to say that those who have faith in God cannot be subjected to any injustice. Faith in God emboldens a man and a true Satyagrahi need not fear anybody on earth. He begins to realise value of brotherhood and love.

We may thus conclude Gandhiji's views about religion and God by saying that he had great love for both these ideas but his views in this regard were broader than what is generally understood by religion or God. For him, Ram and Rahim were two names of the same Creator and both preached love, truth and brotherhood. If both these views are taken in their true sense then alone politics can become a very healthy and interesting game worthy of participation by those who wish to make politics a profession.

Gandhiji was one of those political thinkers who believed that self-sacrifice, satyagrah or non-cooperation could bow even the mightiest empires in the world. For him to shake the empire and to check violence only a true satyagrahi or noncooperation fighter was the most powerful authority. He believed that violence brings with it hatred and a spirit of taking revenge whereas in non-violence there was no such thing. He suggested that satyagrah was as a powerful weapon for fighting against a powerful enemy.

New Form of Agitation

Satyagraha: A Powerful Weapon : According to Gandhian philosophy satyagrah was the most powerful weapon for fighting against imperialism or a powerful enemy. By satyagraha he meant adhering to truth under all circumstances. A true satyagrahi should believe in God and ahimsa. For Gandhiji violence is untruth while non-violence truth. By ahimsa he also meant that no one should be injured and there should be no hatred in thought, speech and action. According to him, a true non-violent fighter hates evil and leaves his opponent because for him it is not the man but the institution which is to be hated. A true non-violent fighter or a satyagrahi is bound to leave credit for himself in the minds of the others and leaves nothing bitter behind him. General Smuts, once said to Gandhiji, "I often wish that you took to violence like the English strikers and I think we would know at once how to dispose of you. But you will not injure even the enemy. You desire victory by self-suffering alone and never transgress your self-imposed limits of courtesy and chivalry. And that is what reduces us to sheer helplessness."

Satyagraha and Passive Resistance Differences : For Gandhiji it was futile to think that many weapons were needed to win over an enemy. An enemy can only be won by love and affection. *In* his own words, "My non-violence does not admit running away from danger and leaving dear ones unprotected. Not knowing the stuff of rich non-violence is made, many have honestly believed that running away from danger every time was a virtue compared to offering resistance, specially when it was fraught with danger to one's love. As a teacher of non-violence, 1 must, as far as it is possible for me, guard against such an unmanly belief." For him, Ahimsa had deep bearing not on body but on soul. Not the evil doer but evil should alone be hated. A satyagrahi should have high ideals. He should not confuse satyagrah with passive resistance because whereas a passive resistor tries to put his opponents in an embarrassing position, a satyagrahi extends affection and love to his opponent to convince him about his demands. A satyagrah can be in various forms namely

(a) *Non-cooperation* : By non-cooperation Gandhiji meant that those who were doing injustice or oppressing should be non-co-operated. They should not be given any support from any corner and the oppressor should feel himself alone. It is in such a situation alone that an oppressor will be obliged to listen patiently to the demands of the opponent. It requires courage and self-sacrifice because it is a weapon in which a non-cooperator is also required to make sacrifices and if he is not prepared for them, he cannot reach the goal. A non co-operator should have moral strength to face all odds and should have so much moral strength that the opponent feels convinced about it.

(b) *Civil Resistance* : For Gandhiji another method of fighting against a powerful enemy was that of civil resistance. He was opposed to armed resistance but what he pleaded for was that the people should not obey unjust and anti-social laws. The people should be bold enough to declare their intention to disobey cruel and unjust laws. They should openly defy such orders and should be ready to go behind the bars and suffer such cruelties as the oppressor might inflict upon them but should carry on the struggle till the time the unjust law was abrogated and replaced by a just law.

(c) *Strike* : According to Gandhiji strike was another weapon for fighting against the oppressor. He pleaded that the workers should organise themselves in each industry to fight against the industrialists. He, however, made it clear that such organisations should only aim at getting their rights and equal status and should not have hostility against the capitalists. He favoured the idea of strikes, if these were organised on nonviolence. He felt that strike was an effective instrument if it did not aim at destruction and sabotage. The workers must realise that machinery and wealth are national property and owner is only the custodian of national wealth. The destruction of machinery was unhealthy and should not be justified on any grounds.

(d) *Fasting* : Gandhiji felt that the sense of the persons in power can most effectively be touched by fasting but fasting person should be highly elevated while observing this method. Fasting is a success only when the person going on fact is spiritually disciplined and true to his cause. An ordinary person cannot achieve his object but will be a failure. He, therefore felt that fasting, if taken in its real spirit, is bound to touch the better sense of the opponent.

(e) *Hijrat* : According to Gandhiji if a person cannot tolerate injustice of the oppressor and also feels that he has not the power to become a good Satyagrahi, for him, the best method was that of *Hijrat* or leaving one's ancestral place. In other words he should not reconcile himself to injustice but should leave the state of such an oppressor. Gandhiji felt that it was not weakness but required great strength. For him it was not an ordinary thing to leave one's ancestral place where one was born, brought up and the land with which he had affection. His associations with his country, relatives and friends will be completely broken and that step required boldness which only a few could take.

Application of Ideas

For quite some time it was considered that Gandhian philosophy and methods of struggle could not be put into actual practice and provided no practical solution against oppression. But as the time has passed these methods have established their effectiveness and we find that through these methods Gandhi ji was in a position to relieve Indians from their miseries in South Africa and also could win freedom for India from their miseries in mightiest empire. These methods, however, require proper disciplining and training of mind, which if one has there is no doubt about the justification of these methods for fighting against any oppression. Therefore, to doubt the effectiveness of these methods is not justified at all.

Gandhiji came on the political scene in India after his return from South Africa and within no time he caught the imagination of the people. He won freedom for India and was in a position to oblige the mightiest colonial power in the world to leave our land but without any hatred or ill-will. He stood for a stateless and classless society based on the system of decentralization and Panchayati Raj. He was basically very close to communist philosophy and thus some of the thinkers have said about him that 'Gandhism is nothing else but communism minus violence.' In the following paragraphs we shall examine the truth of this statement.

6

Gandhi's Philosophy

Gandhian Political Ideologies : Gandhism political philosophy has ushered in a new era in the history of political thought. It made the world believe that even the greatest political problems could be solved only by personal sacrifices and making the opponent realise the excesses and mistakes committed by him. Under it personal sacrifice in the right direction was far more effective a weapon than any other method for fighting against the opponent. For Gandhiji, non-violence or ahimsa was the most suitable reply for violence and force. For him, non-violence was a creed as well a faith.

Gandhiji wanted to establish an ideal society in which Panchayati Raj based on real democratic principles will flourish. He felt that democracy could not come from above but must start from down below and go upward. In Gandhism, religion has a definite place and Gandhiji did not wish to separate religion from politics. In his own words, "It is the permanent element and human nature which counts no cost too great in order to find full expression and which leaves the soul beyond restless until it has found itself known its maker and appreciated the true correspondence between maker and himself."

In his economic ideals, he was a socialist but of a different nature. He did not believe that force should be used to snatch superfluous wealth from the rich for distribution among the poor but he appealed to the capitalists that they themselves should give their wealth to the community and the poor so that it could be put to proper He followed the ideals of persuading the enemy, rather than hating them. For him it was not the man but the institution which was bad and as such the former and not the latter should be hated. Gandhism believes in the use of pure Swadeshi rather than Videshi. He believed in the policy on non-cooperation, civil resistance, strikes, gain on fast and even migrating to another country as weapons against the opponent for obliging him to accept the legitimate demands of the oppressed.

Gandhism is not communism minus violence as some of the thinkers make us believe. Both, of course, believe in a classless society and also believe that capital is a theft but they do not go beyond that. The Marxists believe in the use of force whereas in Gandhism force has no place. Similarly in Marxism end justifies the means whereas Gandhism believes that right means should be used to get lasting ends.

An Ideal Life

Mohan Das Karam Chand Gandhi was born on 2nd October 1869 at Porebunder in Kathiawar. His father was Dewan of the State and mother, a devoted religious lady. He was married at the early age of 12. He was a shy and mediocre student but very obedient and punctual. He could impress his teachers by his shyness and obedience. It was at the age of 19 that he was sent to England with a vow neither to touch wine nor woman nor eat meat there. It was, of course, a very difficult task not suited to his temperament and, therefore, decided to remain an Indian gentleman. Under the influence of his religious mother he spent quite a lot of his time in studying Bhagwat Gita and many other religious books. Gandhiji's life career can broadly be divided into three stages namely.

1. Before his return to India from South Africa;
2. From 1921 to 1947; and
3. From 15th August, 1947 to 30th January, 1948.

During the first period of his career he practised the ideals which he wished to follow in his subsequent life. Till then he was not quite well-known to Indian multitudes. He had then not come to the fore-front to mould the thought and imagination of the people. During the second period of his life career he put into actual practice what he had so far been practising. By this time due to his work in South Africa he had earned great reputation and Indian masses were most willing to extend their hand of co-operation to him. It was during this period that he dominated the whole political life of India.

It was his one-man guidance which was most valuable and most willingly responded to by the multitudes in India. It was also during this period that he successfully guided India to the path of freedom and achieved that with minimum of bloodshed. He forced one of the most powerful colonial and imperial powers in the world to leave the soil of India with no ill-will or bitter feelings.

During the third phase of his life Mahatma Gandhi straggled to end that hatred which the partition of the country had brought with it between the two manor Indian communities, namely the Hindus and the Muslims. As usual he preached the noble cause of Hindus-Muslim unity and was assassinated while fighting for this ideal cause. His death was lamented all over the world and glowing tributes were paid to him after he was no more to guide India in her future development.

First Phase of Gandhiji's Life : On his return from England Mahatma Gandhi started his practice at Rajkot but subsequently he shifted to Bombay. It appears that Nature had destined him for a very noble cause and soon an opportunity came when for a professional work he had to go to South Africa on behalf of a Muslim firm. Though he had no intention of stay there and had planned to come back soon after his business commitment was over yet due to the pitiable conditions of Indians of all communities there, he had to prolong his stay even after he had finished his commitment there. He saw with great dissatisfaction the discriminatory treatment being meted out to Indians. He decided to struggle for legal equality for his countrymen.

But before he could give a call to his people he himself practised the method of Satyagraha, inner purification and self-discipline. He had to labour hard for successfully implementing this new weapon on a foreign soil but credit goes to him for successfully practising them in his future struggle.

He called upon the Indians there to disobey all discriminatory laws. He asked the people to disregard Asiatic Registration Act which required all Asiatics to give their thumb impression and to register themselves. He even led a deputation to England but found that only Satyagraha could solve the problem. Thousands were sent to jails and Gandhiji was the leader of all this movement. Ultimately his determination won and justice prevailed over injustice. All discriminatory laws were repealed and Gandhiji was successful in his noble mission.

Second Phase of Gandhiji's Life : In 1914 Gandhiji returned to India with all honour that he had won during his 20 years stay in south-Africa and decided to guide Indian political life. It goes to his wisdom that he did not immediately plunge into Indian politics and was rightly advised to listen more and speakless. After fully assessing the situation in India he decided to enter Indian politics. First of all he was a very strong supporter of the British sense of justice and said, "I discovered that the British Empire had certain ideals with which I have fallen in love and one of those ideals is that every subject of this British Empire has the freest scope for his energies and honour and whatever he thinks is due to his conscience. And I have found that it is possible for him to be governed least under the British Empire. He even supported the cause of

Indians contributing their maximum in men, money and material in British army in the First World War.

He, however, justified his action that an enemy in danger and difficulty should not be embarrassed in any way. He had so much love for British sense of justice that in their support in the First World War he organised an ambulance corps in London. In 1918 he wrote to the Viceroy, "If I could make my countrymen retrace their steps, I would make them withdraw all Congress resolutions and not whisper Home Rule or responsible Government during the pendency of the war. I would make India hand over all her able bodies sons as a sacrifice to the empire at this critical moment; and I know that India by this very act, would become the most favoured partner and racial distinctions would become a thing of the past."

It was, however, in 1920 that his confidence in British sense of justice was rudely shaken and he became a non-co-operator. After the close of the war when India was expecting better treatment and greater share in the running of the administration, the country was given the Rowlatt Act followed by a massacre at Jallianwala Bagh and the constitutionally fighting country was given the most unsatisfactory reforms known as Montague-Chelmsford Reforms. Above all, the Muslims of India had also been betrayed and the integrity of Khilafat in Europe was not maintained. He himself has written that, "Event that have happened during the past month have confirmed me in the opinion that the imperial Government have acted in the khilafat matter in an unscrupulous, immoral and unjust manner, and have been moving from wrong to-wrong in order to defend their immorality. I can retain neither respect nor affection for such a Government.

Your Excellency's light hearted treatment of official crime, your exhorbation of Sir Michael O. Dwyer, Mr. Montague's despatch and above all the shameful ignorance of Punjab events and the callous disregard of the feelings of the Indians betrayed by the House of Lords, have filled my greatest misgivings regarding the future of the empire, have estranged me completely from the present Government and have disabled me from rendering, as I have hitherto whole heartedly rendered, my total co-operation."

After having completely lost his faith in British impartiality Gandhiji entered Indian politics with his full vigour and strength. He was determined to win India's freedom through his weapon of non-violence and passive resistance which he had successfully practised in South Africa. He also felt that Hindu-Muslim unity was most essential for Indian freedom and decided to struggle for it as well. In 1924 a special meeting of the Congress was organised in which Gandhi ji said, "Non-violence is the first article of my faith and it is the last article of my faith but I had to make my choice ; I had either to submit to a system which I considered has done irreparable harm to my country, or incur the risk of the mad fury of my people bursting forth when they understood the truth from my lips." Gandhiji, however, had to give up his experiment when Chauri Chaura incident took place in U.P. where a few constables were burnt alive and this shocked his faith in the people. In this way, Gandhiji's first attempt to lead the nation to freedom through non-violence was not a success to the expected extent.

Gradually, Gandhiji took the country with him towards independence and he dominated the whole Indian political life. He was put behind the bars but nothing deterred him from his decided path. In 1931 he went to London as the sole representative of Indian National Congress but he found that the conference was in no mood to give freedom to India. He also found that disruptive elements were knowingly being introduced on the conference table with certain motives to slow the progress', of India's winning freedom. In 1942 Gandhiji started his famous Quit India movement which opened the eyes of the Britishers and made the rulers realize that India was now not going to tolerate any injustice. Gandhiji was the main moving force behind the Congress when subsequent negotiations with the British delegations, including the Cripps

Mission Plan, Wavell Plan, Cabinet Mission Plan or the Mountbatten Mission Plan were put forth before India. It was his efforts and under his guidance that Indian National Congress could successfully negotiate with one of the world's greatest imperialist powers.

Gandhiji was, however, much shocked to learn that the Hindus and the Muslims were fighting with each other on political issues. He could easily see that a great sacrifice was required to introduce harmony and end communal fury and hatre between the two communities which the political leaders had implanted in the minds of the people during all these years.

The hatred which expressed itself in Noakhali where there was a slaughter of Hindus and events in Bihar where there was some reaction against the Muslims, shocked Gandhiji. He went at both the places and decided to go on fast until the people of both the communities decided to discard communal hatred as a political weapon. Similarly on September 7, 1947 there were riots in Delhi and Gandhiji had to adopt the same method. The response was very encouraging.

Third Phase of Mahatma Gandhiji's Life : It is unfortunate that the father of the nation, who so much sacrificed for, guided so ably the nation, could not reap the fruits of independence He could hardly breathe for a few months in free India when his end came. He started with the very basis assumption that the Hindus and the Muslims must live together as brethren for the prosperity of India. He, therefore, demanded that all mosques which had been converted into temples or where people had begun to reside after migration from Pakistan should be returned to the Muslims. He also pleaded that a sum of Rs. 55 crones, due to Pakistan, should be given to that country. It is unfortunate that some of the orthodox Hindus could not understand the lofty ideal behind Gandhiji's idea and on 30th January, 1948 when he was going to attend a prayer meeting, an orthodox Hindu, Nathu Ram God say, shot him dead.

Gandhiji's death shocked many. He was, perhaps, the first non-official citizen of a country whose death was mourned even by U.N.O. High tributes were paid to him on his death and he is still remembered and will always be remembered for the ideals which he preached. In the words of Naginder Nath Gupta, "There were willing hearts in India waiting for his call and they at once realised the nature of struggle that lay ahead of them. Since then the struggle of national freedom in India has grown ever wider and today it comprehends the entire nation, it has been a glorious record, which is being added day after day, of sacrifice and suffering of women that vied with men in offering themselves as sacrifices at the altar of liberty and that was only due to Mahatma Gandhiji." According to Sir Stafford Cripps, "There has been no greater spiritual leader in the world in our own times than Mahatma Gandhi." Acharya Kripalani said about Gandhiji, "Mahatma is more right when he is wrong than we are when we are right."

Dr. Rajendra Prasad said, "Mahatma Gandhi's movement operated both horizontally and vertically. He took up causes which were not entirely political but which touched very intimately the life of large masses of people." Dr. Stanley Jones said about Mahatma Gandhiji, "He is stronger in death than he was in life. Millions around in the world are now interested in the Mahatma and his ideas - millions who would have only given him a passing glance had he not died for his ideals-martyr for the things for which he lived." Leon Blum, a French socialist, wrote about him, "I never saw Gandhi, I do not know his language, I never set foot in his country and yet I feel the same sorrow as if I had lost some one near and dear. The whole world has been plunged into mourning by the death of this extraordinary man." According to Lord Halifax, "I suppose there could be few men in all history who by their personal character and examples have so deeply influenced the thought of their generation."

Before we actually discuss the basic principles of Gandhian philosophy, it is interesting to discuss whether there is any separate 'ism' as Gandhism. Normally by 'ism' we understand a set philosophy given and preached through a set of literature readily available to the masses. We also believe that these basic ideas have been brought close together and adjusted in such a fashion that these do not contradict each other. If this is the sole test of a 'separate `ism', perhaps few might like to say that Gandhism does not exist at all. The critics will try to plead that Gandhiji in many of his movements the course of action was not always predetermined.

In fact, in Gandhism one is bound to find that it was an experiment which was being carried out constantly and as such his whole philosophy was on an experimental basis only this, but like an ,ism' Gandhian philosophy cannot be fully appreciated on the basis of theory but one is obliged to have practical knowledge of the Gandhian way of life. Not only this but like a philosopher Gandhiji did not coin or originate new ideas. Even Gandhiji himself used to say that "I am not giving any new `ism'." In his own words, "There is no such thing as Gandhism and I do not claim to have originated any new principle or doctrine. I have simply tried in my own way to apply the eternal truths to our daily life and problems.

The things I have formed and conclusions I have arrived at, are not final. I may change them homely. I have nothing to teach to the world. Truth and non-violence are as old as hills. All I have done is to try experiments in both on as vast a scale as I could do. In doing so I have sometimes erred and learnt by my errors ; well, of my philosophy, if it might be called by that pretentious name is done in what I have said, you will not call it Gandhism ; there is no ism about it."

But all that does not appear to be very convincing to say that Gandhism was not an 'ism' at all. Subsequent study will reveal that Gandhiji had certain basic principles of his philosophy which had no contradictions but were consistent. The ideas of noncooperation and non-violence were coined by him. Similarly he gave a new technique of fighting against the powerful nations. It was his basic idea which was given for the first time that a true and non-violent individual has nothing to fear even from a mighty empire based on violence, force and having all government authority under its control. He tried to see that these basic principles were consistently followed. His philosophy has come to stay and is being preached and made available to the modern generation in a very systematic form. It shall, therefore, be much safe to say that there is a separate Gandhism. If Gandhiji himself said that there was no separate Gandhism that was only due to his greatness.

Philosophy of the Mahatma

Gandhiji came on the scene of India and soon caught the imagination of the masses. His philosophy was very simple. He drew his philosophy from different sources. For Gandhiji most important source of inspiration was Bhagwat Gita. He found solution to every problem in Gita. He learnt from Gita that one should act for getting the results.

Gita in actual life, thus made him a man of action. From Gita he also picked up the philosophy or self-control, which he followed throughout his life. Again it was Gita that gave him the philosophy that truth was infallible and gives everyone courage and strength, even against the most powerful enemy. It is truth which gives man even mindedness and a balanced thinking and relieves from worries and pressures of life. It makes life ideal and happy.

From Buddhism and Jainism, Gandhiji picked up the philosophy of non-violence. He was also influenced by Rukin's 'Unto this Last.' It was from here that he learnt that only such economy was good which looked after the welfare of all. Then he learnt that all had equal right to earn their livelihood and life of a worker is both worth living and enjoying.

On Gandhiji influence of Tolstoy was in no way less. In was from him that he learnt that tyrannical government should be refused to be obeyed. He expounded the philosophy of non-resistance on this very basis.

In this way, Gandhian philosophy drew its inspiration not from one but from many sources and when it came out in practical shape from Gandhiji, it was a sound composite philosophy, which stood the test of time even against the mightiest empire of the world, in India's freedom struggle.

Gandhiji was a practical thinker and as such it has rightly been said about him that he was a great Karmayogi. It was his faith that theory should follow the practice and this he applied while discussing the future of his state. He left very much to the practice and as such he only gave broad outlines of the society which he wanted to have at any future date.

Gandhian View of State

Gandhiji firmly believed that the present state was unwanted because it was a highly centralized organization. Not only this, he even condemned the state because it was based on force and as such believed that every thing should be achieved only by forceful methods. For him the state has many evils and was deeply rooted in violence. Since it is based on force and is centralized it is bound to crush individual freedom. Gandhiji felt that the modern state was becoming an end in itself but it was forgetting that an individual was an end while state was only means to an end. He attached greatest significance to individual than to the state.

Critical View

Gandhiji felt that in the present set-up state authority had been centralized and the power passed on a few individuals and there was every danger that such power might be misused. As early as in 1931 he wrote, "To me political power is not an end but one of the means enabling the people to better their condition in every department of life. Political power means capacity to regulate national life through national representatives. If national life become so perfect as to become self-regulated, no representation is necessary.

There is then a state of enlightened anarchy. In such a state every one is his own ruler. He rules himself in such a manner that he is never a hindrance to his neighbour." He also felt that a stage must come when the authority of the state small not be wanted and it will change its very character and then instead of centralization it will pass on to decentralization. That decentralized state will be the real democracy based on most democratic principles. To quote him again, "I look upon an increase in the power of the state with greatest fear, because although while apparently doing good by minimising exploitation, it does the greatest harm to mankind by destroying individuality which lies at the root of all progress. We know of so many cases where men have adopted trusteeship but nowhere has the state really lived for the power. The state represents violence in a concentrated and organized form."

7

Role of Communism

A close study of Gandhian philosophy is bound to reveal that Gandhism and Communism agree on some basic principles. For example both Gandhiji and Karl Marx wanted to have a classless society in which there would be no distinction between the rich and the poor and everyone would be appreciated by the qualities which he possessed. For them South class consciousness had created rift in the society and resulted in exploitation of the poor by the rich. Similarly, both believed that state was based on violence and in its present form it had no justification to exist.

Both even went to the extent of saying that it was an evil institution and Karl Marx believed that ultimately it was bound to wither away. Not only this, but both had identical views about capital. For both of them, capital was a theft and a few people in the society had no right whatsoever to hold the money with them and thus deny their use for collective welfare. The capital should be used for social welfare and those who possessed money should be obliged to part with that and they should work in the spirit that they were only the trustees of the wealth which belongs to the nation as a whole.

Karl Marx and Gandhiji both had a very soft corner for the down-trodden and the poor. Karl Marx used to say that history of hitherto existing struggle is that of class struggle in which the labourers and the poor are being constantly exploited by the rich who control the means of production. He therefore, gave the slogan workers of the world unite and it is in that unity alone that the depressed classes will come up and have their soft corner for the downtrodden and low castes in the society. According to him the so called scheduled castes are a part of our society. He lived and worked among them and for them.

Through his 'Harijan' he tried to plead their cause vigorously and saw that in all walks of life they were given due representation. Similarly both believed in the concept of social equality meaning thereby that all should be given equal opportunities for getting justice and the doors of judiciary should not be closed on a particular class simply because they could not afford to purchase justice. He thus stood to preach with Marx that there should be political and economic equality.

No doubt prima facie there is much similarity between Gandhism and communism but there is a vast difference between the two. Gandhi ji had deep faith in religion and believed that politics without religion was barren and both should work side by side. It is religion which brings life to politics. He himself, used to say that "I am first a religious man then a political man." On the other hand. Marx believed that religion had no place in politics and both should be separated from each other. For him religion was opium for the people and also a method for making the people fatalist. He felt that it was a method through which the capitalists tried to contend the poor and he discarded religion altogether. Similarly we find that Gandhiji had faith in the existence of God which, he said, was a mysterious force but all-powerful and was guiding our affairs. On the other hand, Marx did not believe at all in the existence of God and for him man was the architect of his own fate and there was no heavenly power to guide the destiny of man.

Again, we find that Gandhian political philosophy was based on spiritualism whereas Marxian philosophy was based on materialism. For Marx, man was only means to an end whereas for Gandhi ji man was an end in itself. Both, therefore, had an altogether different approach to the problem of individual liberty. For Marx State is above everything else whereas for Gandhiji state stands for realization of man's personality. We also find that Marx stood to take the fullest advantages of discoveries and inventions of science. He therefore, pleaded that there should be dependence on large-scale industrialization. On the contrary, Gandhiji pleaded for decentralization and believed that there should be the system of cottage industries and modern large-scale industry should exist only as an interim measure till the man was ready to discard this.

Gandhiji believed in right means for having a lasting and durable end. For him proper means were necessary for proper ends. If the means are not good, ends cannot be good. He, therefore, stressed on means saying that if proper means were followed, good ends would automatically be achieved. On the other hand, Marx did not believe in this idea. For him ends justified the means and, therefore, our aim should be to achieve ends, no matter whether means were just or unjust. We also find that Gandhiji had a different view about the evil-doer and the evil. For him one should hate the evil and not the evil-doer, because evil-doer always is only an instrument and has been forced to commit crime under circumstances created by the society. He, therefore, believed that it was capital and not the capitalist, which should be hated. On the contrary Marx believed that both the evil and evil-doer should be hated. He, therefore, hated both the capital and capitalist. In his society there was no place for capitalists because they represent an evil institution and as long as they exist, social justice cannot be achieved.

Gandhiji was a very strong and ardent believer of non-violence. For him one should be non-violent both in thought, speech and action. For him, even if the property earned by a particular individual is to be snatched that should be by persuasion only and not by forced. For Gandhiji *ahimsa*, was not only a method of struggle but creed. On the contrary Marx believed that there was no harm in using violence. No doubt, he suggested that violence should not be used as a primary method for securing the ends, but for all purposes he felt, that unless force was used there was no possibility of setting the modern evil institutions of state and capitalism on proper lines.

Marx, therefore, stressed on violence rather than non-violence. We also find that Gandhian philosophy does not believe in embarrassing the opponent but what Gandhiji intended was that the opponent should be made to realise his mistake. On the other hand, Marx believed that the enemy should be put in a most embarrassing position so that he is obliged to agree to the demands put to him.

We can, therefore, safely conclude that Gandhism is not Communism minus violence but it is something beyond that. Both prima facie agree on certain principles but as they proceed the differences also widen up. It is quite evident that they do not agree at all on the means for achieving the ends set forth by them. Gandhian philosophy which is combination of politics with religion has made Gandhiji one of the most important personalities of our modern age.

Mahatma Gandhi was one of the most dynamic personalities of our times who moulded the very outlook of the world. His greatness, however, is not for his winning the freedom for India or that he was the pioneer of non-violence and non-cooperation movement but it was something more than that. He contributed both in India and to the cause of world at large. It is his many sided contribution that gave him the title of Mahatma and on whose death even the U.N.O covered its flag.

Role in India

Gandhiji's contribution to Indian political thought was, of course, immense. It was through him and through his efforts that the national movement in India changed its very character. He struggled hard in India to see that the two great communities, namely the Hindus and the Muslims, live together like brethren forgetting all their differences. He also struggled to see that all minorities got their differences. He also struggled to see that all minorities got their due and the majority did not ride rough shod over´the minorities. We also find that he took up the cause of down-trodden and hard-pressed and saw that India became a casteless society in which there was no question of high and low. He tried to see that there was dignity of labour for all, and all got equal wages for equal work. He also found that as long as the poor used intoxicating goods, they could not get their due status in the society. This made him plead for total prohibition all over India. Not only this but he preached the use of swadeshi goods to relieve India of economic dependence. Similarly he had a hand on the pulse of the nation and pleaded the system of decentralization and *Panchayati Raj* which alone, in his opinion, could give real democracy to a big country like India. He introduced Wardha Scheme of education which was more utilitarian than the system of education preached by the British government.

Role in World

But his contribution is not to India alone In fact tie was for the whole world. He was the person who for the first time believed and preached that religion and politics must go hand in hand. He boldly said that unless that was done politics could not become a healthy game. Again we find that he laid emphasis on truth and proper means for achieving right ends. In the words of Lord Boyd Orr, "Truth and truth is attained by contemplation; justice for all men, freedom for all nations to develop their own resources according to their agency; freedom for individuals within nations that is complete freedom, no matter what colour, creed, what religion or political use they have; freedom from disease, hunger and poverty; in a word complete freedom for all so that each individual could attain his highest innate capacity for physical, psychological and cultural well bring. And the striking feature of Gandhiji's principle was that these great ideas could only be attained by non-violent measures. That I think was the most important part of the Gandhian teaching in our deliberations."

Non-violence, as a Philosophy

Gandhiji's another contribution to political thought is his philosophy of non-violence, non-cooperation and satyagrah. He felt that with the help of these weapons even the greatest and the most powerful enemy could be defeated without leaving any bitterness behind it. He surprised the world when he said that weapons were not needed for over-throwing an empire but what was needed was a true mind having real faith in God or in other words in becoming a true satyagrahi. Gandhiji then also contributed by saying that man was an end in itself and it was only soul for which the state should care. All state activities should move with the sole object of raising moral and economic life of the subjects. One cannot forget Gandhiji's contribution towards political thought when he said that it was difficult to separate a man into his religious and secular aspects. It was rather an impossible task and as such must go side by side complementing rather than contradicting each other.

The Tributes : High tributes have been paid to Gandhiji both by Indian as well as world leaders. Dr. John Haynes went to the extent of saying that Gandhiji was the greatest man in the world after Jesus Christ Roman Rolland said, 'Mahatma Gandhi has raised up three hundred million of his fellow men, shaken the British Empire and inaugurated in human politics, the most powerful movement that the whole world has seen for nearly two thousand years." Sir Stafford Cripps said, "There has been no greater spiritual leader in the world in our own times." Lord Halifax said about Gandhiji, "I suppose there could be few men in all history who by their own personal character and example have been able deeply to influence the thought of their generation." Dr. Radhakrishnan had said about him. "Great teacher appears once in a while. Several centuries may pass by without the advent of such a one. That by which he is known in his life. He first lives and then tells others how they may live likewise. Such a teacher was Gandhiji." Dr. Rajendra Prasad said about Gandhiji, "Mahatma Gandhiji's greatest contribution, however, does not consist in making masses of India politically self-conscious and organising them on a scale they had never before been organised. To my mind his greatest contribution to Indian politics and perhaps to the humanity in the world at large lies in the unique method which be has prescribed and employed for fighting wrong."

***Conclusion* :** We may, however, conclude with Allen that, "it was the merit of Gandhi that, while revealing to his personalities of single human being in an age of organisation and machinery and the masses he put those powers to the highest use. In him we saw what can be accomplished, not by the self assertive, will, but by the will wholly, dedicated to God and the good of men. He possessed the only valid coin of authority, not that which should precise others that it may rise but that which lift there to its own level."

8

Mass Movements

Problems Related to Society **:** A social problem is defined as a situation confronting a section of society having injurious consequences. No one individual is responsible for the appearance of a socially problematic situation and the control of this situation is also beyond the ability of one person. This responsibility of solving such problems in a democratic society is placed upon the society at large. To find a solution, various processes in the society leads to the rise Social Movements.

The social problems however change with the passage of time. What was not a social problem a few decades ago, may become a crucial social problem after two decades. Social change creates new conditions in which a new issue comes to be identified as a social problem.

However question arises is, what social problem which led to Social Movements? Horton and Seshe define social problem as "a condition affecting a significant number of people in ways consider undesirable about which it is fell that something can be done through collective social action."

Social problem also involves a value judgement, a feeling that a condition is detrimental and requires change.

States in the Development of a Social Problem

Fuller and Myres have referred three stages through which the problems pass in the process of being defined and solved.

1. *Awareness :* In this first stage people become convinced that the problem exists and something can be done about it.
2. *Policy Determination :* As awareness spreads to a larger section of society, possible solutions are discussed.
3. *Reform :* As basic solutions and policies are decided upon, the stage of action is reached.

Similarly Spector and Kitsuse have also formulated some stages. Initially people agitate against a given situation for a redressal of their grievances. When the group in power acknowledge the existence of a problem, the problem acquires legitimacy. To the extent to which the bureaucrats look for solutions of the problem and the extent to which they are able to satisfy vested interests will determine whether the agitation will take the form of a movement or not. The defective policies of the decision matters and their disinterestedness rekindle the feelings of the angered people and they start a movement to force the power-holders for solving the problem. Thus arises a New Social Movement.

Role of Farmers

Kisan Sabha, Telengana and Naxalbari : Peasant movements occupy an important place in the history of social unrest in India though the aims and objectives of these movements differ in nature and degree from region to region.

It is in this sense that these movements also aimed at the unification of the peasants of a region, development of leadership, ideology and a peasant elite. Through these movements emerged a new power structure and peasant alliance. The genesis of peasant movements rests in the relationship patterns of different social categories existing within the framework of feudal and semi-feudal structure of our society. Recent movement created a stir in the total relationship pattern of a community or society. The peasant movement developed resistance to the act of suppression by landlords and brought unification among the peasants. Peasant movements are movements of a category exhibiting the characteristics of social movements in general as well as some general characteristics of their own. The peasant movements do not take into account the whole society or even the whole community. The participants in such movements are mainly peasants but the non-cultivator groups align with them for their own benefit or for the benefit of the peasants through which they gain. Though these movements develop their own leadership from the peasant ranks they tend to get leadership from city elites as well.

Parth Nath Mukherji has made a study of Naxalbari movement and the peasant revolt in North Bengal in Darjeeling district and the regions are Phansidewa, Naxalbari and Khoribuari. There are both tea plantations and paddy cultivation. He analyses the peasant uprising against the background of the communist movement in India.

The Communist Party of India (Marxist) which itself was born in 1964 when it split from the Communist Party of India, developed two strands; one which argued that the situation in India was not yet ripe for revolution and the other led by a most articulate group of Siliguri sub division of Darjeeling district under the leadership of Charu Majumdar. Ideological pressures for radicalization of CPI (M) politics were exerted by the Darjeeling District Committee. Even among the radicals there were those who favoured participation in the elections while the others proposed to shun the elections and socialize the masses against it. The former held to the primacy of the land problem and recommended mass struggles to solve it.

The Naxalbari peasant movement is related to the Tebhaga movement of Bengal where the Bengali weavers were exploited. Over a period of time, numerous struggles against such exploitation led to the emergence of Krishak Sabha. But such movements also suffered from various weaknesses.

The weakness of the movement was, there were two kinds of leadership. The two kinds of leadership weakens the movement. On the one hand, there was the urban based leadership which claimed superior knowledge and status with regard to the manner in which the movement should be conducted. Among the rural leaders there were the indigenous rural leaders. (e.g. Punjab, Rao Naresh Aich) and co-opted rural leaders like Kanu Sanyal, Panchang Sarkar, and urban leaders like Charu Majumdar. When most of the rural leaders were in prison, the leadership passed into the hands of the urban leaders who were interested in systemic changes rather than a mere just redistribution of the produce. Charu Majumdar shifted the focus from narrow economic demands to capture of power. He wanted the annihilation of class enemies which in effect was indistinguishable from secret assassinations. As a result he drove the movement underground.

Ranga Rao made a study of Peasant Movement in Telengana based on both secondary sources and fieldwork. He places the Communist led peasant movement in the wider context of other social movements which sprang up in Telengana in the beginning of the 20th century. The Telugu Literary Movement introduced ideas of renaissance and was against the Nizam's establishment. Under the influence of the Indian National Congress and the Arya Samaj, the Telegana elite gave a new direction to the activities of the Andhra Mahasabha in the 1930. They mobilized the public for the abolition of forced labour, untounchability and other social evils. They also demanded equal educational and economic opportunities and equal political representation for the Hindus.

The peasant movement in Telengana brings out one interesting point that it is not enough if economic conditions are ripe for such a movement. Narayana Reddy says that while "similar conditions prevailed in Madhya Pradesh and Rajasthan it was the added presence of the Nizam as a ruler from a minority religious group, lack of civil and religious liberties and the lack of correct understanding of the socio-economic situation prevailing in Hyderabad State by Communists that helped a Movement to develop. Ranga Rao adds that it was other structural factors like improvement in the economic and social conditions of the people followed by a period of reversal and oppression that made the peasants, rich and poor take part in the campaign of non-co-operation against the Nizam's government under the collective leadership of the congress, the Communist Parties and the Andhra Mahasabha.

Many of these movements have also been changed over time and exist today in some form or the other in some places of India. These movement did not have a solid and unified aim all over India and hence its nature and struggle was also different from region to region.

Role of Backward Castes

Self-Respect Movement: The self-respect movement sowed its seed during the Indian freedom struggle movement. This movement formed a party of the many social reforms occurred during the Indian freedom movement. Perivar E.B. Ramaswami was the leader of this movement. It was a popular movement which occurred in Tamil Nadu in 1925. It was the movement basically to improve upon the socio-economic conditions of the low caste Tamils. Later, it had a profound political implication.

This movement had the following objectives

* Inculcation and dissemination of knowledge of the political education.
* Right to lead life with dignity and self-respect and do away with the exploitative system based on superstitions and beliefs.
* Abolition of the practices of many social ills.
* Establishment and maintenance of homes for orphans and widows and opening educational institutions for them.
* This movement gained popularity in no time and became a political platform. At present, its legacy has

been taken over by various political outfits of Tamil land such as the D.M.K. parties.

Backward Castes Mobilisation in North India : The Backward classes have been deprived of many social, economic, political and religious privileges. These people were responsible for providing manual labour such as agricultural labour The untouchables occupied the lowest position among the backward class and were subjected to extreme form of exploitation.

While the presence of structural conditions of relative deprivation provided only the necessary context for the genesis of protest movements, certain external influences provided the sufficient conditions to create an awakening among them. The Christian missionaries were the first group to organize a programme for them. The missionaries not only converted them to different denominations but initiated a broad-based programme involving English education, and setting up of orphanages and other special welfare measures. Those of the depressed classes who were converted to Christianity soon developed a different lifestyle from their contemporaries. They received English education and were recruited to various government jobs.

A further impetus was provided by the national movement which provided an ideology of egalitarianism and support social movements which revolted against discrimination of any kind. Then there were the reform movements organized by the upper castes which initiated programmes of education and welfare for the Backward Classes. These movements being liberal were against many orthodox brahmanical practices including their attitudes towards the untouchables. Finally, the British abolished slavery and introduced an egalitarian system of law, liberal education and notions of representative government. All these developments provided a favourable climate for the genesis of social movements, with distinct ideologies and leadership, among the Backward Classes.

They began to organize themselves in different parts of India, establishing new identities based on diverse ideologies.

These ideologies could include ideology such as castes belonging to the other backward classes claiming a higher Varna status through a reinterpretation and recasting of appropriate mythologies of origin. For example, several castes-such as the Ahirs in many parts of North India, the Gopas in Bengal, the Gollas in A.P. and Karnataka and the Konars in Tamil Nadu-claimed descent from the Yadav dynasty to which Lord Krishna belonged. In the second decade of the present century, they organized themselves into an All-India Yadava-Association. In parts of North India especially in Bihar, the Yadavs were in conflict with the Bhommiya Brahmins.

The rejection of Brahmnical ideology and culture was other protest movements. The Dravida Kazhagam Movements in Tamil Nadu idealized the Dravidian culture and religion and attacked the Aryan Culture and religion.

The Mahar movement under the leadership of Ambedkar abandoned Hinduism altogether and embraced Buddhism. The Mahars formed an important section of the scheduled castes of Maharashtra constituting about 10 per cent of that state's population. They se[illegible]s village watchmen, messengers and removers of cattle caresses. These services were hereditary and were paid for in kind. The Mahars were also weavers, petty traders, carpenters and cultivators.

Thus they occupied a low position in the caste and occupational hierarchy and as such suffered from many religious, economic, educational and political disabilities. Thus the ideology of the Mahar movement reflects a total rejection of the religion of the Hindus which was identified with hierarchy and inequality. Mahars now belong to a religion which stands for egalitarian values and hence they are superior to the caste Hindus. This is another strategy to gain self-respect and esteem on the one hand and to protest against the religion of the upper castes on the other. The civil rights ideology, based on democracy, motivated the Backward Classes to evolve campaigns to fight for equality in educational, economic and political opportunities. Thus the leaders of the SNDP and the

Mahar movement agitated for their basic civil rights. They also incorporated the religious-cultural ideology in this approach seeking to gain respect and honour. The ideology of class conflict provides another secular source for establishing a separate identity as the exploited class.

The Dalit Panther movement, fashioned after the Black Panthers of America, emerged among the Mahars of Bombay and Poona in 1972. Its spokesmen were Namdeo Dhasal, Raja Dhale and J.V. Pawar, all eminent literary men. It clashed on the frustration that the urban youth were experiencing when faced with diverse forms of discrimination against the untouchables and the oppressed. According to its manifesto, the Dalit Panthers included all the revolutionary parties seeking to destroy the Hindu Caste system. Its declared enemies were the landlords, capitalists and money-lenders. It aimed at an all round revolution. In the ideology of the Dalit Panthers, class struggle cannot be separated from an anti-caste Hindu attitude. Thus the protest ideologies of the Backward Classes movements reveal four organizing principles :

(1) reinterpretation of myths of origin or of one's own religion.

(2) rejection of Hinduism and Aryan religion and culture,

(3) civil rights and

(4) class conflict.

The SNDP movement exemplifies the principle of reinterpretation as a theme of the protest ideology. Sri Narayana Guru Swamy established a set of beliefs, rituals, temples and priests which was parallel to that of the upper castes. The world-view of his reinterpreted Hinduism was both enlightened and simple, on the basis of which Izhavas were able to claim a new identity with honour, esteem and self-respect.

Similarly the Ahirs systematically reinterpreted the Yadava myth of origin of their castes in legitimizing their superior status. This was backed by protest against the status that was accorded to them by the dominant groups backed by religion.

They not only achieved self-respect and honour but also gained access to the religious goods and services of the twice-born castes which they had long been denied. The new ideology provided the language of protest and aggression against the opposition groups.

New identities are established not only on the basis of a religious cultural ideology, but also on the basis of a secular one, with civil rights and class conflict themes. The former, when viewed as an attempt to claim equality of status through democratic means, is exemplified by many backward class movements fighting for basic secular rights such as right of admission to schools, right of recruitment to government jobs and right of adult suffrage. For example, these programmes were part of the SNDP and Mahar movements. The leaders of these movements adopted both religious-cultural and civil rights ideology simultaneously in their efforts to attain equality of status with the dominant groups on the ritual and the secular planes.

Among the Backward Classes, the Dalit Panthers adopted the ideology of class conflict and anti-caste Hindu feeling. The new identity that emerged based on these two principles enabled the young urban Mahars to attack the upper caste Hindu capitalists. Thus both secular class conflict and religious-cultural principles can be seen as transformations. All these movements arose due to the extreme exploitation of the lower castes by upper castes and the lower castes were subjected to frequent oppression and exploitation over a period of time.

9

The Constitution

Indian Constitution

According to the traditional classification followed by the political scientists, constitutions are either unitary or federal. In a unitary constitution the powers of the Government are centralised in one government viz., the Central Government. The provinces are subordinate to the Centre. In a federal constitution, on the other hand, there is a division of powers between the Federal and the State Governments and both are independent in their own spheres.

There is a difference of opinion amongst the constitutional jurists about the nature of the Indian Constitution. One view is that it is a quasi-federal constitution and contains more unitary features than federal. The other view is that it is a federal constitution with a novel feature adopting itself to national emergencies. The view of the framers of the Constitution is that the Indian Constitution is a Federal Constitution. Dr. Ambedkar, the Chairman of the Drafting Committee, observed thus, "I think it is agreed that our Constitution notwithstanding the many provisions which are contained in it whereby the Centre has been given powers to override the Provinces (States) nonetheless, is a *Federal Constitution*".

But some constitutional jurists hesitate to characterize the Indian Constitution as federal. It is, therefore, necessary to ascertain *firstly*, what federal constitution is and what are its essential characteristics, and secondly, to examine whether our Constitution possesses those characteristics.

Federal Aspect : "By the Federal Principles", Prof. Wheare observes, "is meant the method of dividing powers, so that the *general* and *regional* Governments are each within a sphere coordinate and independent. Both the federal and the Regional Governments are coordinate and independent in their spheres and not subordinate to one another".

The American Constitution is universally regarded as an example of federal constitution. It establishes dual polity or dual form of Government, *i.e.*, the Federal and the State Governments. The powers of both the Central and the State Governments, are divided and both are independent in their own spheres. The existence of coordinate authorities independent of each other is the gist of the federal principle.

Prof. Wheare, after giving the above definition as to what the federal principle is, himself proceeds to examine whether the American Constitution satisfies the above test. He observes: "Are we to confine the forms to cases where the federal principle has been applied completely and without exception? It would not be sensible to do this. After all, the Constitution of the United States itself, as originally drawn up contained at least one exception to the federal principle in that the Senate was composed of representatives selected by the Legislatures of the State. Thus a part of the general Government of the United States was dependent to some extent upon a part of the regional Government. This exception to the federal principle was maintained in law until 1913: Yet the American Constitution from 1787-1913 was and must be called a "federal constitution" for the federal principle was predominant in it.

Thus the criterion is *"the federal principle predominant in the constitution!* If so, that constitution may be called a "federal constitution". If, on the other hand, there are so many modifications, in the application of the federal principle that it ceases to be of any significance, then the constitution cannot be termed as federal. This appears to be the most instructive and responsible way in which to use the term 'federal constitution'. It seems essential to define federal principle rigidly, but to apply the term 'federal constitution' more widely. Thus Dr. Wheare accepts that exceptions are permissible provided federal principle is predominantly retained in the Constitution.

Constitution of the Federal Nature

A federal constitution usually has the following essential characteristics:

(1) *Power Distribution* : The distribution of powers is an essential feature of federalism. Federalism means the distribution of the powers of the State among a number of coordinate bodies each originating in and controlled by the Constitution. The basis of such distribution of powers is that in matters of national importance, in which a uniform policy is desirable in the interest of the units, authority is entrusted to the Union, and matters of local concern remain with the States.

(2) *Constitution as a Supreme Body* : A federal State derives its existence from the Constitution, just as a corporation derives its existence from the grant by which it is created. Hence, every power, executive, legislative or judicial whether it belongs to the nation or to the individual State is subordinate to and controlled by the Constitution. The Constitution in a federal State constitutes the supreme law of the land. Prof. Wheare says "that those two institutions—the supreme constitution and the written constitution are then, essential institutions to a federal Government. The supreme constitution is essential if Government is to

be federal; the written constitution is essential if federal Government is to work well."

(3) *Constitution in a Written Form* : A federal constitution must almost necessarily be a written constitution. The foundations of a federal State are complicated contracts. It will be practically impossible to maintain the supremacy of the Constitution, unless the terms of the Constitution have been reduced into writing. To base an arrangement of this kind upon understandings or conventions would be certain to generate misunderstandings and disagreements.

(4) *No Flexibility* : A natural corollary of a written constitution is its rigidity. A constitution which is the supreme law of the land must also be ridge. In a rigid constitution the procedure of amendment is very complicated and difficult. This does not mean that the constitution should be legally unalterable. It simply means that the power of amending the constitution should not remain exclusively with either the Central or State Governments. A constitution of a country is considered to be a permanent document. It is the supreme law of the land. This supremacy of the constitution can only be maintained if the method of amendment is rigid.

(5) *Authority of Courts* : In a federal State the legal supremacy of the Constitution is essential for the existence of the federal system. The very nature of a federal State involves a division of powers between the Central and State Governments under the framework of the Constitution. It is, therefore, essential to maintain this division of powers between the two levels of Governments. This must be done by some independent and impartial authority above and beyond the ordinary bodies whether federal or State legislatures existing under the constitution. The judiciary has, in a federal polity, the final power to interpret the constitution and guard the entrenched provisions of the Constitution.

The Indian Constitution possesses all the essential characteristics of a federal constitution mentioned above. The constitution establishes a dual polity, a system of double Government with the Central Government at one level and the State Government at the other. There is a division of powers between the Central and the State Governments. Each level of Government is supreme in its own sphere. The Constitution of India is written and is supreme. The provisions of the Constitution which are concerned with federal principles cannot be altered without the consent of the majority of the States. The Constitution establishes a Supreme Court to decide disputes between the Union and the States, or the States *inter se* interpret finally the provisions of the Constitution.

But, as said earlier, some scholars hesitate to characterise the Indian Constitution as truly federal because according to them in certain circumstances the Constitution empowers the Centre to interfere in the State matters and thus places the States in a subordinate position which violates the federal principle. They, therefore, use such expressions for it as 'quasi-federal", 'unitary with federal features' or 'federal with unitary features'. In the opinion of Prof. Wheare: 'The Constitution establishes a system of Government which is almost quasi-federal..............a unitary State with *subsidiary federal features rather than a federal State with subsidiary unitary features*'? Jennings has characterised it as 'a federation with a strong centralising tendency'.

Let us now examine what are those provisions of the Constitution which are produced in support of the above argument and how they modify the strict application of the federal principle. In the following matters, it is pointed out, the Indian Constitution contains the modifications of the federal principle:—

(1) *Governors Appointment* : The Governors of the States are appointed by the President (Articles 155 and 156) and answerable to him this is, however, not a matter of much significance, for, the Governor is only the

constitutional head of the State who shall normally act on the advice of his Ministers. There are provisions in the Constitution under which the Governor is required to send certain State laws for the assent of the President. The President has power to veto those State laws *e.g.* Arts. 200, 288(2). But whatever be the letter of the Constitution, in practice there are not many examples where the President has vetoed the State Laws. The only example has been the *Kerala Education Bill.* But here also the Centre obtained the advisory opinion of the Supreme Court before sending it back to the State Legislature for suitable amendments in the light of the Court's opinion.

(2) *Parliament Empower Legislate in the National Interest :* Under Art. 249 Parliament is empowered to make laws with respect to every matter enumerated in the State List if the Rajya Sabha passes a resolution by 2/3 majority that it is necessary in the national interest. There cannot be any objection to this provision: First, no one will deny that if a subject in the State List assumes national character. Parliament should make a law on it. In normal course this cannot be done unless the Constitution is amended. But in this provision we have devised an expedient way by which without formally amending the Constitution we can achieve the desired effect, namely, the acquisition by the Centre of the power to administer and legislate upon a subject which has assumed national importance. Secondly, it should also be noted that this power is given to Parliament by the Council of States itself by passing a resolution supported by 2/3 majority of-the members present. Thus, in effect by this device the Constitution is amended by the agreement of majority of the States. We, therefore, fail to understand how Article 249 places the State in subordinate position.

(3) *Form of New State and Alter Boundaries of Existing States:* The Parliament of India may form new States; it may

increase or diminish the area of any State and it may alter the boundaries or name of any State (Art. 3). The very existence of the State thus depends upon the sweet will of the Union Government. The power conferred on Parliament to make territorial adjustment is better explained on the historical basis. The Government of India, for the first time, establish federal polity in India. It deliberately created the constituent units of the federation although they had no organic roots in the past. The framers of the Constitution were well aware of the peculiar conditions under which and the reasons for which the States were formed and their boundaries were defined and so they deliberately accepted the provisions in Article 3 with a view to meeting the possibility of the redistribution of the State territory after the integration of Indian States. The provisions in Art. 3 take into account the fact that the Constitution contemplated readjustment of the territories of constituent States which might arise in future.

(4) *Provision of Emergency* : The Constitution envisages three types of emergencies: (1) emergency caused by war or external aggression or armed rebellion (Art. 352); (2) emergency caused by failure of constitutional machinery in States (Art. 356); and (3) financial emergency (Art. 360). When the proclamation of emergency is made under Art. 352, the normal distribution of powers between the Centre and the States undergo a vital change. Parliament is empowered to make laws with respect to any matter enumerated in the State List. The Centre is empowered to give directions to any State as to manner in which the State's executive power is to be exercised. Further, the President may by order direct that all or any of the provisions of Arts. 278 to 279 relating to distribution of revenue between the Centre and the State shall take effect with such exception or modifications, as he thinks fit. Under

Art. 356, if the President is satisfied that Government of a State cannot be carried on in accordance with the provisions of the Constitution he can dismiss the State ministry and dissolve the Legislature and assume all the functions of the State. Thus the normal distribution of powers between the Centre and the States, which is the basic element of a federal constitution, is completely suspended. It is alleged that these provisions enable the Union Parliament to convert the Union into a unitary State which vitally affects the federal character of the Indian Constitution.

Has Indian Constitution a Real Federal Status? "The correct view", observes Dr. V.N. Shukla, "is that emergency provisions which come into operation only on the happening of the specific contingencies, do not modify or destroy the federal system. It is rather a merit of the Constitution that it visualises the contingencies when the strict application of the federal principle might destroy the basic assumption on which our Constitution is built. The Constitution by adopting itself to a changed circumstances strengthens the Government in its endeavour to overcome the crisis. In an emergency the behaviour of each federal Constitution is very much different from that in peace time. Though the Constitution of the U.S.A., Australia and Canada do not expressly provide for enlargement of federal power during the periods of emergency, but during the two World Wars, the defence power of the Federal Government was given so extended an interpretation by the courts that these countries behaved more likely unitary than federal State. For the above reasons we maintain that the Indian Constitution is federal in nature. Prof. Wheare has coined a phrase 'quasi-federation' as applicable to India but he has nowhere defined what a 'quasi-federation' is. "It is not necessary to use such a vague term 'quasi-federal' to characterise it". The term 'quasi-federal' is extremely vague as it does not denote how powerful the Centre is, how much deviation there is from the pure 'federal model' or what kind of special position a particular quasi-federation occupies between a unitary State and a federation proper. The fundamental principle of federation is that the powers are distributed between the Centre and the States and that is done by the Constitution. That is what the Constitution does. The States do not depend upon the Centre, for, in normal times the Centre cannot intrude. It may be that the Centre has been assigned a larger role than the Sates but that by itself does not detract from the federal nature of the Constitution, for it is not the essence of federalism to say that only so much, and more power, is to be given to the Centre.

Prof. Wheare appears to feel that the American Constitution is truly of federal type. He says 'among examples of federal constitutions there may be mentioned those of the United States, Switzerland and Australia'. It may, however, be clearly understood that the nature of federalism is more of historical growth based on a nation's necessity. To accept the same pattern of federalism in all countries is well nigh impossible. With all respects to Prof. Wheare, we may tell him that federalism varies from place to place, and from time to time depending on so many factors—historical, geographical, economical and political. So what is good for America is not necessarily good for India. The people of a country can take in only the required dosages, otherwise they may stunt or destroy their growth. Federalism is not like the set pattern of coats to wear. It is a clock of varying organised pattern befitting each wearer and helping him to the next and superior stages of federalism. India's federalism is unique and good for itself. America's federalism is not perfect as it is stated to be. It has got its own drawback. Indian Constitution is sufficiently federal. It is not less federal than American federalism which on paper is of higher degree but in the actual practice the leaning is towards centralisation of national interest. The term 'quasi' is a misnomer. *India is federal and America is more federal* in the outline of the Constitution. In practice there is not much difference between the two.

It may be that we deviated in respect of certain matters from the strict federalism as operating in the U.S.A. or

Switzerland, but the reasons are obvious. The Indian Constitution makers defined the Indian federal structure not with an eye on theoretical but on practical considerations in designing federalism. Under the impact of world wars, international crisis, scientific and technological progress and developments and the emergence of the ideal of social welfare State, the whole concept of federalism had been undergoing a change for sometime throughout the world. There are centralising tendencies in evidence in every federation and whether it is in U.S.A. or in Australia, strong and powerful national governments have emerged in every federation. The framers of the Indian Constitution took note of these tendencies and kept in view the practical needs of the country designed on federal structure not on the footing that it should conform to some theoretical, definite or standard pattern, but on the basis that it should be able to subserved the need of the vast and diverse country like India. The Indian Constitution, therefore, constitutes a new bold experiment in the area of federalism.

In short, it may be concluded that the Constitution of India is neither purely federal nor purely unitary but is a combination of both. It is a union of composite State of a novel type. It enshrines the principle that inspite of federalism, the national interest ought to be paramount. Thus, the Indian Constitution is mainly federal with unique safeguards for enforcing national unity and growth.

Constitution by Indians : The right of the people to determine the form of government under which they would live and to frame their own constitution, despite repeated disavowal by the British Government, was finally conceded in March, 1942 when Sir Stafford Cripps brought to India reform proposals of the War Cabinet. The Cripps Proposals were rejected, but the right of Indians to frame their own constitution through a Constituent Assembly was established. It was reiterated in the March 15, 1946 statement of the Prime Minister, Clement Attlee. While recognising India's right to independence, he said, "......What form of government is to replace the present regime is for India to decide, but our desire is to set up forthwith the machinery for making the decision."

In pursuance of the Prime Minister's statement elections to the Constituent Assembly were held in July, 1946. The Muslim League won all but seven of the seats reserved for Muslims and the Congress secured 203 of the General seats. The Congress had also succeeded in capturing one Sikh and four Muslim seats, thus, making a tally of 208 seats out of a total of 296 seats allotted to the Provinces. The Indian States were to have 93 seats. The representatives of the States of Baroda, Bikaner, Jaipur, Jodhpur, Rewa, Udaipur and Patiala entered the Assembly in April, 1947. Representatives of States, other than Jammu and Kashmir, and Hyderabad, Junagadh and two more States, entered the Assembly subsequently. Jammu and Kashmir and Hyderabad came in after the accession of these States in October, 1947 and November, 1948 respectively.

The Constituent Assembly was a galaxy of top-ranking leaders of the Congress and the Muslim League, veteran statesmen, seasoned administrators, eminent jurists, in fact, people drawn from all walks of life and all parts of the country. In the selection of its candidates for election to the Constituent Assembly, the Congress adopted two basic norms: (i) that the Congress candidates should represent the country as a whole and various-viewpoints within the Party itself must find due representation; and (ii) due care should be taken to bring on its list candidates capable of representing country's dynamism irrespective of party affiliations. It was, accordingly, ensured that persons of exceptional ability outside the Congress Party found places in the Constituent Assembly, and that minority communities were justly represented. The Cabinet Mission Plan had guaranteed seats for Muslims and Sikhs only and no provision was made for the representation of other minorities, such as, Parsis, Anglo-Indians, Indian Christians, members of the Scheduled Castes and even women. In some cases, instructions were issued by the Congress Working Committee to the Presidents of the Provincial Congress Committees to recommend the names of specified persons for nomination. All minority communities were represented usually by the members of their choice. The Indian Christians had seven members, the Anglo-Indians three and Parsis three. After the partition the total number of representatives of the minorities, including Muslims, was 88 out of 233 seats allotted to the Provinces; 37 per cent of the total population of the Provinces. There was hardly any shade of opinion not represented in the Constituent Assembly.

After partition the Congress majority in the Assembly jumped to 82 per cent. There was no conceivable opposition. The twenty-eight Muslim League members from the non-Pakistan Provinces, who took their seats in the Assembly, were separately divided among themselves. The Muslim League was "suspect" in India and Pakistan having been created there was no motivating force which could bind them together in a cohesive body. Nor was there any dynamic leader to whom they would have looked for guidance. Their only aim was to safeguard the interests of the Muslims who had not opted for Pakistan. They still feared Hindu domination and, therefore, turned to Nehru and the Congress leadership for the protection of the interests of their community. The Constituent Assembly was the Congress. At the Centre and in the Provinces there were Congress Governments too. As Granville Austin has said, "The Assembly, the Congress, and the government were, like the points of a triangle, separate entities, but, linked by overlapping membership, they assumed a form infinitely meaningful for India."

The Constituent Assembly met as scheduled on December 9, 1946. The Muslim League boycotted its deliberations, although the December 6 statement of the British Government had accepted the Muslim League's interpretation of the grouping clause. Jawaharlal Nehru moved the Objectives Resolution on December 13, 1946 and described it as a "solemn pledge to the people" which they would redeem in the constitution that they would frame. On the motion of M. R. Jayakar's amendment the discussion on the Objectives

Resolution was postponed so as to enable representatives not only of the Muslim League, but of the Indian States, too, to participate in the deliberations of the Assembly.

The Assembly was adjourned till January 20, 1947, but the Muslim League continued with its boycott when it met after the adjournment. After the acceptance of partition the position was entirely changed. Jinnah and the league leadership agreed that the League members of the Assembly from the non-Pakistan Provinces should participate in its deliberations, and play their part in the framing of the future constitution of India, with a view to securing the interests of the Mussaunans, who were to remain in India, by providing effective safeguards. When the Assembly met for the fourth session on July 14,1947 the Muslim League members from the non-Pakistan Provinces took their seats and declared themselves as "loyal and law-abiding citizens of India." Now, the Constituent Assembly was not bound by the provisions of the Cabinet Mission Plan. It was, competent to chalk out its own course and to establish a federation of its own choice, with as strong a Centre as desired.

Challenges for the Farmers of Constitution

But partition had made the task of the Constitution-makers tremendously arduous. The problems they had to tackle were many and difficult to resolve. They had to devise a scheme of government for 400 million people in no way homogenous and alike. There were scores of communities speaking different languages, professing different faiths, practising different customs, following different traditions and emphasising different cultures. The demand of the Muslim League for the division of India on religious basis, culminating ultimately in slicing territories in the West and the East, had completely changed the pattern of the political set-up originally contemplated. The first task of the Constitution-makers, therefore, was to adequately provide for the unity and integrity of the country in the presence of a foreign State within the very compound of India.

The creation of Pakistan did not mean the total exit of the Muslims from India. More than ten per cent of the total population of the country was left on the Indian side of the border and that, too, in the same Provinces from where the cry that Islam was in danger was raised first. Having been left leaderless, and forsaken by their own co-religionists whose battle they had fought, these political orphans were to be rehabilitated with adequate guarantees for the protection of their religion and culture. The object was to instil in them the sense of belongingness to India and the faith of a unified nation. Together with the problem of the Muslims, and equally important, was the problem of near about forty-million untouchables, numerous other minority groups, backward people and areas, like tribes and tribal areas, who were to be protected from the centuries old oppression and suppression.

Then, there was the baffling problem of the Indian States, 562 in number. The declaration of lapse of Paramountcy on transfer of power had created an intriguing situation. The States were left free "to enter into a federal relationship with the successor Government or Governments or failing this, enter into political arrangements with it or them." Interpreted in terms of law, the Memorandum prepared by the Cabinet Mission on "States, Treaties and Paramountcy" and endorsed by the Mountbatten Plan left any Prince or a combination of Princes free to declare his or their independence and even to enter into negotiations with any foreign power and thus become islands of independent territory within the country. In fact, some States, such as Hyderabad-and Junagadh, had begun to flirt with foreign States. Junagadh, a small State in Kathiawar, acceded to Pakistan, and Pakistan accepted the accession, even though the population of the State was predominantly Hindu. Apparently, the Nizam of Hyderabad desired to maintain an independent status. Envoys from the Nizam's court, together with intermediaries, like Sir Walter Monckton, went silently to and from Delhi "carrying terms and proposals, feelers and conditions." By November, 1947, no more than a Standstill

Agreement could be secured from him, prolonged negotiations failed to persuade His Exalted Highness to accede to India.

The position of the Indian National Congress was clear enough on the issue of Indian States. On July 15, 1947 the All-India Congress Committee categorically rejected the claim of some of the States and the theory of Paramountcy. Speaking at this meeting Nehru said that the States have only two alternatives : they could join the Union of India either individually or in groups. "There is no third way out of the situation—third way meaning Independence or special relation to a foreign power." Coupland had aptly said, "India could live if its Muslim limbs in the north-west and north-east were amputated but could it live without its heart ?" The heart of India was its Princely States. The foremost concern of the Government of Independent India was to conserve the heart of India.

Immediately after the plan to partition and grant of Independence on August 15, 1947 was announced, the Interim Government decided to set up a State Ministry to deal with the problem of Indian States. This Ministry was placed under the charge of Sardar Vallabhbhai Patel. By August, 1947, all the 562 States, with the exception of Hyderabad, Jammu and Kashmir and Junagadh, had been persuaded by a combination of cajolery and firmness, to sign instruments of Accession and Standstill Agreements which had the effect of surrendering their powers in the three fields of foreign relations, defence and communication, and maintaining unchanged all arrangements in other matters.

The unity of what had been left as India after the partition was so vital that the Government of India "could not view with equanimity and trifling with it." The people of Junagadh forced the Nawab to flee to Karachi and in November 1947 the Muslim Dewan of the State was compelled to invite the Government of India. Junagadh became a part of the Union of India as a result of plebiscite in February, 1948. In Hyderabad the situation became explosive as a result of disorder that broke out inside the State, fanned by the Communist-led peasants of Telengana and the ugly acts of a violent fanatical group of Muslim militants, Razakars. Even raiders from Hyderabad made incursions into Indian territory. Indian troops were, consequently, ordered to enter Hyderabad and after four days of 'police action' the Nizam capitulated. He agreed to accede to the Indian Union in November, 1948 and became the nominal head of the State.

Along with Hyderabad, Kashmir was another problem. The Maharaja of Jammu and Kashmir refused to accede either to Pakistan or India prior to August 15, 1947. In October, 1947 the Pathan tribesmen from Pakistan raided Kashmir and threatened its capital, Srinagar. The Maharaja in desperation sought military aid from India which was given only on his agreeing that the State of Jammu and Kashmir should accede to India. For the Government of India it was announced by Lord Mountbatten as Governor-General that "as soon as law and order have been restored in Kashmir and her soil cleared of the invader, the question of the accession should be settled by reference to the people." Although a cease-fire was agreed upon on January 1, 1949, through the good offices of the United Nations, the Kashmir question has been the major issue in dispute between India and Pakistan ever since. The cease-fire line has became a *defacto* frontier.

The work accomplished by Sardar Vallabhbhai Patel in the States Ministry rationalised the political map of India by the merger or the consolidation and integration of the Indian States. It was a silent revolution and India was unified as never before in her history. No fewer than 216 smaller States were abolished as separate units and merged into the Provinces. States numbering 275 in all were integrated to form five new Unions with a Rajpramukh as the head of a Union of States. The Rajpramukh was chosen by the States integrated into a Union. Sixty-one States were brought under direct Central administration either as separate units or in consolidated blocks. The States of Hyderabad, Mysore and Jammu and Kashmir were left unaffected by these changes.

The White Paper on Indian States had said that Indian independence would have no meaning if the people of the States did not have the same political, social and economic freedom, as those enjoyed by the people of the Provinces. All the Princely States, save for a few enlightened States, such as Mysore, were notoriously backward and even feudal. The makers of the Constitution had therefore, to devise means to make them as viable and sizable units with democratic institutions. The process of integration and democratization began after their accession to India.

Aims and Goals

Important Objectives : To forge unity out of numerous diversities, both natural and artificial, was therefore, the foremost task of the Constitution-makers. But their real and stupendous task was, as Jawaharlal Nehru explained in the Constituent Assembly, "to free India through a new constitution, to feed the starving people and to clothe the naked masses, and to give every Indian the fullest opportunity to develop himself according to his need." On the mid-night of August 14, 1947 Nehru in a moving speech called upon the members of the Constituent Assembly to take a pledge of dedication of service to India and humanity. "Long ago," he said, "we made a tryst with destiny, and now the time comes when we shall redeem our pledge not wholly or in full measure, but very substantially........." To the people of India, Nehru made a fervent appeal "for cooperation in the great adventure of building the noble mansion of free India where all her children may dwell." The task of the Assembly was to devise a constitution that would serve the ultimate goal of social revolution, "of national renaissance." Simple drafting of the fundamental rights and moral precepts of a preamble were only a parchment of paper unless the political machinery established by the constitution did not foster or at least permit a social revolution to reach the destination.

The basic aims and objectives of the new State of India find their expression in the Objectives Resolution approved by the

Constituent Assembly on January 22, 1947 and the most significant statement of such aims and objectives is found in the Preamble to the Constitution of 1950. Thus, the foundation of the constitutional structure was laid by the Objectives Resolution which prescribed:

(1) This Constituent Assembly declares its firm and solemn resolve to proclaim India as an Independent Sovereign Republic and to draw up for her future government a Constitution; ....

(2) Wherein all power and authority of the Sovereign Independent India, its constituent parts and organs of government, are derived from the people; and

(3) Wherein shall be guaranteed and secured to all the people of India justice, social, economic and political; equality of status, of opportunity, and before the law; freedom of thought, expression, belief, faith, worship, vocation, association and action, subject to law and public morality; and

(4) Wherein adequate safeguards shall be provided for minorities, backward and tribal areas, and depressed and other backward classes; and

(5) Whereby shall be maintained the integrity of territory of the Republic and its sovereign rights on land, sea, and air according to justice and the law of civilised nations; and

(6) This ancient land attains its rightful and honoured place in the world, makes its full and willing contribution to the promotion of world peace and the welfare of mankind.

These fundamental Objectives, which were to guide the deliberations of the Constituent Assembly, may, thus, be stated:

(1) that India is to be an independent sovereign Republic;

(2) that it is to be a democratic Union with equal level of self-government in all the constituent parts. "There cannot be," as Nehru emphasised, "different standards

of freedom as between the peoples of the states and the people outside the states;"

(3) that all power and authority of the Union Government and Governments of the constituent parts is derived from the people;

(4) that the constitution must strive to obtain and guarantee to the people justice based upon social, economic and political equality, equality of opportunity and equality before the law;

(5) that there should be freedom of thought, expression, belief, faith, worship, vocation, association and action, subject to law and public morality;

(6) that the constitution should provide just rights for minorities, backward and tribal areas, and depressed and other backward classes so that they may be equal participants in and recipients of social, economic and political justice; and

(7) to frame a constitution which should secure for India a due place in the comity of Nations and to contribute to the promotion of world peace and the welfare of mankind.

With well-defined objectives before them the Constituent Assembly established eight major Committees to provide bricks and mortar for the constitutional structure. Either Patel, Nehru or Prasad chaired each of these committees and in many.cases the other two or Azad, were present. With seven other Assembly members, these leaders constituted an inner circle in the Committees of the Assembly. The inner circle demonstrated the inter-locking of the three organisations-the Party, the Assembly and the Congress Governments at the Centre and the Provinces-for with one exception all were also members of the Congress or of the Central Government. After partition, the Constituent Assembly was a one-party body in an essentially one party country. In other words, the Assembly was the Congress and the Congress was India.

The Drafting Committee appointed by the resolution of the

Constituent Assembly on August 29, 1947 submitted its report on February 21, 1948. The Draft Constitution was presented to the Constituent Assembly on November 4, 1948, for consideration, thereby providing a sufficiently long opportunity to the public, the press and the Provincial Legislatures to discuss it and focus public opinion. Its first reading comprised general discussion which commenced on November 4 and continued till November 9. Then began the second reading or consideration of the clauses of the Draft and it continued from November 15, 1948 to October 17, 1949. As many as 7,635 amendments were tabled out of which 2,473 were actually moved and discussed. The Assembly again sat on November 14, 1949, for the third reading of the Draft and it concluded on November 26. On this date the Constitution received the signatures of the President of the Constituent Assembly and it was declared passed.

The final session of the Constituent Assembly was held on January 24, 1950. It unanimously elected Rajendra Prasad the first President of the Republic of India under the new constitution which came into force on January 26, 1950. This date was specifically chosen for the inauguration of the Indian Republic, as it was on January 26, the Indian National Congress had passed the historic resolution at its Lahore session to win independence. Since then this resolution was repeated every year at public meetings all over the country till India became independent in 1947. It was the Congress Expert Committee, presided over by Nehru, that set India to her present Constitution. This Committee was appointed by the Congress Working Committee to prepare materials for the Constituent Assembly and six of its eight members had been elected to that body. Vallabhbhai Patel was not a member of the Committee, but he attended many committee meetings. Other invitees were V. K. Krishna Menon, A. Appadorai, Mridula Sarabhai, and Raja Hathee Singh. The Committee drew widely upon the mature experience of advanced democratic countries. The Union Constitution Committee ransacked all the known constitutions of the world. They borrowed freely from the Government of

India Act, 1935, although they deviated from it wherever they believed it was necessary.

Relevant Characteristics

Seven of the decisions regarding the nature of the new State which were made with due consideration, but without significant opposition were : India should have a written constitution, it should be a federal State; it should be a republic; it should have a parliamentary democracy; it should be a member of the Commonwealth of Nations; it should be a secular State; and, it should be a Welfare State.

Written Form of Constitution

For a federal State the constitution must almost necessarily be a written constitution which defines the relations between the Central Government and the regional Governments, demarcates the sphere of each, and is paramount to the constitutions of regional Governments, if each component part of the union has its own separate constitution. To base the arrangements which are inherent in a federal polity "upon understandings and conventions," as Dicey said, "would be certain to generate misunderstandings and disagreements." Moreover, the demand for Constituent Assembly and the making of constitution by that body postulates that it must be a written constitution.

There were other compelling reasons for India to opt for a written constitution and that, too, for an elaborate and detailed document. India inherited a written constitution in the Government of India Act, 1935, one of the longest pieces of legislation ever enacted by the British Parliament. This Act, supplemented by the Indian Independence Act, 1947, another elaborate measure of the British Parliament with certain amending statutes passed by the Constituent Assembly of India, gave the Indian Union a working constitution till 1950 when the new Constitution became operative. The Constitution-makers thoroughly familiar with the provisions and implications of the 1935 Act, and with the practical experience of the machinery of Government then available instinctively borrowed profusely from it and in many cases entire Sections from the Act were transferred to the new Constitution. The members of the Assembly believed that to effect a smooth transfer of authority from the British Indian Government to the Government of India a variety of details should be included in the constitution in order to preserve administrative continuity and efficiency. At the time of Independence, India inherited a well-established system of constitutional law. "To have recreated this body of law in the form of legislation to be passed after drafting a constitution of broad principles seemed to Assembly members a difficult if not a dangerous proposition."

Then, the task of the Constitution-makers was pre-conditioned by inescapable factors of previous regime and the politico-economic set up of the vast sub-continent. Highly divergent elements had to be welded together and units widely differing from one another were to be brought together in an organic unification. These differences created difficulties in the legislative and administrative set-up and the Constitution originally provided for four distinct types of units-Part A, Part B, Part C, and Part D of the First Schedule—on a different constitutional level. Moreover, the unity of what was left as India was so vital a necessity for the political strength, full economic development, and the cultural expression of the people that the Constitution-makers followed the precedent of Canada and prescribed, in the federal polity they established a full dressed constitution for the States comprising the Indian Union. The Constitution also elaborately dealt with the complicated problem of relations between the Union and the States as well as inter-State co-ordination and adjudication of disputes relating to water of inter-State rivers or river valleys. Not oblivious of the centrifugal forces that worked in India from the dawn of her history and in order to checkmate any recurrence of fissiparous tendencies arising out of various divergent elements in the Indian social life, the Constitution-makers armed the Union with adequate powers to meet any contingency whenever any grave threat, internal or external, appeared or was likely to appear threatening the unity and security of India. Rajendra Prasad gave a matter of fact analysis in his observations to the Constituent Assembly on November 26, 1949. He said, "India today needs nothing more than a set of honest men who will have the interest of the country before them. There is a fissiparous tendency arising out of various elements in our life. We have communal differences, caste differences, language differences and so forth."

Referring to the detailed nature of the constitution, Prasad observed, "The Constitution has gone into great details regarding the distribution of powers and functions between the Union and the States in all aspects of their administrative and other activities. I do not wish to pass any judgement on this criticism and can only say that we cannot be too cautious about our future, particularly when we remember the history of the country extending over many centuries." The problem relating to public services, special classes, like Anglo-Indians, Scheduled Castes and Scheduled Tribes required in the opinion of the Assembly members, special constitutional provisions and they were duly provided. Similarly, the question relating to official language and regional languages has been specifically dealt with in the Constitution. Provisions relating to higher judiciary were also included so as to put its independence beyond the reach of Parliament. The Constitution embodies an elaborate List of Fundamental Rights as also the Directives Principles of State Policy. Some of these rights are unknown to other constitutions and their inclusion was necessitated by the peculiar conditions and circumstances prevailing in India. The theme of social revolution runs throughout the proceedings of the Constituent Assembly and in their efforts to achieve that end an elaborate Bill of Rights was engrafted on the parliamentary system of government and a federal system was supplemented by provisions for centralization of power whenever national interests demanded the strength of the unitary system.

The Constitution of a country cannot be divorced from the

facts of history. It is, therefore, not surprising that the Constitution-makers would have produced quite a comprehensive document which at places entered into comparatively detailed provisions. The predominance of the lawyer element in the making of the Constitution might have been another contributory factor. But as K. C. Wheare explained, "in the long process by which the Government of India Act, 1935 was framed, the people in Britain learned much of the difficulties of making a Constitution of India, and any one who followed the discussions of these years, in which Indians and British alike strove to devise a good government for India will be slow to criticise the work with which the Indian Constituent Assembly has done. It has been a tremendous task and to have produced a constitution at all which can command so wide a measure of agreement is a great achievement.

The constitution as finally emerged out of the Constituent Assembly consisted of 395 Articles and Eight Schedules. The Ninth Schedule was added by the Constitution (First Amendment) Act, 1951, and the Tenth by the Constitution (Fifty-second Amendment) Act, 1985. The total number of amendments so far made is 74 and many more are on the anvil. No other constitution in the world is so long. President Neelam Sanjiva Reddy in his broadcast to the nation on the eve of 32nd anniversary (1979) of the Independence Day bemoaned the "steady and cumulative deterioration of standards in public life and public morality" and the contempt with which principles of life had been compromised and the basic values of life treated. He considered that the time was ripe now for enlightened public opinion in the mainstream of national public life "to review the provisions of the Constitution in the light of working it over for the last three decades." No other Constitution in the world is so long and detailed, even ponderous, as the 1950 Constitution of India in its present shape. M. V. Kamath humorously remarked in the Constituent Assembly. "The emblem, and the crest that we have selected for our Assembly is an elephant. It is perhaps in consonance with that, our Constitution is the bulkiest that the world has produced."

10

Indian Parliament

Government of People

The predominant aim of the Constituent Assembly members when framing the legislative provisions of the constitution, was to create a basis for the social and political unity of the country. They chose to do this by welding the diversified Indian elements and interests into one mass electorate having universal, adult suffrage and by providing for the direct representation of the voters in the popular assemblies.

This bold step completely overturned the constitutional pattern left by the British rule. The Executive and Judicial provisions of the Government of India Act, 1935, were adapted to India's needs by the Assembly with some major changes of substance, but with few of form. It was not so with the legislative provisions. These had to be entirely remade to incorporate the aims and objectives the nation had set before it.

Under the Act of 1935, not only did the Provinces lack even a semblance of popular government, but the small electorate that existed was thoroughly fragmented. The franchise was restricted by property, educational and other qualifications to near about 15 per cent of the entire population and this narrow electorate was split into not less than thirteen communal and functional sectors for whose representation seats were reserved, and that too with weightage in many cases, in the various legislative bodies. Election to the Lower Chamber of the Central Assembly was indirect on the basis of communal and functional electorates consisting of the members of the Provincial Assemblies. Evidently, the members of the Constituent Assembly could not hope to succeed in their mission to achieve national unity and stability "by perpetuating a system of government that accentuated existing cleavages in Indian society and tended to create new ones." In their efforts to remove all such cankers from the body politic of the country the Assembly members decided to provide universal adult franchise and joint electorates, by replacing communal electorate. There was to be neither weightage of representation for minorities nor reservation of seats, except for Scheduled Castes and Backward Tribes and that, too, for a short period.' The Lower Chambers, both at the Centre and in the States, were to be directly elected by adult suffrage. Only the Upper Chambers, at both levels, were to be, in part, indirectly elected. The members of the Council of States (Rajya Sabha) were to be elected by the members of the State Assemblies whereas the Legislative Councils, except for those nominated, were to be elected from territorial constituencies by special electorates of the members of municipal, district and other forms of local government, of the university graduates and of teachers in Higher Secondary Schools. The restrictions on the powers of the Legislatures, as under the 1935 Act, were removed and all powers exercised by parliamentary bodies in federal representative democracies were given.

Sovereign Body

Parliament is the name given by the Constitution to the Union Legislature and it consists of the President and two Houses known respectively as the Council of States (Rajya Sabha) and the House of the People (Lok Sabha). The President is a constituent part of Parliament just as the Monarch is in Britain. But the American President is not a constituent part of Congress. The Constitution of the United States provides, "All legislative powers herein granted shall be vested in the Congress of the United States, which shall consist of a Senate and a House of Representatives."

Though the Constitution of India adopts the language of Britain in describing its Legislature at the Centre, and makes the President, like the Monarch of that country, a constituent part of Parliament, yet the Indian Parliament is not sovereign Legislature like the British Parliament. It functions within the bounds of a written Constitution setting up a federal polity and a Supreme Court invested with the power of judicial review. The legislative competence of Parliament is limited, during normal times, to the subjects enumerated in the Union List and the Concurrent List in the Seventh Schedule of the Constitution. Besides, its supremacy within its own sphere of jurisdiction is limited by the Fundamental Rights guaranteed to the citizens in Part III of the Constitution. Article 13 Clause (2) prohibits, subject to specified restriction, the State from making any law which would take away or abridge any of the Fundamental Rights. Where the State makes a law in contravention of the Fundamental Rights, that law shall, to the extent of contravention, be void.

In Britain no formal distinction is made between constitutional and other laws and the same body, Parliament, can change or abrogate any law whatsoever and by the same procedure. The Constitution of India, on the other hand, makes a distinction between statutory law and constitutional law and prescribes a special procedure for amending the latter as incorporated in Article 368. The Supreme Court held in *Keshavananda Bharati v. The State of Kerala* that Article 368 does not enable Parliament to alter the basic structure or framework of the Constitution. The term basic structure is a vague and general term and the Judges themselves did not offer a common agreed meaning. Some included Fundamental Rights and federation in the concept of basic structure while others saw no limit to the amending power of Parliament. The Constitution (Forty-second Amendment) Act 1976, provided that Parliament had full power to amend the Constitution and no Amendment made under article 368 could be questioned in any Court on any ground. The validity of the Forty-second Amendment was questioned and in May 1980 the Supreme Court struck down in the *Minerva Mills* case Section 55 of the Amendment incorporated in Clauses (4) and (5) of Article 368 as it altered or destroyed the basic structure or framework of the Constitution. It was affirmation of the *Keshavananda Bharati* case (1973) judgement. Unless this Judgement is reversed by the Court on the review application of the Union Government or a new amendment of the Constitution is enacted and the Supreme Court upholds that amendment, the power of Parliament cannot extend beyond the limitations placed by the Constitution and the Supreme Court.

Despite these limitations on the authority of Parliament, it is the pivot on which revolves the whole machinery of the Government. Its legislative competence embraces a large field and its financial powers are vast. Its sanction is also necessary for declaring war and making peace. Parliament and the State Legislatures have equal rights to make laws in respect of subjects in the Concurrent List, but if a law enacted by a State Assembly is not in conformity to the law passed by Parliament, the law made by Parliament prevails. Parliament can also legislate on any subject in the State List if the Council of States declares by a resolution that it is necessary in the national interest to do so. During Emergency all restrictions on the legislative and financial jurisdiction of Parliament disappear.

Parliament of Bicameral Nature

One of the most vexing questions of Political Science, wrote B. N. Rao in his *Constitutional Precedents* was the problem of second chambers. The first bicameral legislature was established in New Delhi under the Government of India Act, 1919, but the Upper House was never intended to have a federal role in the sense of providing for equal representation to the various Provinces. In 1919, the federal issue did not arise and the Government of India was constructed on the basis of devolution of authority from the Centre. In the federal structure as envisaged by the Nehru Report, the Upper House would have existed primarily to provide an opportunity for reconsideration of legislation in a "somewhat cooler atmosphere" than that obtaining in the Lower House. Such a precaution was considered especially necessary owing to the existence of sharp communal differences that had been marked in the working of the Lower House at the Centre as well as in the Provinces. The Nehru Committee rejected the argument that in a federal polity the constituent units should be equally represented in the Upper House, as in the United States' Senate, "in view of great differences in size and population of our Provinces." Yet it did recommend the number of representatives assigned to small Provinces could be increased so that their relationship to the great Provinces should not be "wholly disproportionate." The Committee felt that as the members of the Upper House were to be elected by the Provincial Legislatures, it would give the Provinces a feeling of being represented at the Centre.

The same reasons for not having equal representation of the constituent units in the Upper House were cited by the Federal Structure Sub-Committee at the Round Table Conference. The Sub-Committee added that it doubted if equal representation "would commend itself to general public opinion." The Government of India Act, 1935, gave expression to this view point. The Sapru Committee made no recommendations on the subject, and, thus, the issue came to the Constituent Assembly.

The Union and Provincial Constitution Committees considered the question of second chambers in the meetings separately held in June 1947. The Union Constitution Committee was in favour of an Upper House of the State legislatures. Provincial representation was to be one member for each million of population upto five millions and one for each two millions of population thereafter. The maximum representation of a Province was to be twenty. The Report of the Union Constitution Committee is silent for its rejection of equal representation of the constituent units. It may, however, be surmised the members of the Committee agreed with the views expressed in the Nehru Committee Report and at the Round Table Conference. They might also have feared, as B. N. Rau did, that if they allowed equal representation to all units of the Federation, the Provinces "would be swamped" by the Princely States when they acceded to the federation.

The Constituent Assembly considered the report of the Union Constitution Committee during July and August 1947. The debate centred on the role of the second chambers in modern democracies and the necessity of any Upper House in a federal Legislature was discussed only once and that too cursorily. N. Gopalaswami Ayyangar told the Assembly that "the need for a second chamber has been felt practically all over the world wherever there are federations of any importance." Dealing with the role of the second chambers, he said, "After all, the question for us to consider is whether it performs any useful function. The most that we expect the Second Chamber to do is perhaps to hold dignified debates on important issues and to delay legislation which might be the outcome of passions of the moment until passions have subsided and calm consideration could be bestowed on the measures which will be before the Legislature; and we shall take care to provide in the Constitution that whenever on any important matter, particularly matters relating to finance, there is a conflict between the House of the People and the Council of States, it is the view of the House of the People that shall prevail.

Therefore, what we really achieve by the existence of this Second Chamber is only an instrument by which we delay action which might be hastily conceived, and we also give an opportunity, perhaps to seasoned people who may not be in the thickness of the political fray, but who might be willing to participate in the debate with an amount of learning and importance which we do not ordinarily associate with House of the People. That is all that is proposed in regard to this Second Chamber. I think, on the whole, this balance of consideration is in favour of having such a Chamber and taking care to see that it does not prove clog either to legislation or administration. It is significant to note that Ayyangar made no attempt to justify the existence of the Council of States on any of the grounds which are generally responsible fur establishing a second chamber in a federation, especially giving equal representation to the federating units. The new Constitution also did not reflect it. Nor do the powers and functions of the Council of States demonstrate its federal character as a custodian of the interests of the constituent units.

Role of Upper House (Rajya Sabha)

Composition of Rajya Sabha and its Organisation : The Constitution fixes the maximum strength of the Council of States (Rajya Sabha) at 250 including 12 nominated by the President to represent literature, science; art and social service. The maximum number of seats is 34 in the case of Uttar Pradesh and the minimum is 1(one) each for Sikkim, Nagaland, Manipur, Tripura, Meghalaya and Mizoram. The representatives of States are elected by the elected members of their Legislative Assemblies in accordance with the system of proportional representation by means of the single transferable vote. In the case of the Union Territories, members are chosen in such a manner as Parliament may by law determine.

The principle of nomination was the subject of a good deal of criticism in the Constituent Assembly. Some members characterised it as an undemocratic and reactionary element of membership in a democratic republic. Representation of the States on the basis of population and inclusion of nominated members, it was contended, violated the federal principle too. During the early Constitution-making debate an amendment to establish a single chamber was moved, although it was defeated. When in the later debate on the Draft Constitution an attempt was again made for a single Chamber Legislature,

Ananthasayanam Ayyangar defended the Upper House as a way to utilise the services of persons of intellectual capacity and experience of affairs without imperilling the administration. But all such arguments were in favour of bicameralism, and not in defence of the composition of an Upper House in a federation. Nor could it be claimed that the Council of States so constituted would serve as a defence for smaller States. The Council is a continuous body and is not subject to dissolution. Its life is for six years, one-third of the number of members retiring after every two years.

Qualifications for Membership : To be qualified, a candidate for election to the Council of States should be :

(a) a citizen of India, and makes and subscribes before a person authorised by the Election Commission an oath and affirmation that he will bear true faith and allegiance to the Constitution of India as by law established and that he will uphold the sovereignty and integrity of India;

(b) not less than thirty years of age; and

(c) possessing such other qualifications as may be prescribed by Parliament. Under the Representation of the People Act, 1951, a candidate for election to the Council must be a parliamentary elector in the State from which he seeks election.

The qualifications required for eligibility to the Council of States are the same as those required for the House of the People except that the age in the case of the latter must not be less than twenty five years. The framers of the Constitution thought that higher qualifications would tend to give greater dignity to the House and, at the same time, higher average ability. The functions, observed Ambedkar, that a member "is required to discharge in the House require experience, certain amount of knowledge and practical experience in the affairs of the world, and I think if these additional qualifications are accepted, we shall be able to secure the proper sort of candidates who would be able to serve the House better than a mere ordinary voter might do."

Chairperson : The Vice-President of India is the ex-officio Chairman of the Council of States and finds a close parallel in the Vice-President of the United States who is the President of the Senate. The Vice-President of India like his American counterpart, is not a member of the House and both have no right to vote except in the event of a tie. But the President of the Senate is just a moderator. He cannot control debate through the power of recognition; he must recognise the members in the order in which they rise. The Chairman of the Council of States in India enjoys an exalted position. He recognises members to the floor, allots time, 10 decides point of order, maintains order and relevancy in debates, puts questions and announces results. The American Vice-President permanently relinquishes the office of the President of the Senate on his succession to Presidency, but the Vice-President of India fills only a casual vacancy and reverts to his original office of Chairman as soon as the contingency of his acting President is over.

The Council of States elects a Deputy Chairman from amongst its own members and he presides at the sittings of the House in the absence of the Chairman or during any period when the Vice-President is acting, or discharging the functions of the President. In the absence of both the Chairman and the Deputy Chairman from any sitting of the House such person, as may be determined by the Rules of Procedure of the Council of States, acts as Chairman. If no such person is present, some other member as the Council may determine acts as Chairman.

The Chairman may be removed from office by a resolution of the Council of States, provided at least fourteen days notice for the intention to move such a resolution has been given, by a majority of all the then members of the Council, and agreed to by the House of the People. While such a resolution of removal is under consideration of the Council, the Chairman neither presides at any sitting of the Council nor can he exercise a casting vote in case of equality of votes, but he has the right to vote on such a resolution on the first instance. He has the right to speak in, and otherwise to take part in the proceedings in the Council. The Deputy Chairman is also subject to removal in the like manner, except that the resolution of his or her removal does not require the agreement of the House of the People as it is necessary in the case of the Chairman. The salaries and allowances of the Chairman and the Deputy Chairman are determined by Parliament and are charged on the Consolidated Fund of India. The office of the Vice-President carries no salary by itself.

Functions of the Rajya Sabha

Functions Related to Legislation : The process of making laws is the business of the Parliament as a whole, that is, the President, the Council of States (Rajya Sabha) and the House of the People. The House of the People by itself can do nothing, although the actual powers exercised by the President and conferred on the Council of States (Rajya Sabha) are subject to specific limitations. All Bills, other than Money Bills, may originate in either House and no Bill can become a law unless agreed to by both the Houses and assented to by the President. It means that the power of initiating legislation on any non-Money Bill belongs to the Council of States and the House of the People, and such a Bill in order to become law must be agreed to by both the Houses. When a Bill is amended in either House, such amendment must be agreed to by both the Houses. In case of disagreement made in the Bill, the President may summon both the Houses in a joint sitting for the purpose of deliberating and voting on the Bill. At the joint sitting questions are decided by a majority of the members of both Houses present and voting. A Bill thus agreed to and passed is deemed to have been passed by both Houses. The method of joint sitting also applies when a Bill is passed by one House and sent to the other but is not passed within six months after its reception by the other House, excluding any period of prorogation or adjournment over four days.

The Council of States (Rajya Sabha), thus, possesses coordinate legislative powers with the House of the People. Unlike the Parliament Act of 1911 as amended in 1949, in Britain, there is nothing in the Indian Constitution which may limit the legislative powers of the Council of States. On the other hand, the Council of States may press an issue to the extent of summoning joint sitting of the two Houses for the resolution of any disagreement. The Banking Service Commission (Repeal) Bill was passed by the House of the People (Lok Sabha) on December 5, 1977, but rejected by the Council, of States (Rajya Sabha) three days later. The President summoned a joint session of the two Houses to meet on May 16, 1978 to consider the Banking Service Commission (Repeal) Bill. It was the first joint session of Parliament since May 1961 when the two Houses met to resolve differences over the Dowry Prohibition Bill. But in a joint sitting the position of the Council of States becomes weaker as its membership is in a minority of 1 to 2 (250 to 544) with membership of the House of the People. The Council can, at most, delay legislation passed by the House of the People for a period not exceeding six months. It cannot permanently kill it.

Functions Related to Finance : The position of the Council of States (Rajya Sabha) in respect of Money Bills is definitely inferior to that of the House of the People (Lok Sabha). The Constitution defines a Money Bill and it is expressly provided that the decision of the Speaker of the House of the People (Lok Sabha) whether a Bill is a Money Bill or not shall be final. The Constitution prescribes that a Money Bill shall not be introduced in the Council of States and it is barred from rejecting or amending a Money Bill. After a Money Bill has been passed by the House of the People (Lok Sabha), it is transmitted to the Council of States (Rajya Sabha) for its "recommendations" within a period of fourteen days. It is for the House of the People to accept or reject such "recommendations." In case it rejects the "recommendations," the Bill is deemed to have been passed by both Houses in the form in which it was passed by the House of the People. If the Council of States does not return to the House of the People within fourteen days a Money Bill with or without its recommendations," it is deemed to have been passed by both Houses in the form in which it was passed by the House of the People.

The right to vote supplies is perhaps the greatest privilege of a legislative body and under the Constitution this right is the exclusive privilege of the House of the People. The Council of States simply discusses the budget. Demands for grants are not submitted to the Council.

Functions Related to Administration : The Council of States does not control the Executive as the Constitution makes the Council of Ministers responsible to the House of the People. In fact, control and responsibility go together. But the Council of States can influence the Executive in two ways. First, by eliciting information about the actions of Government and secondly, by criticism aimed at the Government. The most effective instrument by which the Council of States seeks information from the Government is through the instrument of oral or written questions together with supplementaries. The normal occasion for criticism of the Executive is debate on a motion of adjournment and the Council shares this privilege with the House. The policy of the Government is really under review when laws are made and the motion of thanks on the address of the President is being discussed. In order to defend the policy of the Government, Ministers are there and some of them are appointed from among its members. The Constitution permits a Minister, who is not a member of the Council, to speak in, and otherwise to take part in its proceedings, though he has no right to vote in that House. The Council, however, cannot bring about the downfall of the Government as the Constitution makes it responsible to the House of the People alone. But the Council amended the President's address to Parliament in January 1980 by the combined strength of the Opposition which commanded a majority. This was the first time since the promulgation of the

Constitution in 1950 that the President's address had been so amended and it set an unusual precedent.

Functions Related to Constitution : The Council of States exercises constituent functions along with the House of the People. A Bill to amend the Constitution may originate in either House. But all Constitution-amending Bills, except the Constitution (Fortieth Amendment) Bill, 1975, have been initiated in the House of the People. A Bill amending the Constitution under article 368 must pass in each House by a majority of not less than two-thirds of the members of that House present and voting. But if such amendment seeks to make any change in Article 54 (election of the President), Article 75 (manner of election of President), Article 73 (extent of executive power of the Union), Article 162 (extent of executive power of the State), Article 241(High Courts for Union territories), or Chapter IV of Part V (the Union Judiciary), Chapter V of Part VI (High Courts), or Chapter I of Part XI (Legislative relations between the Union and the States), or any of the Lists in the Seventh Schedule, or any representation of States in Parliament, or the provisions of Article 368 (amendment of the Constitution) the amendment also requires to be ratified by the Legislatures of not less than one-half of the States by resolution to that effect passed by those Legislatures before the amendment Bill is presented to the President for assent.

The Constitution does not prescribe any procedure for settling differences between the two Houses in case of disagreement on an amendment Bill. The procedure prescribed in Article 108 in case of disagreement on ordinary legislation does not apply to Bills amending the Constitution. Hari Chand is of the opinion that the House of the People represents the will of the people and, consequently, the will of the people crust prevail and the Council of States must not become an obstacle in the way of the popular Chamber. "Moreover, in case the amendment relates to any of the entrenched provisions, the interests of the States are not in danger, because the amendment would require ratification by at least half the States Legislatures and the States can take care of their interests better than the Upper House." But this is not a correct appraisal. The Council of States defeated the Constitution (Twenty-fourth Amendment) Bill, 1970, though by only a fraction of vote, and, again, in 1977 discussion on the Forty-third Amendment Bill was postponed till the next session of Parliament apprehending stout opposition by the Congress (I) which then commanded a majority in the Council. The Opposition also successfully thwarted the Constitution (Forty-fourth Amendment) Bill which was intended to amend the distortions wrought by the Constitution (Forty-second Amendment) Act, 1978, as viewed by the Janata Government and had been passed by an overwhelming majority in the House of the People.

Miscellaneous Functions : The miscellaneous functions of the Council of States are:

(1) The elected members of the Council of States participate in the election of the President of India. The President is elected by an Electoral College consisting of the elected members of both Houses of Parliament and the elected members of the Legislative Assemblies of the States.

(2) The President is liable to be impeached and a resolution to impeach the President may be moved in any House of Parliament and such a resolution must be passed by two-thirds majority of the total membership of that House. When this has been done, the charge is investigated by the other House or by a Court or Tribunal to which that House may refer the Impeachment charge to be investigated. A vote by two-thirds of the total membership of the House which investigates it is necessary for the impeachment to succeed. It means that if the Council of States initiates proceedings of impeachment the House of the People investigates the charge, and if it is initiated by the House the Council investigates and the impeachment,

succeeds if the investigating House passes a resolution by a two-thirds majority of its membership. The Council of States, thus, enjoys co-equal powers with the House of the People in the process of impeachment of the President.

(3) The Vice-President of India is elected by an electoral college consisting of the members of both Houses of Parliament and may be removed from his office by a resolution of the Council of States and agreed to by the House of the People.

(4) A Judge of the Supreme Court or a High Court may be removed for misbehavior or incapacity on the address passed by both Houses of Parliament, supported by a majority of the total membership of, and a two-thirds majority of the members present and voting in each House. Here, too, the powers of the Council of States are identical to those of the House of the People. Agreement of the Council is also necessary if action is to be taken against the Chief Election Commissioner, Comptroller and Auditor-General of India and the members of the Union Public Service Commission.

(5) The report of the Union Public Service Commission, the Comptroller-General, the Scheduled Castes and Tribes Commission and the Finance Commission and are considered both by the Council and the House.

(6) If the Government makes a proposal to take an appointment from he purview of the Union Public Service Commission, both the Houses must agree to its exclusion.

(7) The Council may declare by a resolution, passed by two-thirds majority of its members present and voting, that it is necessary or expedient in the national interests that Parliament should make laws with respect to any matter enumerated in the State List. Such a resolution remains in force for a period not exceeding one year.

(8) The Council is also empowered under Article 312 to create one or more All India Services, if the House of the People declares by a resolution supported by not less than two-thirds of the members present and voting that it is necessary or expedient in the national interest to do so.

(9) The approval of the Council of States is necessary for the continuance of a Proclamation of Emergency (Article 352), failure of constitutional machinery in a State (Article 356), and financial emergency (Article 360), beyond the specified period of time. If the House of the People stands dissolved when a Proclamation is issued or it is dissolved before the expiry of the specified period of time the Council of States alone is to judge the necessity of the continuance of a Proclamation issued under either of the aforesaid Articles. If it does not approve, the Proclamation ceases to operate.

(10) Every Order made by the President suspending the enforcement of Fundamental Rights is required to be laid before each House of Parliament.

(11) The delegated legislation made and rule framed thereunder by various Ministries must be approved by both Houses.

Role of the Upper House : The Council of States was intended to be less powerful and influential than the House of the People and this is in accordance with basic principles which govern the functioning of the Parliamentary system. The Constitution does not give to the Council specific powers to control the Executive. A motion for lack of confidence in the Government cannot be moved therein. It has, no doubt, the right to seek information from the Government through the instrument of questions and supplementaries, to discuss and criticise its policy through debates, and to draw attention to matters of urgent public importance, through the "calling attention" motions but the Council can not plague the Ministry and oust it from office. The Constitution recognises and ordains the collective responsibility of the Council of Ministers to the House of the People alone.

The Council has coordinate powers with the House of the People in ordinary and amending legislation only in theory. It cannot veto legislation passed by the House of the People, but can only delay it. If the differences between the two Houses cannot be settled in the ordinary process of the legislation the President may summon a joint sitting of the two Houses where the will of the House of the People prevails because of its numerical superiority. In matters financial, the Council is absolutely powerless, even not at par with the British House of Lords. Money Bills originate in the House of the People and if a question arises whether a particular Bill is a Money Bill or not, the decision of the Speaker is final. The House of the People simply transmits a Money Bill to the Council for "recommendations" and it is required to return it within fourteen days of its receipt. If it is not returned within the specified time or returns it with "recommendations" which are not acceptable to the House of the People, the Money Bill is deemed to have been passed by both Houses, in the form in which it was originally passed by the House of the People. Demands for grants are not submitted to the Council; sanctioning of public expenditure is the exclusive right of the House of the People.

The Council does not even serve the purpose of a federal second chamber. Neither the critics of a Second Chamber in the Constituent Assembly nor its supporters did advance a single federal argument. The well-accepted practice of a federal polity is to make the Upper Chamber a representative House of the constituent units and its constitution is based upon equality by representation irrespective of the size and population of the federating units. The Council of States does not accord equal representation to the States of the Union of India. It is not, at the same time, the voice of the States and has no power to safeguard their interests. The justification of the Council of States, remarks Morris-Jones, "has always been in terms of 'second thought' rather than 'State rights." On no occasion the federal conscience of the members of the Council of States revolted whenever the State Assemblies were dissolved; even nine Assemblies twice at one stroke in 1977 and 190, without any valid reason or cause and contrary to the expectations of the framers of the Constitution.

It does not, however, mean that the Council of States occupies the same pitiable position as French Council of Republic under the Constitution of the Fourth Republic. Nor is it so ineffective as the Canadian Senate. "There is a misconception," wrote B.D. Jatti, Vice-President of India, "about the powers of the Rajya Sabha in financial matters." It is true, he says, that Money Bills cannot be introduced in the Council and it is deemed to have been passed by both Houses if the Council does not make any "recommen-dation" within fourteen days and if "recommen-dations" are made it is up to the House of the People to a accept or reject such "recommendations."

But the Constitution also provides that the Union Budget is to be laid before both the Houses of Parliament and it is discussed in the Council also, although the demands for grants are to be made only in the House of the People. A practice has, however, come into vogue that the Council of States discusses the working of three or four important Ministries as it chooses during the Budget session. The reports of the Comptroller General relating to the accounts of the Union are also laid before both Houses. The Council of States is also represented on two of the financial committees of Parliament-the Committee on Public Accounts, and the Committee on Public Undertakings.

The Council of States has, thus, a fairly adequate opportunity in influencing and even shaping the financial affairs of the country. It has not hesitated to recommend quite a number of amendments in the Income-Tax Bill, 1961 and the House of the People accepted all the proposed amendments.

The Council of States significantly performs the function of influencing the Government and weightage is given to the views expressed on the floor of the House by elder statesmen and eminent parliamentarians. Since the Council is smaller in membership and less worried by the pressure of work, the debates in the Council are less frequently subject to time control through time limits. The Council provides a calmer atmosphere where members can debate controversial questions in well-informed and objective manner. The debates are often outspoken marked by dignity and a remarkable responsiveness of public opinion. The tradition of dignified debates, observed, B.N. Banerjee, "which was built up by the House is the result of a happy combination of circumstances not the least of which is the fact that the five Chairmen of the Rajya Sabha so far are among the most eminent person experts in their own lines." All these persons "have given an aura of dignity to the atmosphere of the House by conducting the proceedings with judicious combination of firmness and flexibility."

The co-equal powers of the Council of States on constitutional amendments are of great importance. The House of the People cannot by itself amend the Constitution unless the Council agrees to such a change. The provisions of Article 108 governing the joint sittings of the two Houses in case of disagreement do not apply to Bills amending the Constitution. The Constitution (Twenty-fourth Amendment) Bill, 1970, which was passed by an overwhelming majority in the House of the People, was defeated in the Council of States by only a fraction of vote and, consequently, the amending Bill fell through. Apprehending stout opposition to the Constitution (Forty-third Amendment) Bill, 1977, its discussion was postponed till the next session of Parliament. The Council refused to adopt the Constitution (Forty-fourth Amendment) Bill 1978 except with five amendments. The Congress Opposition stalled on April 11, 1977 the final passage of the two official Bills, one to extend the term of Goa, Daman and Diu and Mizoram Assemblies, and the other to extend the term of the Delhi Metropolitan Council. Intervening in the discussion on a non-official Bill moved by the Communist Member Bhupesh Gupta seeking to amend Article 368 to provide that in the event of a disagreement between the two Houses over an amendment Bill of the Constitution there should be a joint session for resolving the differences, the Law Minister said that such suggestions were considered in 1971 and found unnecessary.

Even with regard to ordinary legislation referred by the President to a joint sitting of the two Houses under article 108, B.N. Banerjee, the Secretary-General of the Council of States, rebutted the argument that the views of the House of the People will invariably prevail because of its numerical superiority. He explains that the critics of the Council of States "ignore the fact that a disagreement which may arise on important issues may not be the House qua *the House* but may arise on the basis of policies and approaches of the different political parties in the two Houses on the various issues. It is possible to contemplate a situation in which the decision of the Lok Sabha may be outvoted in joint sitting of two Houses. There have been only two joint sittings of both Houses so far in order to resolve a deadlock on the Dowry Prohibition Bill in May 1961, and on the Banking Service Commission (Repeal) Bill in May 1978. In the Dowry Prohibition Bill one of the most important amendments, which the Council of States had been insisting from the, beginning and the House of the People had been refusing to accept, was adopted at a joint sitting in May 1961.

The Constitution confers on the Council two special powers exclusively exercised by it and not shared with the House of the People. As stated earlier, Parliament is empowered to legislate with respect to any matters on the State List of the Seventh Schedule if the Council of States declared by a resolution that it is necessary or expedient in the national interest that Parliament should make laws thereon. Again, under Article 312 if the Council passes a resolution declaring that it is necessary or expedient in the national interest to create one or more All-India services common to the Union and States, Parliament will have the power to create by law such services. The Council of States twice passed such resolutions in 1961 and 1965. The resolution passed on December 6, 1961 recommended the creation of Indian Service of Engineers, the Indian Forest Service and Indian Medical and Health Services. On March 30, 1965 the Council passed a resolution for the creation of the Indian Education Service, though both these resolutions have not been implemented so far.

As a body which is not subject to dissolution but which perpetually renews itself every two years, the Council of States symbolises the permanence and continuity of Parliamentary institutions of the country. This continuity acquires a special significance when the House of the People stands dissolved and the Council of States is to discharge the Constitutional obligation under Articles 352, 356 and 360 relating to declaration of Emergency either due to war or external aggression or armed rebellion or threat thereto; breakdown of the constitutional machinery in a State; or financial Emergency.

These specific constitutional provisions make the Council of States an integral part of the machinery of Government. It is true, that the Council of States was not designed to view with the House of the People, but it was not also the intention of the Constitution-makers to render the Council to play the "humble role of an unimportant adviser" or an occasional check on hasty legislation. In practice, the Council has, from the beginning of its career, played its role effectively in the affairs of the State and has vigorously focussed the attention of the Government on many matters of special importance in the life of the nation. In 1969, the Council passed the resolution that "this House is of the opinion that Government should take legal and other steps for the abolition of privy purses and privileges of ex-rulers before presentation of the general Budget in the coming February session of Parliament." The Council also acclaimed the nationalisation of the fourteen banks. The vigilant members of the Council made persistent demands during discussions for inquiring into the charges against the

Punjab Chief Minister Partap Singh Kairon, grant of industrial licences to the Birlas and the affairs of Dharam Teja and Jayanti Shipping Company. Likewise, public attention on alleged irregularity in respect of import licences to some firms of Pondicherry was focussed for the first time through a starred question on August 27, 1974. Again, on August 10, 1978 the Council of States adopted a resolution demanding a probe into allegations of corruption against members of the families of Prime Minister Morarji Desai and Home Minister Charan Singh. The Chairman, B.D. Jatti, pointed out that the motion was necessarily a "recommendation" and it was for the Government to accept or not. When the Government decided not to accept the "recommendation", the Council asserted itself in a way thwarting the proceedings of the House compelling the Prime Minister to announce the Government's decision to refer the charges as contained in the resolution of the Council to the Chief Justice eventually leading to Vaidialingam probe which indicted the close relations of Desai and Charan Singh. The important committees, like the Committee on subordinate Legislation and Committee on Government Assurance have always played an effective role in influencing and supervising the administrative actions of the Government. The Committee on Petitions has proved to be a useful forum for ventilating the grievances of the public and getting redressed. B.D. Jatti, the former Vice-President of India and the Chairman of the Council, asserted that the Council of States "by its record of work has proved to be an effective force and I can say with confidence that in the years to come the critics of the second chamber are bound to find themselves in negligible minority.""

The Council of States has certainly belied the apprehensions of the critics of bicameralism in the Constituent Assembly that the Council will be "a clog in the wheel of progress of India", or that it could serve to keep the capitalistic outlook safe in India and that it would be a "unnecessary drain on our poor economy." The world has come a long way from Abbe Sieyes who disfavoured bicameralism with the epigram : "If a second chamber dissents from the first, it is mischievous; if it agrees-it is superfluous" Democracy proved that neither it is mischievous nor superfluous. The role and relevance of bicameralism has now veered round to John Stuart Mill who wrote, "A majority in a single Assembly ....easily becomes despotic and overweening, if released from the necessity of considering whether its acts will be concurred by another constituted authority." India has along tradition of its assemblies going down to the post-Vedic period and that heritage finds expression in a verse from Mahabharata inscribed on the opening page of "Twenty-five years of Rajya Sabha" brought out by the Rajya Sabha Secretariat in 1977.

That's not an Assembly where there are no eldermen,

Those are not elders, who do not speak with righteousness.

But there is one aspect against which the Council of States must guard itself. While welcoming the sixty-four new members of the Council of States on April 6, 1960, Vice-President Radhakrishnan called upon them to fight "inertia, obscurantism, reaction and superstition." These are the evils from which second chambers suffer in general and invite a widespread demand for their abolition. The Council of States should not be allowed to become a political prisoners' home. Law-making is a specialised job; and a modicum of technical knowledge and a certain intellectual ability are essential even to understand the problems that confront Legislatures in our times. The criterion laid down in the Constitution for nominations is a partial indication of what is expected of a second chamber. But it is evident from the nominations so far made that to a great extent the intentions of the framers of the Constitution have not been realised. The Congress did not always consciously try to fill the nominations with a corpus of special knowledge such as cannot be ensured in the House of the People. Nor have the indirect elections of the remaining members introduced a body of seasoned parliamentarians, who might import into the debates "an amount of learning and importance", as

Gopalswami Ayyangar argued in the Constituent Assembly. According to Morris-Jones the Council of States has three outstanding merits : "It supplies additional political positions for which there is a demand, it provides some additional debating opportunities for which there is occasionally need, and it assists in the resolution of the legislative time table problems." It is, accordingly, incumbent on all political parties to help the Council of States to play its requisite role by sending to it members whose party grading may be low but I.Q. is high.

"But the House of the Elders is no longer elderly, feels the Chief Reporter, S. P. Agarwal, of the Council who retired recently after covering the Upper House for over thirty years. His observations are relevant to the atmosphere that now prevails in this House as compared to 1952, when it began its career. The first ten years of the Council of States were the House's finest hours. During this period there was hardly an occasion to call the House to order. Even if a member spoke for an hour he was heard with respect and without interruption. Points of order were rare. According to Agarwal there were less than a dozen expuctions during this period. Members themselves withdrew any word they felt was unparliamentary.

But the change began in the early seventies and "the Rajya Sabha today has become more youthful. It is now vibrating with the situation prevailing outside in the country. The quality of the debate as also the composition is not as merited today as it was in the past. A major time of the House is lost in personal and party squabbles. Scant attention is paid to the rules of procedure and the rulings of the Chairman are invariably defied. Use of unparliamentary language and unruly behaviour rule the day. There are "half a dozen expunctions in every session" and not a day passes without an order that a Member's speech should not be recorded. The practice of ordering the House reporters not to take notes as the Member refuses to listen to the Chairman's entreaties to be seated has become "in vogue" since seventies. Walk-ups is a normal feature.

But the most disturbing development is the defiance of the Chairman's rulings and often use of in decorous language on his observations and comments on minor points at issue or when the Chairman performs his duty to protect the right of a Private Member in seeking more information on a question raised. Such an attitude of the parliamentarians and more so of seasoned Members of the House and Ministers, too, not only undermines the authority and dignity of the Chair, but the prestige of the House itself. A sharp clash between the Chairman, M. Hidayatullah, and the leader of the Janata Party of the House marked the start of the proceedings on September 15, 1981. Seconds after the Chairman occupied his seat and called for the first question, Piloo Mody stood up to ask him when he and some of his colleagues could raise certain issues in his (M. Hidayatullah's) presence in the House. The Chairman told him that he did not have to guarantee his presence in the House, but "You can certainly come to my chamber and raise anything you want." When Mody sharply insisted that the members of the House were entitled to raise matters in the House in his presence and not in his chamber, the Chairman reminded him, "Nobody seems to have told you that you are sometimes inclined to be rude." Mody retorted, "I am inclined to be rude as I am recipient of rudeness also. I hope you will take it in the same spirit., "

But Pranab Mukherjee's behaviour, who was the Finance Minister and the Leader of the House, reveals more than it can be described. On November 2, 1982, the Chairman intervened on behalf of a Member who was not satisfied with the Finance Minister's replies to a question on World Bank loans to developing countries. The Minister replied that he had already given the requisite information. But the Chairman did not agree with him. The Minister thereupon became sharp in his reply. The Chairman told him, "There is such a thing as politeness." Mukherjee retorted, "Yes, that is why I do not want, that you should come between me and the Member." The Chairman reminded him, "I will, that is why I am sitting in the Chair." Mukherjee curtly replied, "I will accept your ruling without any question ..... But don't have a running commentary. Let me answer the question in my own way. "

Relevant proceedings of the Constituent Assembly suggest that rewarding talent was not the sole aim of the Constitution-makers in providing for nominated members. They visualised the Council of States as a mechanism for moderating, rather than rivalling or thwarting the House of the People (Lok Sabha). One member likened the Upper Chamber to the saucer that might cool the beverage in a cup but which could never threaten the cup. If the Council of States was to mellow the Lower House's emotions with fresh reflection, the nominated members were to be of a special value as they were expected to add a component wisdom that was not only specialised but also detached and non-partisan. But this precious expectation has not been fulfilled as nominations have now degenerated into party spoils.

Even biennial elections to the Council of States are being fought strictly on party lines and selection of candidates is made purely on party considerations. Those who, per chance, were non-party nominees they did not remain aloof from active politics and many formally joined the ruling party as it was rewarding to do so. The Anti-defection law is now a great deterrent, but such nominations are not likely to disappear altogether. The voting pattern of most others shows that they have generally sided with the Government whatever be the merit of the measure under consideration. Independence and talent are guarantees against the principle of nomination in vogue.

Lower House verses Upper House : Jawaharlal Nehru gave a succinct exposition about the relations of the Council of States and the House of the People. "Under our Constitution," he explained, "Parliament consists of two Houses, each functioning in the allotted sphere laid down in the Constitution .... sometimes we refer back to practice and conventions prevailing in the Houses of Parliament of the United Kingdom and even refer erroneously to an Upper House and Lower House. I do not think that is correct .... To consider either of these Houses an Upper House or a Lower House is not correct. Each House has full authority to regulate its procedure within the limits of the Constitution. Neither House by itself constitutes Parliament. It is the two Houses together that are the Parliament in India.

The successful working of our constitution, as of our democratic structure, demands the closest cooperation between the two Houses." The Council has powers similar to those of the House of the People, except in matters financial and responsibility of the Council of Ministers. The party composition of both Houses remained similar till March, 1977 when Congress lost its majority in the House of People but regained its previous position after January 1980, though it did not command a two-third majority. Even the social composition of the Council and the House resembles each other. The Council had its members the galaxy of some eminent personalities who served the Council since it came into existence; Pattabhi Sitaramayya, Sardar K. M. Panikkar, Dr. Tara Chand, Dr. Radha Kumud Mukherjee, Prof. S. N. Bose, B.R. Ambedkar, Alladi Krishnaswami Ayyar, P. N. Sapru, G. S. Pathak, M. C. Setalved, M. C. Chagla, C. K. Daphtary, K. Santhanam, Rama Krishna Rao, Dr. Ramaswami Mudliar, R.R. Diwakar and Bhupesh Gupta are a few of the many more.

The procedure for the conduct of business in both Houses is also not appreciably distinguishable. The Council has a regular question hour 24 and the same half-an-hour discussion procedure as in the House of the People. From 1964 the revised Rules of Procedure provide for discussion on matters of urgent public importance. Petitions for redress of grievances can be made to the Council. A new Committee, namely, the Committee on Subordinate Legislation has since been extended by including within the ambit of its functions various rules, regulations and orders framed in pursuance of the Constitution also. The Committee on Government Assurances has also been set up.

The Government, too, had made an effort to introduce first in the Council of States an increasing number of public Bills. Since 1952 up to the end of December 1974, 312 Government Bills were introduced in the Council. From the analysis of the subject-matter of those Bills it can definitely be said that quite a good number of them were of immense social, educational and legal importance. Apart from the Hindu Marriage and Divorce Bill, 1952, the Hindu Minority and Guardianship Bill, 1953, the Hindu Succession Bill, 1954 and the Hindu Adoptions and Maintenance Bill, 1956, some of the more important legislative measures introduced in the Council were the Working Journalists (Industrial Disputes) Bill, 1955, the Children Bill, 1959, the Foreign Marriage Bill 1963, the Press Council Bill, 1963, the Banaras Hindu University (Amendment) Bill 1964, the Jawaharlal Nehru University bill 1964, the Monopolies and Restrictive Trade Practices Bill, 1967, the Medical Termination of Pregnancy Bill, 1969, the Code of Criminal Procedure Bill, 1970, the Foreign Contribution (Regulation) Bill, 1974. The Constitution (Fortieth Amendment) Bill, 1975 was also initiated in the Council of States.

The Council of States, thus, started its career on the same lines as the House of the People. But being a chamber primarily intended for reflection, its members had the psychological realisation of its inferiority and, consequently, they felt frustrated. There had been also vehement critics of bicameralism who strongly pleaded for its abolition. But, "it is the habit of institutions," as Morris-Jones had remarked, "to give birth to loyalties. The Council, therefore, tried to assert itself in order to remove the impression of its inferiority. A bitter rivalry between the two Houses soon developed despite the dominating position of one party in both Houses.

The first clash between the two Houses occurred during the Budget session of 1953 when the Council of States refused to accept the position of subordination by disallowing the Law Minister, a member-Minister of the Council, to appear before the House of the People, on its call, to clear some misunderstanding that had arisen on the Income-Tax (Amendment) Bill, 1952. The Council of States thereupon passed a resolution that "this Council is of the opinion that the Leader of the Council (Law Minister Biswas) be directed not to present himself in any capacity whatsoever in the House of the People."

It angered the members of the other House and they asserted that Ministers were responsible to the House of the People and doubted the propriety of the Council's resolution." There would have been an open rupture if the tactful intervention of the Prime Minister had not saved the situation.

Soon there was another occasion for conflict. In January 1953 the Rules Committee of the Council of States sent its proposals with regard to the Public Accounts Committee to the House of the People. It had suggested that the Council should have either a Public Accounts Committee of its own, or seven of its members should be added to make it a joint committee of both Houses. The Public Accounts Committee passed a resolution that a joint committee of the two Houses or a separate committee of the Council "would be against principles underlying the Constitution." The Rules Committee of the House of the People, which considered the proposal of the Rules Committee of the Council, agreed with the opinion expressed by the Public Accounts Committee in its resolution. The matter would have ended there, but the motion of the Prime Minister in the House "to recommend to the Council of States that they nominate seven members to associate with the Public Accounts Committee of this House" brought the issue in the open. The motion of the Prime Minister did not envisage a Joint Public Accounts Committee of two Houses, yet it caused a good deal of criticism and resentment in the House of the People. It was on the assurance of the Prime Minister that the Committee would be a Committee of the House of the People under the control of the Speaker and that the financial powers of the House were in no way threatened that the motion was finally passed in December 1953 and the seven members of the Council of States joined the Public Accounts Committee in

May 1954. Similar difficulties arose with regard to the composition of Joint Committees of both Houses and somewhat sullenly the House of the People agreed to the proposals of the Council of States.

The Chatterjee incident engendered still more excitement and resentment. N.C. Chatterjee, a Member of the House of the People, was reported to have said that the Upper House, "which is supposed to be a body of elders, seems to be behaving irresponsibly like a pack of urchins." The question of privileges was raised in the Council of States and the Chairman directed the Secretary of the Council to ascertain the facts. The House members objected to the letter of the Council Secretary inquiring from N. C. Chatterjee whether the report was correct. The Speaker held that the Secretary's letter was more "in the nature of a writ" and suggested that the reference to this particular issue, and the general problem of procedure in such cases be made to a joint meeting of the Privileges Committees of both Houses. The Council agreed to the Speaker's suggestion and the two Privileges Committees worked out an acceptable procedure for cases where a member of the House commits a breach of the privileges of the other.

The Chairman of the Legislative Council (Rajya Sabha) M. Hidayatullah, while interpreting Rule 187 relating to the rights and privileges of the members of the Upper House on the Parliamentary Committee on Public Undertakings gave his ruling, July 1982, that members of the Council on this Committee were "associate members." As a consequence of this ruling the Opposition members of the Council in Public Undertakings Committee and the Public Accounts Committee resigned *en bloc.* The opposition members unanimously demanded that Rule 187 be so amended as to remove the anomaly at the earliest. The Speaker of the House of the People in his ruling on the issue recalled what Jawaharlal Nehru had said on May 13, 1953 in support of the motion for association of members of the Council of States with the Public Accounts Committee and observed, "It has been ceaseless endeavour" to live up to

Nehru's sagacious counsel "in letter and spirit". Intervening in the discussion, Finance Minister Pranab Mukherjee assured the Council, on August 2, 1982, that it would not be difficult to sort out the matter on the basis of the usages, practices and conventions and the Speaker's ruling of July 28, 1982 that members of both Houses of Parliament were equal in every respect.

These disputes brought into prominence the question of the utility of the Council of States. A Private Member moved a resolution in the House of the People in April, 1954 demanding the abolition of the Upper House. Some Members of the House belonging to the Congress Party and the Leftists advanced the same old familiar argument that the Council of States was a stronghold of reactionary elements and a device to flout the voice of the people. One Member spoke about "the mad drive towards equalisation of powers and functions." Some argued for the retention of the Council of States but urged that its members should be chosen differently.

The Government view was that the Council of States had not been given a fair trial and that it was too early to pronounce a judgement on its utility. Once again, after two decades, Niren Ghosh, Marxist member of the Council, while welcoming B.D. Jatti, on assuming the office of the Vice-President of India and, as such, Chairman of the Council on August 31, 1974, on behalf of his Party, said that the Council of States represented the States of the Union and the nationalities of the Union and accordingly, deserved to be "upgraded" in its parliamentary powers. He suggested that the Constitution be so amended as to give equal powers, to the Council of States and the House of the People.

Unless it is acceptably proved that democracy does not need a second chamber, and more so a federation, it is not democratic to urge for its abolition. Institutions are always reluctant to vanish and it does not seem likely that public opinion could be made to agree to the liquidation of the Council of States. But enjoyment of identical powers and functions by both of Houses means a sheer duplication and the advantages of such a system of legislature are questionable. Democracy has decidedly made the representative Chamber a predominant partner, and the second Chamber is created to exercise a moderating influence, a counterpoises to democratic fervour, a safety which lies to sober second thought and, consequently, a check on hasty and ill-considered legislation. It serves as a brake, but not too tight a brake which may lead to an open rupture between the two Chambers.

The intention of the framers of India's Constitution was significantly clear on this point and the Constitution itself is quite specific about it. Once this point is appreciated by both the Houses the cause or causes of conflict, if any, are sure to disappear and each House will shine within its allotted sphere of functions.

Incredible as it may seem, even a former Prime Minister is known to have told some senior Members of the Council of States on more than one occasion that the "Lok Sabha is the real Parliament. We are directly elected by the people not indirectly. Whom does your House represent ? It should be abolished." He altogether forgot that India is a federation for which second Chamber is the prerequisite condition as it represents the States, its constituent units.

Such like utterances create confusion and friction without realising the repercussion on the body politic. Morris-Jones has succinctly said, "What is certain is that peaceful co-existence is difficult if the two Houses continue to desire to perform the same functions."

If their roles are not soon distinguished, "the tradition of rivalry will soon become established and the Council will continue to attract a large number of persons who would have been more readily found themselves in the House of the People." The practice of rivalry is most wasteful exercise of political energies "and it can only serve to lower Parliament as a whole in public esteem," he added.

B. D. Jatti foresees an important role that the Council of States may play in the body politic of the Country. He maintains, "In view of the present political set-up in the country a situation may arise when the governments in a number of States may be run by political parties other than the party at the Centre and this will have its impact on the Rajya Sabha. Then the Rajya Sabha will have an important role to play in handling the problem of federal adjustment."

Role of Lower House (Lok Sabha)

Its Composition and Organisation : The House of the People (Lok Sabha) is the representative Chamber of Parliament of India. It had a maximum membership of 525; not more than 500 members chosen by direct election from territorial constituencies in the States and not more than 25 members from the Union Territories chosen in such a manner as Parliament by law provided. The Constitution (Thirty-first Amendment) Act, 1973, increased the upper limit for representation of the States to 525 and set the limit for representation of the Union Territories at 20. The Goa, Daman and Diu Reorganisation Act, 1987, necessitated further change in the composition of the House of the People. Article 81 now provides that subject to the provisions of Article 331, relating to nomination of not more than two members of the Anglo-Indian Community the House of the People shall consist of

(a) not more than five hundred and thirty members chosen by direct election from territorial constituencies in the States, and

(b) not more than twenty members to represent the Union Territories, chosen in such manner as Parliament may by law provide.

A person is qualified to be chosen to fill a seat in the House of the People if he :

(a) is a citizen of India, and makes and subscribes before some person authorised in that behalf by the Election Commission an oath or affirmation according to the form set out for the purpose in the Third Schedule to the Constitution;

(b) is not less than twenty-five years of age; and

(c) possesses such other qualifications as may be prescribed in that behalf by or under any law made by Parliament.

In the case of a seat reserved for the Scheduled Castes in any State, a candidate for election to the House of the People should be a member of any of the Scheduled Castes, whether of that State or of any other State and should be a elector for a parliamentary constituency: In the case of a seat reserved for Scheduled Tribes in any State, he should be a member of any of the scheduled Tribes, whether of that State or of any other State and should be an elector for any parliamentary constituency.

A person is disqualified for being chosen as, and for being a member of either House of Parliament :

(i) if he holds any such office of profit under the Government of India or the Government of any States as is declared by Parliament by law to disqualify its holders;

(ii) if he is of unsound mind and stands so declared by a competent court;

(iii) if he is an undischarged insolvent;

(iv) if he is not a citizen of India, or has voluntarily acquired the citizenship of a foreign State, or is under any acknowledgment of allegiance or adherence to a foreign State; and

(v) if he is so disqualified by or under any law made by Parliament.

Article 103 deals with the decision on questions as to disqualification of members. Originally, it provided that all questions about the disqualification of a person would be decided by the President in accordance with the opinion rendered by the Election Commission. The Constitution (Forty-second Amendment) Act, 1976, substituted a new Article providing that the question whether a member had become subject to any of the disqualifications mentioned in Article 102 (1) or as to whether a person, found guilty of a corrupt practice at an election to a House of Parliament under any law made by Parliament was disqualified, including the question as to the period of disqualification, would be decided by the President after consulting the Election Commission. The Election Commission might hold any inquiry for this purpose as it deemed fit. The decision of the President in this respect was final.

The Constitution (Forty-fourth Amendment) Act, 1978, omitted Article 103 as inserted by the one restoring the original position. It now provides that the question whether a member has become subject to any of the disqualifications mentioned in Article 102 (1) shall be referred to the decision of the President and his decision shall be final. But before giving any such decision, the President shall obtain the opinion of the Election Commission and act according to such opinion.

The Union Constitution Committee had recommended a term of four years for the House. The Drafting Committee accepted the opinion of de Valera, and changed it into five years. The Draft Constitution in a footnote explained the justification for this change. It said, "The Committee has inserted 'five years' instead of 'four years' as the life of the House of the People as it considers that under parliamentary system of government the first year of a Minister's term of office would generally be taken up in gaining knowledge of the work of administration and the last year would be taken up in preparing for the next general election, and there would thus be only two years for effective work which should be too short a period for planned administration."

Speaker's Office

Speaker's Office : The House elects its own Speaker from among its members to preside over its sittings and conduct its proceedings. The Speaker vacates his office if he ceases to be a member of the House. He may at any time resign from his office or may be removed on a resolution passed by a majority of all the then members of the House. Fourteen days' notice for moving such a resolution is required to be given. The Speaker does not vacate his office on the dissolution of the House; he continues in office until immediately before the first sitting of the reconstitued House after the dissolution.

The Constitution also provides for the office of the Deputy Speaker and he performs the duties of the Speaker when the latter is absent or while the office of the Speaker is vacant. In Britain the Speaker is indispensable and without him the House can not meet. In India, on the other hand, the Constitution definitely provides, that while the office of the Speaker is vacant the duties of the office shall be performed by the Deputy Speaker. And if the office of the Deputy Speaker, too, happens to be vacant, then, the duties of the office of the Speaker shall be performed by such member of the House, as the President may appoint for the purpose. When both the Speaker and the Deputy Speaker are absent from any sitting of the House one of such members as may be determined by the Rules of Procedure of the House acts as Speaker. The Rules of Procedure and Conduct of Business in Parliament, 1950, provide that at the commencement of the Parliament or from time to time as the case may be, the Speaker nominates from amongst the members of Parliament a panel of not more than six chairmen any one of whom may preside in the absence of the Speaker and the Deputy Speaker when so required by the Speaker or in his absence by the Deputy Speaker. If none of the chairmen of the panel be available, the House may choose one of its members to act as Speaker. Neither the Speaker nor the Deputy Speaker is to preside while a resolution for his own removal is under consideration, although he is entitled to be present, speak in and otherwise to take part in the proceedings of the House. He shall also have the right to vote but only in the first instance on such resolution or on any other matter during such proceedings. But he does not exercise a casting vote in the case of an equality of votes.

The Constitution gives to the Speaker only a casting vote to be exercised in the case of equality of votes. This provision incorporates the British convention that the Speaker of the House of the Commons does not vote except in case of a tie. But the British Speaker usually endeavours to give the casting vote in such a way that it does not make the decision final, thereby extending to the House another opportunity to consider the question.

The Constitution provides that the Speaker and the Deputy Speaker shall receive such salaries and allowances as may be determined by Parliament and they are charged on the Consolidated Fund of India.

Speaker's Position : The office of the Speaker is of much dignity, honour and authority. Like the Speaker of the British House of Commons, the Speaker of the House of the People (Lok Sabha) interprets the will of the House and speaks for it as well as to it. He is the custodian of the dignity of the House and an impartial arbiter in its proceedings. Speaking in the Constituent Assembly of India (Legislative), on March 8, 1948, on the occasion of the unveiling of the portrait of the late V.J. Patel, the Prime Minister observed: "Now, Sir, specially on behalf of the government, may I say that we would like the distinguished occupant of this Chair now and always to guard the freedom and liberties of the House from every possible danger, even from the danger of executive intrusion. There is always that danger—even from a National Government that it may choose to ride roughshod over the opinions of a minority, and it is there that the Speaker comes to protect each single member, or each single group........ Vithalbhai Patel.... laid the foundations of those traditions which have already grown up round the Chair .... I hope that those traditions will continue, because the position of the Speaker is not an individual's position or an honour done to an individual. The Speaker represents the House. He represents the dignity of the House and because the House represents the nation, in a particular way, the Speaker becomes the symbol of the nation's liberty and freedom. Therefore, it is right that should be an honoured position, a free position and should be occupied always by men of outstanding ability and impartiality.'

Vithalbhai Patel may be regarded as the first Speaker in India, though his official designation was the President of the Legislative Assembly, who laid the foundations of the office by following the British traditions. Immediately after his election to the Chair in 1925, he declared himself a no party man and rigidly abstained from any kind of political activity. He had established such a firm reputation as a Speaker and his position was so unchallenged that in spite of the many remarkable rulings he gave which were not to the liking of the Government of the day he was unanimously elected to the Chair both by the official and non-official members of the Assembly of that day. And when the urge to participate in the Civil Disobedience Movement of 1930 came Patel resigned from his office. But the Congress was the first to violate the conventions associated with the office of the Speaker in Britain and so scrupulously observed by Vithalbhai Patel. Mohammed Yakub succeeded Patel, but he was there only for a session. Ibrahim Rahimtula, who succeeded Yakub soon after his election to Chair, resigned for reasons of health. Then, came Shanmukham Chetty. But at the next General Election, Shanmukham Chetty was opposed and defeated by the Congress candidate.

Since then, the retiring Speakers have always been opposed in the General Election and the Speakers themselves, till the election of N. Sanjiva Reddy, retained their active party affiliations. On May 17,1967 when Reddy was elected Speaker of the Fourth House of the People, he observed, "My office requires of me to be impartial and judicious in the conduct of my work. I can assure you with all the force at my command that I will try to live up to this requirement and maintain the high traditions set by my predecessors. As a necessary corollary to this resolve, I resign my membership of the party (Congress) to which I had the honour to belong for 34 years. So long as I occupy this Chair it shall be my endeavour to see that all sections of this House get an honest impression that I do not belong to any party at all." When Gurdial Singh Dhillon was elected Speaker in August 1969, he resigned from the Congress Party in Parliament but continued to be a member of the Congress Party.

N. Sanjiva Reddy resigned from the Speakership in 1969 and was nominated the Congress candidate for the Fourth Presidential election. Reddy was again elected the Speaker of the Sixth House of the People as a Janata Party candidate. But this time he did not resign from his party. He took, on the other hand, active part in the party politics. Reddy disclosed the mind of his Party when he told the newsmen at Hyderabad on April 9, 1977 that the Forty-third Constitutional Amendment Bill, which sought to reduce the term of the House of the People and the State Assemblies to five years, was introduced in Parliament with the Presidential election in mind. He also said that the Bill was introduced to "respect the feeling of Mr. Jayaprakash Narayan who wanted the States also to go to polls. Addressing a public meeting at Tirupati on April 12, 1977, Reddy asked the Janata Party workers to find out what was wrong with their campaigning in the South. He asked the rural youth, especially the educated, to tour the villages and explain to the people why the Janata Party was voted to power in the North and how the unity of the country should be preserved. "There is no question of North versus South in elections," he added.

The Congress Working Committee in a resolution determined that the Speakers, both in the States as well at the Centre, should keep back from Congress election. But this decision of the Working Commute did not imply that they could remain members of the Congress Party. This point was further made clear by G.V. Mavalankar, Speaker of the First Lok Sabha. Speaker maintained, the speaker in India is not today absolutely out of the political arena as the speaker of the

House of Commons though with very extensive limitations on his activities. He may continue to be a member of his Party, but he should not take part in the affairs of the party, particularly in regard to matters which are likely to come before the House for discussion and decision. We have also considered it proper that he should not take sides in public controversies in respect of matters likely to come before the House. In short, he should not identify himself with any propaganda or express any opinions which are likely to embarrass his position as the presiding authority or is likely to create an impression that the Speaker is a partisan."

Mavalankar admitted that the logical corollary of the Speaker's position in Britain is that his seat is not contested in the General Election and he is elected Speaker so long as he wishes to be so elected irrespective of his party affiliation. But "with the present state of political consciousness of public life in India," Mavalankar added, "it is too much to expect that people with different ideologies will all respect the convention of not contesting the election of the Speaker and it is this aspect which very seriously affects the adoption in toto of all British conventions in respect of the office of the Speaker. "

Mavalankar considered the British precedent an ideal to be reached in course of time. Mavalankar followed the middle course between the two schools of thought in India; the new school which urged the impartiality of the Chair does not depend on the nature of the Speaker's outside activities and accordingly, did not accept the British model of absolute severance from politics, and the older orthodox school which insisted on the adherence to the British model and emphasised that impartiality demanded sincere attempts to break previous political connections. According to Mavalankar's middle course, the Speaker may not be a partisan yet he still remains a party man and is the choice of his party. But every party man has his own prejudices and the prejudices of a promoted politician are, indeed, very strong. The Chair, under such circumstances, cannot command that much reverence as it does in Britain for its impartiality. The result was the first motion of no-confidence moved against the Speaker on December 18, 1954. It was condemned by the Prime Minister as "vicious" and he described the Opposition responsible for it as "incompetent and frivolous." The motion was lost on a voice vote, but it had a lesson. It gave a setback to the dignity of the Chair and, as such, to the dignity of Parliament.

The Socialist Member of Parliament, Madhu Limaye, gave a notice, on March 3, 1975, of a no-confidence motion against Speaker Gurdial Singh Dhillon "for having lowered the prestige of the office." It was also signed by Piloo Mody (BLD) and S.N. Mishra (Congress O). Listing thirteen charges against the Speaker, Madu Limaye, inter alia, accused Dhillon for having wilfully abolished the right of the members to raise points of order and having "continually and arbitrarily" disallowed, in total violation of the rules, questions highly embarrassing to the Government. It was also alleged that the Speaker constantly interrupted even those members who were speaking with his permission and not letting them complete their submissions.

The notice was subsequently withdrawn for reasons best known to Madu Limaye and his associates. But the result of such motions of no confidence against the Speaker and especially charging him for having lowered the prestige of office by partiality towards the Government is disastrous. Such ugly scenes, as disorderly defiance of Speaker's rulings, interruptions by raising irrelevant points of order and staging a walkout had become a common feature of the proceedings of Parliament prior to the Sixth House of the People elections. Speaker Hukam Singh, addressing a conference of Presiding Officers on October 29, 1966, stressed the need for finding a "'permanent and lasting" solution of the problem of "repeated disorders" in Parliament and State Legislatures. Satyanarayan Singh, Union Minister for Parliamentary Affairs, called for a "Pathological diagnosis" of the causes of disorderly scenes in India's Legislatures President Giri, in his inaugural address to the Speakers' Conference in New Delhi, in December 1970, raised the question whether any useful purpose was served by framing codes of conduct for legislators. "No member of Parliament or of a legislative body", he said "can hope to impress his constituents by some act of his or some sensation" which makes headline news. But the majority of the Legislators, the President observed, do not share this view. "In any event", he further added, "there is no evidence that any member has in the slightest degree impaired his career by being the storm centre of disorderly scenes in Parliament or a State Legislature. Otherwise it is difficult to see why noisy interruption of parliamentary proceedings is becoming more and more frequent after each successive election." The Speaker's continued association with his party is an undeniable and a potential cause of such a vicious circle. When sitting Speakers, as Gurudial Singh Dhillon can be switched over to ministerial, posts, there is ample justification for lack of confidence in the impartiality of the Speaker and distrust thus caused breeds disorderly scenes and unruly members.

But Balram Jakhar, Speaker of the Seventh House of the People, excelled his mentor Gurdial Singh Dhillon. *The Tribune* reported that the Speaker joined five Congress (I) leaders from Punjab on April 30, 1980 in Delhi "to screen the list of seekers of the party tickets" and in doing so had "violated" one of the "most sacrosanct conventions of the democratic form of government." It caused not a few eyebrows to be raised among veteran parliamentarians and sparked a controversy in the whole country. Despite the rebuttal of Darbara Singh, the Punjab Chief Minister, Gurdial Singh Dhillon and Satpal Mittal, two other participants in the meeting, confirmed the Speaker's presence and sought to make it a non-issue by adding that Jakhar was there "merely" for consultation in regard to the party candidates for the Assembly segments forming his parliamentary constituency. Once the Speaker was elected on party ticket, Dhillon argued among other things, "the party's claim to utilize his services was natural." Whatever be the justification, Jakhar's presence in a party meeting for the selection of party candidates for the Assembly poll is a matter of serious concern for the future of the parliamentary system in which the Speaker occupies a key position. The image of his independence and impartiality is shattered and what happens everyday on the floor of the House is its clear testimony.

The House of the People (Lok Sabha), on April 15, 1987, rejected by a voice vote the no-confidence motion against Speaker Balram Jakhar. The motion specifically brought out the charge that the Speaker had bared Parliament from discussing vital constitutional and procedural issues and the burning problems of the day; the obvious reference was to his ruling of March 19, 1987 as a result of which members were not permitted to raise a discussion on the relationship between the President and the Council of Ministers under Article 78 of the Constitution. The Speaker had also ruled that even during the discussion on a motion of censure or no-confidence directed against the Council of Ministers "the relationship between the President and the Prime Minister or the Council of Ministers, including the advice tendered or exercised or correspondence exchanged between them cannot be allowed to be brought in to influence the debate." Madhu Dandavate, Janata member, described during the acrimonious discussion of the motion of no confidence the ruling of the Speaker as a piece of "misrepresentation of the Constitution, rules of the House and precedents." Such an accusation, whether legally correct or not, certainly reflects on the dignity and impartiality of the Speaker and erodes his authority.

In the Eighth Lok Sabha no Party commanded a majority. But the Janata Dal and its National Front Allies could count on the avowed support of the Left Parties and the BJP and were thus assured a working majority in the House. Rabi Ray was elected the Speaker, though much against the wishes of V. P. Singh. It goes to the credit of Rabi Ray that he did act with exemplary impartiality during his all too brief term as Speaker. He was even called upon to give a ruling on the question of disqualification of certain members who violated the anti-defection law by crossing the floor which he did with objectivity.

The election of Shiv Raj Patil as Speaker of the Tenth Lok Sabha without a contest was rather dramatic as his success was assured the moment the Bhartiya Janata Party, the main Opposition Party in the Lok Sabha with a strength of 117, expressed itself in favour of support to his candidature. From the beginning the Congress (1) was keen that its nominee should occupy the key post notwithstanding its minority status. Yet it did not make any serious effort to reach consensus on this matter, particularly with the Janata Dal and the Left who had all along persisted with the candidature of Rabi Ray. Having come to realise that Ray did not stand a chance of making the grade the National Front finally decided not to press its claim describing the understanding between the Congress and the BJP as a clandestine arrangement and an opportunistic idea. It was the contention of the Prime Minister P V. Narasimha Rao, that it was imperative for the Congress (1) to bag the Speakership "if the Government is to run" implying thereby that a smooth functioning was next to impossible if the post went to a candidate belonging to some other parry.

In fact, there has been no precedent of an Opposition candidate occupying the office of Speaker so far and the ruling Party must have felt that it should not give up its right if it even meant making certain compromises in achieving the desired goal. This indeed was the refrain of the Prime Minister when he categorically asserted that they had to brush aside all inhibitions and do everything that was needed to ensure that the ruling Party candidate was elected Speaker whatever the cost might be. Two important results emerge from this. The first is that unlike Britain, Speakership in India is a post not an institution and, secondly, the post of a Speaker is partisan institution as its incumbent must be a partyman.

Functions of the Speaker : The functions and authority of the Speaker in India resemble more or less to those of the Speaker of the British House of Commons. He speaks for the House and to the House and, as such, is the principal spokesman of the House. Messages on behalf of the House and to the House are sent or received with the authority of the Speaker. All Bills passed by the House are authenticated by his signatures before they are sent to the Council of States for its consideration or the President for his assent. He receives all petitions, appeals, messages and documents addressed to the House and all orders of the House are executed through him.

Communications from the President to the House are made through the Speaker. When a message from the President, whether with respect to a Bill pending in Parliament or otherwise, is received by the Speaker, he reads it to the House and gives necessary directions in regard to the procedure to be followed for the consideration of matters referred to in the message, and in giving those directions he may suspend or vary those to such extent as he may deem necessary. Similarly, all communications from House to the President are made through the Speaker in the form of a formal address after a motion has been made and carried by the House.

The Speaker presides over the sittings of the House and conducts its proceedings. He decides who shall have the floor and all speeches and remarks are addressed to the Chair. He proposes and puts the necessary questions and announces the results. In consultation with the Leader of the House, the Speaker determines the order of business, the time to be allotted for different kinds of business, and sees that it is taken up and finished according to the Time Allocation Orders. He is the final judge to decide on the admissibility of questions, resolutions and motions. He must also certify, under Article 110 of the Constitution, whether a Bill is a Money Bill or not. Every Money Bill, when it is transmitted to the Council of States is so certified by him, as also when it is presented to the President for his assent. The Speaker does not vote except in the case of a tie.

The Speaker does not take part in the deliberations of the House except in the discharge of his duties as the presiding officer of the House. He may, however, either on a point of order, or on a request made by a member, address the House at any time on a matter under consideration with a view to help and aid members in their deliberations. Such instances are rare, 44 but whenever he addresses the House those expressions are not to be taken in the nature of a ruling.

The Speaker exercises his powers and functions partly under the Constitution and partly under the Rules of Procedure of the House. He has also the power to deal with all matters which are not adequately provided for in the Rules of Procedure. He has, in fact, done so quite frequently and now all such precedents have been embodied in book form as Directions of the Speaker and are made available to the members of the House. The Speaker maintains perfect order and decorum in the House and has wide powers to check disorder, irrelevance and unparliamentary language or behaviour. A member who shows disrespect to the Chair by not obeying his order may be punished by suspension from the service of the House, and any reflection on the action or character of the Speaker for his ruling is a grave breach of order which will receive immediate and serious reproof. If the Speaker is of the opinion that a word or words used in the debate are defamatory or indecent, or unparliamentary or undignified, he may, in his discretion, order that such word or words be expunged from the proceedings of the House. He may direct any member guilty of disorderly conduct to withdraw from the House, or adjourn or suspend the business of the House in case of grave disorder. However, when strong feelings exist or are aroused in the House, there are times when the Chair can appropriately be deaf or indeed blind."

The Speaker announces the closure of debates, is the guardian of the privileges of the House and protects the interests of the minorities. He also protects the encroachments by the Government. When Ministers tend to encroach upon the rights of the members or refuse to answer questions, or circumvent the answers, or do not give sufficient information, it is, then, to Mr. Speaker that the members appeal to safeguard and enforce their rights against the Executive. Various powers are conferred on the Speaker in relation to questions to Ministers. Though the guiding principles regarding admissibility of questions are laid down in the Rules of Procedure, their interpretation is vested in the Speaker. He may also vary the Question Hour, waive the rules relating to notice of questions, and permit a question to be asked at short notice if it relates to a matter of public importance and is, in his opinion, of an urgent character. Provision has been made in the Rules for half-an-hour discussion on matters arising from the answers to questions provided they are of sufficient public importance, but the decision as to whether a matter conforms to the requirements of the relevant Rules rests with the speaker.

The Speaker also decides about the admissibility of resolutions and motions. He decides whether a motion expressing want of confidence in the Council of Ministers is in order, and whether a "cut" motion is or is not admissible under the Rules. His consent is required to a motion to adjourn the House for the purpose of discussing a definite matter of public importance, to a motion for discussing a matter of general public interest, and to any motion for adjourning the debate on a Bill. His consultation is also necessary for the presentation of petitions to the House, for calling the attention of a Minister to any matter of urgent public importance and for any member to point out a mistake of accuracy in a statement made by a Minister or any other member of the House. Further, the consent of the Speaker is required by a Minister desiring to make a personal statement explaining the reasons of his resignation from his office. The Speaker's permission is likewise necessary if a member of the House wants to make a personal explanation. He can refer any matter to the Privileges Committee.

But the chief function, and an arduous too, of the Speaker relates to the judicious conduct of debates. He fixes a time limit for speeches, selects amendments to a Bill or resolution to be discussed by the House. The Speaker is, in fact, "lord of the debate." He must see that the debate centres on the main issue before the House and members do not wander accidentally or deliberately, in the realm of irrelevance. Then, there are constant appeals to him for his ruling on point of procedure and his ruling is final which must be accepted without demur. They constitute precedents which are collected for future guidance and cannot be questioned on a substantive motion. It is said of the Speaker of the British House of Commons that the Prime Minister "can do nothing right, but Speaker can do nothing wrong." This is, however, not true in India. Defiance of the rulings of the Speaker is rule now rather than an exception. When, Speakers do not eschew party connections and are active participants in the affairs of the party, the respect and obedience which the Chair should command disappears with loss of faith in the independence and impartiality of the Speaker.

The Speaker appoints Chairmen of all committees of the House. "The Speaker", writes S. L. Shakdhar, "is the supreme head of all Parliamentary Committees set up by him or by the House. He issues directions to the Chairmen in all matters relating to their working and the procedure to be followed. He guides them holding periodical consultations with the Chairman and the members. The Speaker reads all reports of the Committees and keeps in touch with their activities. All difficulties and matters of importance are referred to him for guidance and advice." He sees that any notice issued by a Committee or a minute of dissent of a member does not contain any words, phrases or expressions which are argumentative, unparliamentary, irrelevant, verbose of otherwise inappropriate. He may, accordingly, amend it, if deemed necessary, before circulation. The Speaker himself is the ex-officio Chairman of some of the Committees of the House such as the Business Advisory Committee, Rules Committee and the General Purposes Committee.

The Speaker presides over the joint sitting of both Houses of Parliament, whenever the President calls it in the event of the disagreement between the House of the People and the

Council of States and all the rules of Procedure operate in regard to the joint sitting under his directions and orders. However, if at any sitting of the House of the People a resolution for the removal of the Speaker from his office is under consideration, he is not to preside at that sitting. The Constitution also prescribes certain of his duties : he is empowered to adjourn the House or to suspend its sitting in the event of the absence of a quorum; and he is authorised, in his discretion, to permit any member of the House who is unable to express himself in Hindi or in English to address the House in his mother tongue. He has also the power to recognise parties and groups in the House of the People.

The Speaker is the ex-officio President of the Indian Parliamentary Group, which in India functions as the National Group of the Inter-Parliamentary Union and the Main branch of the Commonwealth Parliamentary Association. He nominates, in consultation with the Chairman of the Council of States, personnel for various parliamentary delegations to foreign countries. He may lead these delegations himself. The Speaker is also the Chairman of the Conference of Presiding Officers of Legislative Bodies in India.

The House of the People has its own Secretariat and the conditions of service of persons appointed to the secretarial staff of either House of Parliament are regulated by law of Parliament. The secretariat staff of the House functions directly under the control of the Speaker and is responsible to no other authority. The Speaker also controls the premises of the House and his authority within and without the House is undisputed. He regulates admission of "strangers" and Press correspondents to the galleries and other precincts of the House. Visitors and Press correspondents, after their admission to the galleries, are subject to the discipline and orders of the Speaker. In the event of breach of his orders he may punish them by stopping their admission either for a definite or an indefinite period or, in serious circumstances, involving contempt of the House or its members or the committees, censure them or, in extreme cases, commit them to prison. Summons to offenders are issued under his authority and it is sufficient for the courts if his orders merely state that the person is required to appear before the House on the charge of contempt of the House or a breach of privilege.

The Speaker is, thus, the impartial custodian of the rights of the members of the House. For him the humblest back-bencher is not less than a member, nor is the greatest Minister more than a member. He seldom speaks, but when he does, 'he speaks for the House not to it." The essence of his impartiality lies in the way he maintains an atmosphere of fair play by ensuring that the Opposition have an opportunity to express their views and criticism, yet at the same time, seeing that there is no parliamentary obstruction to hinder the Government in the task of governing the country. The powers vested in the Speaker are intended to enable him that the House functions smoothly and it transacts its business effectively, efficiently and expeditiously.

The Speaker would not, therefore, exercise his powers arbitrarily or in such manner as to prevent the House from functioning as the Speakers of the West Bengal and Punjab Legislative Assemblies did in 1967-68. The Page Committee, while commenting upon the duties and responsibilities of the Speaker and his relations with the House, observed, "The fundamental principle is that the House, subject to the provisions of the Constitution, is sovereign in the matter of its own rules of procedure and conduct of business .... Hence whatever powers have been conferred by the rules on the Speaker are intended to serve one purpose, i.e., the House should be enabled to function at all times in the interest of the country and the powers conferred on the Speaker, should be used by him in the interest of the House." The Speaker must, therefore, possess high and varied qualities of character and intellect. He should be able, vigilant, thoroughly conversant with he Rules of Procedure and precedents, imperturbable, tactful and should possess a sense of humour to relieve not only tension's in the House but also at times to relieve its monotony. This is a gift which may be either natural or cultivated, but it is certainly a weapon of great potency with a wise and capable Speaker. Addressing the 52nd Annual Conference of the Speakers of legislative bodies of India in October 1986, Balram Jakhar, Speaker of the Lok Sabha, likened the Speakers to wild horses whose rider was the State Legislature. "They would want to tame you, but never get tamed. For if you do so, you would be dragged all along." The Speaker should be "firm with a smile."

The Thirty-ninth Constitution Amendment Act, which has since been rescinded, intended to protect the Speaker, because of the dignity of the office that he occupied, from the jurisdiction of the courts in respect of all disputes arising out or in connection with his election to the House of the People.

Functions of Parliament : India is a Union of States and, accordingly, all legislative power is divided between the Union and the States. Parliament has exclusive power to make laws with respect to matters enumerated in the Union List—List I in the Seventh Schedule to the Constitution. With respect to the Concurrent List—List III-both Parliament and State Legislatures have concurrent powers. Subject to the provisions of the Constitution, Parliament has the power to make laws for the whole or any part of India whereas the jurisdiction of State extends to the whole or any part of the State. No law made by Parliament shall be deemed to be invalid on the ground that it will have extraterritorial operation. When a Proclamation of Emergency is in operation, Parliament has the power to make laws for the whole or any part of the territory of India with respect to any matter enumerated in the State List — List II though on the expiry of six months after the Proclamation has ceased to operate such laws cease to have effect. Parliament has also the power to legislate for two or more States by their consent and it is open to other States also to consent to or adopt such legislation. In case of repugnancy between the law of the Union and the law of a State, the former shall prevail. Residuary powers rest with the Union.

The entries in the Union, Concurrent and State Lists are only legislative heads or fields of legislation and, as such, they demarcate the area over which the appropriate legislature can operate. From the classification of matters into the three Lists, competence of the House of the People has been questioned from time to time on particular matters before the House. It is the accepted practice in the House of the People that the Speaker does not give any ruling on a point of order raised whether a Bill is constitutionally within the competence of the House. The House also does not take a decision on the specific question of *vires* of a Bill. The members express their views in the matter and advance arguments for and against the *vires* for the consideration of the House and the issue is decided accordingly. There have, however, been occasions when the Speaker leaving the ultimate decision on the matter to the House has expressed his *own views* on the *vires* of Bills. In order to help the House and the Speaker to decide disputed or complicated legislative proposals before the House, the Attorney-General may address the House on the suggestion of the Speaker or the House itself and give his opinion on the legal and constitutional aspects involved therein.

Functions Related to Legislation : The process of making laws is the business of Parliament as a whole; President, the Council of States and the House of the People.

The House can by itself do nothing, although the actual powers of the President and the Council of States are subject to limitations. A non-Money Bill may originate in any of the two Houses and it must be passed by both Houses if it has to become law. The House of the People, unlike the British House of Commons, has no means to overrule the Council of States. In case of disagreement between the two Houses or if more than six months elapse from the date of the receipt of the Bill by the other House without the Bill being passed by it, the President may summon a joint sitting of both the Houses. If at the joint sitting the Bill is passed by a majority of the total number of members of both Houses present and voting, it shall be deemed to have been passed by both Houses of Parliament. Here lies the supreme position of the House of the People. The will of the House is bound to prevail at the joint sitting on account of its numerical strength.

Functions Related to Finance : "Who holds the purse, holds the power," wrote Madison in the *Federalist*. It is through the control of the nation's purse that the House enjoys real supremacy over the Council of States. The Constitution provides that a Money Bill shall not be introduced in the Council of States. It should originate in the House of the People and when it passes therefrom, it is transmitted to the Council of States for its recommendations. The Constitution further requires that the Council of States should return the Bill to the House with or without its "recommendations" within fourteen days from the date of the receipt of the Bill by the Council. If the House accepts any of the "recommendations" made by the Council, the Bill is deemed to have been passed by both Houses of Parliament with those amendments. If the House does not accept the "recommendations" of the Council, the Bill is deemed to have been passed by both Houses of Parliament in the original form as passed by the House of the People. If a Bill passed by the House and transmitted to the Council is not returned within fourteen days of its receipt, it is deemed to have been passed by both Houses of Parliament, after the expiry of fourteen days, in the form in which it was passed by the House of the People. The Council of States can only delay the enactment of a Money Bill for a period of fourteen days. Demands for grants are not submitted to the Council of States. The sanctioning of expenditure is the exclusive privilege of the House of the People.

Functions Related to Election : The elected members of the Both Houses of Parliament form a part the Electoral College for the election of the President of India; the other part of the Electoral College being the Elected members of the Legislative Assemblies of the States. The Vice-President is elected by the members of an Electoral College consisting of the members of both Houses of Parliament. In the process of election of both the President and the Vice-President the House of the People enjoys co-equal powers with the Council of States.

Functions Related to Executive Control : But the most important function of the House is that of controlling the executive. The Constitution makes the Council of Ministers collectively responsible to the House of the People and the responsibility of the Council of Ministers to the House involves a constant control of the House over the Government; control and responsibility go together. Responsibility of Government means its resignation from office whenever the policy of the Government proves fundamentally unacceptable to the House. An obligation, therefore, rests on the House to exercise a day-to-day scrutiny over the activities of the Government in such a way that fundamental disagreement between the Executive and the representatives of the people will be clear and manifest. If the actual and possible mistakes of the Government were not apparent, the Government might become irresponsible. Control by the House prevents irresponsibility since Ministers are constantly conscious of the fact that they will be called to account.

The House maintains its control in two ways. The first is the constant demand in the House for information about the actions of Government. The second is the criticism that is constantly aimed at the Government in the House. These two methods are closely related to each other and take various forms. The most effective instrument by which the House seeks information from the Executive is the oral or written questions. Any member of the House may, by following prescribed rules, direct questions at Ministers and the Ministers at the beginning of each sitting of the House devote almost an hour to answering questions that have been put to them. The institution of asking questions is as highly developed in India as it is in Britain and is prominently distinguished from some of the Dominion countries, like Australia. It is generally the most interesting part of the proceedings of the House and it provides the time when a member can make his mark and when Ministers, too, can make or mar their reputations. A member may also move for obtaining returns or supplying information on matters of public importance. Information may, again, be obtained by the House regarding the administration by appointing Parliamentary Committees.

The House is also a debating assembly. "A society," writes Laski, "that is able to discuss does not need to fight, and the greater the capacity to maintain interest in discussion, the less degree there is of an inability to effect the compromises that maintain social peace." The most important function of the Opposition is to discuss and criticize matters of administration and policy making and to make the Government to defend its intentions and practices. The best opportunity for the Opposition to criticize governmental policy as a whole is when it debates the reply on the Address of the President to Parliament. Another opportunity is when public finance, more especially proposals for expenditure, are under discussion. At this stage, the action of every individual Minister and his Ministry is under review. Demands for supplementary estimates similarly offer an opportunity for criticism. It must, however, be said that till March, 1977 there was no well-organised strong Opposition to create an effective stir in Government by its criticism.

The Janata Government recognised the worth of responsible Opposition within the framework of a parliamentary system and accorded to the Leader of the Opposition the status of a Minister of the Cabinet rank with all the privileges attached to the office. But after January 1980 the Opposition was in complete disarray and there was no cohesion among the various Opposition parties and groups to present a united front and arrest the vagaries of the Government effectively and in a responsible spirit. Proper restraint on the actions and policies of the Government is not possible under the circumstances, except the pre-planned obstructionist strategy followed by walk-outs.

In addition to these regularly scheduled debates, any member of the House may, after the notice and subject to the rules governing it, move a resolution expressing lack of confidence in the Council of Ministers. Motion for a vote of no confidence is really a crucial occasion in the life of the Government as it decides its fate. So long as a Government can command a comfortable majority, it is not possible for such a motion to get through, still it creates embarrassment the ranks of the Ministry and agitates public opinion. The most normal occasion for the criticism of the Executive is debate on a motion of adjournment. A member may, during a sitting, move the adjournment of the House for discussing a definite matter of urgent public importance. If the Speaker admits the motion, then, a full debate on the issue is held. The policies and actions of the Government are exposed by the Opposition and its lapses highlighted. The Government stoutly defends with reasoned arguments substantiated by authentic official material. If the Government fails to convince the House it must face the consequences.

There is another kind of adjournment motion and it may be called the emergency adjournment motion. It is intended to raise discussion on matters of urgent public importance for a short duration and for calling attention of the Government. No formal motion is allowed. What the Rules require is that a member wishing to raise a debate should give a notice to the Secretary of the House clearly and precisely specifying the matter to be discussed. The notice must be supported by at least two other members. If the Speaker admits the notice, he will fix a day, in consultation with the Leader of the House, for discussion. The duration of the debate does not exceed two and a half hours. What is important to note here is that even a Government which commands an overwhelming majority in the House cannot prevent the ventilation of an important grievance and the Constitution gives to every member freedom of speech in Parliament. The Half-an-Hour Discussion on matters arising out of questions, also, affords opportunities for ventilating grievances. Other opportunities for raising debates include the moving of resolutions and No-Day-Yet-Named motion.

Another device for raising important matters and ventilating whatever has happened and agitating the Members is the 'Zero Hour' practice. It is entirely an Indian innovation and is unknown to the Rules of Procedure and Conduct of Business in the House. Nobody can say how did it originate and acquire the name. But the practice goes back to early 1950 during the tenure of Speaker Hukam Singh. Immediately after the Question Hour and before other business was taken up the Speaker would permit ordinary Members of the House, who otherwise were overshadowed by the presence of a host of veteran parliamentarians, to bring to the notice of the Government important matters and seek redress. The Members, thus, found that their voice counted and began to use the opportunity freely and since it was an interregnum between the Question Hour and the other business to be taken up it came to be known as the Zero Hour.

Originally, it was useful device conducted in an atmosphere of orderly and fruitful proceedings, but soon it declined into a line of disorder, uproar and pandemonium, often unbecoming of Parliament and almost invariably unproductive. On February 17, 1981 the House was adjourned in a state of shock when Congress (I) and Lok Dal Members freely exchanged blows. On August 22, 1978 a Lok Sabha bulletin informed Members that there was no Zero Hour in the Rules of Procedure and Conduct of Business in the House. Anybody desiring to raise a matter of wide public importance had to give appropriate notice under the relevant Rule. "Members are requested not to raise matters without the specific approval and consent of the Speaker." On a Member's plea that it had been the practice of the House and the decision be reconsidered, the Speaker commented, "May I tell you that there is nothing like Zero Hour." Speaker Hegde after consulting leaders of various political parties, offered to substitute five statements each day under Rule 377 after giving due notice to the Speaker and obtaining his consent. That system has worked well. It was, for instance, under Rule 377 in the Monsoon Session in 1979 that the Congress (I) managed to raise the matter of the Desai-Charan Singh correspondence and the related corruption charges, after having tried unsuccessfully to raise it in other forms under other Rules. Consent is given to almost every matter sought to be raised. Despite this outlet for Members' grievances, Zero Hour lives on and thrives amidst uproarious scenes verging on even vilification.

Functions Related to Constituent : The House together with the Council of States has the power to amend the Constitution. A Bill to amend the Constitution may originate in either House and it must be passed by each House of Parliament by a majority of its total membership as well as by a two-thirds majority of the members present and voting. The Constitution, as said before, does not prescribe the method of resolving differences between the two Houses over a proposed amendment of the Constitution. Article 108 relates to the procedure prescribed for resolving the differences over a legislative measure and does not apply to a constitutional amendment.

Miscellaneous Functions : Parliament has the power for the removal of Judges of the Supreme and High Courts on the grounds of proved misbehaviour or incapacity and address for such a removal is required to be passed by each House of Parliament supported by a majority of the total membership of that House and by a two-thirds majority of the Members of that House present and voting. The removal of the Chief Election Commissioner and Comptroller and Auditor-General of India is subject to the same procedure as in the case of Judges. Either of the two Houses may prefer a charge for impeachment of the President. If the charge is preferred by the House, the Council of States investigates to or causes it to be investigated. The impeachment succeeds when the Chamber investigating the charge passes a resolution supported by a two-thirds majority of members present and voting that the charge is sustained. The removal of the Vice-President is only subject to the approval of the House of the People after a resolution to that effect has been passed by a majority of all the members of the Council of States. Approval of both the Houses is necessary at all stages and every time for the continuance in force of a Proclamation of Emergency, under Article 352, Proclamation declaring the failure of the constitutional machinery in a State, under article 356, and proclamation relating to financial emergency, under Article 360, beyond the specified period of time and when its operation is intended to be extended after the expiry of that period. Rules and Regulations made by the various Ministries and Departments under the authority of delegated legislation are approved by both the Houses.

The reports of the Union Public Service Commission, the Comptroller and Auditor-General of India, the Scheduled Castes and Tribes Commission and the Finance Commission are presented to both Houses for their consideration. If the Government makes a proposal to take an appointment out of the purview of the Union Public Service Commission, both the Houses should agree to such an exclusion.

Procedure of Legislation : The Constitution does not prescribe a detailed legislative procedure. It merely says that a Bill, other than a Money or Financial Bill, may originate in either House of Parliament, and a Bill shall not be deemed to have been passed by Houses of Parliament unless it has been agreed to by both Houses, either without amendment or with such amendments only as are agreed to by both Houses. A Bill pending in either House does not lapse if Parliament is prorogued. The dissolution of the House of the People causes the lapse of any bill which is pending in it or which has been passed by the House but is pending in the Council of States. But a Bill which originated in the Council and is still pending there does not lapse on account of dissolution. When the President has notified his intention to summon a joint sitting of both Houses of Parliament, a subsequent dissolution of the House of the People does not cause the Bill to lapse.

The rest is covered by the Rules made by Parliament. These Rules prescribe an identical procedure in both Houses. A legislative Bill is required to be read three times in each House before it can be deemed to have been passed by both Houses of Parliament. An ordinary legislative measure may be introduced either by a Minister or by a Private member. In the former case, it is known as a Government Bill and in the latter case it is classified as a Private Member's Bill. A Government Bill and a Private Member's Bill both undergo an identical procedure. The three readings of a Bill involve four stages. The first reading relates to the motion to introduce a Bill and on its adoption the Bill is deemed to have been introduced. The Bill is also deemed to have been introduced if it is already published in the *Gazette of India*. The second reading consists of two stages. The first stage constitutes discussion of the principles of the Bill and its provisions generally on any of the following motions :that it be taken into consideration; that it be referred to a Joint Committee of both the Houses with the concurrence of the Council of States; that it be circulated for the purpose of eliciting public opinion. Second stage in the Second Reading constitutes clause-by-clause consideration of the Bill as introduced or as reported by a Select or Joint Committee, as the case may be. The third reading refers to the discussion on the motion that the Bill (or the Bill as amended) be passed.

The Bill is, then, transmitted to the other House for its concurrence. A message from the originating House signed either by the Presiding Officer or the Secretary is sent to the other House. The message is read in the House and copies of the Bill are laid on the table. Thereafter any Minister may give notice that the Bill be taken into consideration. The subsequent procedure of discussion and amendment is the same as in the originating House. After the Bill is passed by the receiving House, it is sent back to the originating House with amendments if any. If the receiving House passes the Bill in the same form in which it came from the House of its origin, it is presented to the President for his assent. The President may give his assent thereto, or withheld it, or return it for reconsideration of the Houses, with or without a message suggesting amendments. When the Bill so returned by the President has been reconsidered by both the Houses and is again passed by the two Houses with or without amendments and presented to the President for his assent, the President can no longer withhold it, and must give his assent thereto. A Bill, thus becomes law.

If a Bill passed by one House and transmitted to the other is amended by that House, it goes back to the House where it originated. If the House originating the Bill does not agree to the amendment or amendments or makes further amendments to which the other House does not agree, the President may summon a joint sitting of the two Houses. The Speaker presides and the Rules of the House of the People are made applicable at a joint sitting. Amendments can be moved at a joint sitting, but only such amendments are admissible as have been made necessary by the delay in the passage of the Bill, or may arise out of amendments, if any, proposed by one House and rejected by the other. The decision of the Presiding Officer with regard to the admissibility of amendments is final. The Bill is deemed to have been passed by both the Houses if a majority of the members present and voting at joint sitting agree to it.

A Joint session may also be summoned if a Bill passed by one House is rejected by the other, or if more than six months elapse from the date of the reception of the Bill by the other House without the Bill being passed by it.

Bill Related to Private Members : Since 1965 the last two and a half hours of the Friday sittings are normally allotted for the transaction of Private Members' Business. Private Members' Business consists of Resolutions and Bills. The Speaker decides which of the two are to be dealt with on a particular Friday. In practice, it means that every alternate Friday is made available for Private Members' Bills, the other Friday being devoted to Private Members' Resolutions.

The Procedure in the case of Private Members' Bill is the same as for Government Bills, except for some special features. The notice for leave to introduce a Bill must be accompanied by a statement of objects and reasons, the recommendation and sanction of the President required for the introduction or consideration of the Bill, memoranda showing the financial effect of the Bill, etc. A notice may be disallowed, if it is not complete in any respect or the Bill is otherwise defective. The Speaker has the inherent power to disallow notice of a Bill, if he thinks that it is not proper to include it in the List of Business.

There is a Committee on Private Members' Bills and Resolutions consisting of not more than 15 members nominated by the Speaker for one year. The Chairman is appointed by the Speaker from among the members of the Committee. If the Deputy Speaker happens to be a member of the Committee, he is appointed Chairman automatically. The functions of the Committee are :

(1) To examines every Bill seeking to amend the Constitution before a motion for leave to introduce the Bill is included in the List of business. The Committee since its inception has taken this matter very seriously and laid down certain principles. One of these states that "the Constitution should be considered as a sacred document—a document which should not be lightly interfered with and should be amended only when it is found absolutely necessary to do so..... Such amendments should normally be brought by government."

(2) To examine all Private Members' Bills after they have been introduced and before they are taken up for consideration in the House and to classify them according to their nature, urgency and importance into

two categories: Category A and Category B. Bills in Category A have precedence over those in Category B.

(3) To recommend the time that should be allocated for the discussion of the stage or stages of a Private Member's Bill and also to indicate the different hours at which the various stages of the Bill in a day shall be completed.

(4) To examine every Private Member's Bill which is opposed in the House on the ground that the Bill initiates legislation not within the legislative competence of the House. The Speaker considers such objection prima facie tenable.

(5) To recommend time limit for the discussion of Private Members' Resolutions and the ancillary matters.

Legislation Related to Finance : The principles involved in the financial procedure are essentially the same as followed in the British House of Commons. Financial initiative in both the countries is the exclusive right of the Government. Secondly, the House of the People in India, as the House of Commons, has the exclusive right to vote supplies and to sanction the levy of taxes and imposts. Finally, in both countries, taxation, and appropriation and expenditure from public funds need legislative authorization.

The Constitution provides for a special procedure in regard to Money Bills. A Money Bill may not be introduced in the Council of States and it cannot be introduced without the recommendation of the President. When it is passed in the House of the People, it is transmitted to the Council of States, with the Speaker's certificate that it is a Money Bill and the decision of the Speaker on this point is final. The Council of States cannot reject a Money Bill, but it may, within fourteen days of its receipt, return it to the House of the People with its "recommendations".

The House may either accept or reject all or any of the "recommendations" of the Council of States. If the House of the People accepts any of them, the Money Bill shall be deemed to have been passed by both Houses with those amendments. If the House does not accept any of the "recommendations" of Council of States, the Money Bill shall be deemed to have been passed by both Houses in the form in which it was passed by the House of the People. If the Bill is not returned to the House within fourteen days, it shall be deemed to have been passed by both Houses at the expiration of the stipulated period in the form in which it was passed by the House of the People. When it is presented to the President for assent the provision by which the President may return the Bill to the Houses for reconsideration (Article 111) does not apply.

A Money Bill cannot be introduced or moved except on the recommendation of the President. According to Article 110 a Bill is deemed to be a Money Bill if it contains only provisions dealing with all or any of the following matters :

(a) the imposition, abolition, remission, alteration or regulation of any tax;
(b) the regulation of the borrowing of money or the giving of any guarantee by the Government of India, or the amendment of the Laws with respect to any financial obligation undertaken by the Government of India;
(c) the custody of the Consolidated Fund or the Contingency Fund of India, 58 the payment of money into or the withdrawal of money from any such fund;
(d) the appropriation of moneys out of the Consolidated Fund of India;
(e) the declaring of any expenditure to be expenditure charged on the Consolidated Fund of India or the increasing of the amount of any such expenditure;
(f) the receipt of money on account of the Consolidated Fund of India or the Public Accounts of India or the custody or the issue of such money or the audit of the amounts of the Union or of a State; or

(g) any matter incidental to any matter referred to above from (a) to (f)."

The use of the word "only" at the beginning of the definition of a Money Bill is significant. The Constitution prescribes two conditions for a Bill to be regarded as a Money Bill. Firstly, it must deal with all or any matters contained in Article 110 (i). Secondly, the provisions of the Bill must deal only with such matters and not with any other matter.

It is, therefore, not possible to enact as a Money Bill anything which changes the law in other respects. It must be a Money Bill, pure and simple. A Bill which imposes fines, penalties, or licence fees, or deals with taxes imposed by the local authorities is neither a Money Bill nor a Financial Bill. A Money Bill when it is presented to the President of India for his assent must be accompanied by a certificate of the Speaker that it is a Money Bill. The President shall not withhold his assent from a Money Bill passed by Parliament. This is in pursuance of the supremacy of Parliament in the matter of finance.

It is necessary to distinguish Money Bill from Financial Bills. Money Bills are those which are defined in Article 110 as referred to above. Financial Bills are other Bills containing financial provisions but to which the provisions of Article 110 are not applicable. Financial Bills also cannot be introduced without the recommendation of the President, and must not be introduced in the Council of States. Whereas a Money Bill is transmitted to the Council of States for its consideration and "recommendations" alone and it has no right to amend it, a Financial Bill can be amended by the Council. It rests with the Speaker of the House of the People to determine whether a Bill is a Money Bill or not. The Council of States has no right to question the certificate subscribed by the Speaker that the Bill is a Money Bill.

Budget of Government **:** The Constitution has adopted the fundamental principles governing the British financial system, that is, parliamentary control over the receipt and expenditure of public Money. These principles are :

(1) no tax can be imposed except with the authority of Parliament;

(2) no expenditure can be incurred except with the sanction of Parliament;

(3) no tax can be imposed or expenditure incurred unless asked for by the Executive. It means that financial initiative rests with the Executive alone; and

(4) all expenditure except that specifically charged by any enactment of Parliament requires to be sanctioned on an annual basis. This is called the principle of annuality.

The expenditure for any financial year, the period between April 1 and March 31, must therefore, be sanctioned either totally or in part by Parliament before the expiry of the previous financial year. That is to say, the Annual Financial Statement or the Budget must be passed whether totally or in part before March 31 of each year. The Budget is ordinarily presented to Parliament in the month of February each year in two parts—the Railway Budget and the General Budget. The Railway Budget exclusively deals with the receipts and expenditure relating to Railways and it is separately presented by the Minister for Railways. The General Budget deals with estimates of all the Departments of the Government of India excluding Railways and is presented by the Finance Minister. The procedure in case of the Railway Budget and the General Budget is the same.

The Budget or the Annual Financial Statement, as the Constitution names it, must show separately the expenditure charged on the Consolidated Fund of India and the sums required to meet other expenditure proposed to be made from the Consolidated Fund of India. It must also distinguish expenditure on revenue account from other expenditure. The expenditure charged on the Consolidated Fund of India comprises:

(a) the emoluments and allowances of the President and other expenditure relating to his office;

(b) the salaries and allowances of the Chairman and the Deputy chairman of the Council of States and the Speaker and the Deputy Speaker of the House of the People;

(c) debt charges for which the Government of India is liable including interest, sinking fund charges and redemption charges and the expenditure relating to the raising of loans and the service and redemption of debt;

(d) (i) the salaries, allowances and pensions payable to or in respect of judges of the Supreme Court,

(ii) the pensions payable to or in respect of the Federal court,

(iii) the pensions payable to or in respect of judges of any High Court which exercises jurisdiction in relation to any area included in the territory of India or which at any time before the commencement of the present Constitution exercised jurisdiction in relation to any area included in a Province corresponding to a State specified in Part A of the first Schedule;

(e) the salary, allowances and pension payable to or in respect of the Comptroller and Auditor-General of India;

(f) any sums required to satisfy any judgement, decree or award of any Court or arbitration tribunal;

(g) any other expenditure declared by the Constitution or by Parliament by law to be so charged.

The expenditure charged on the Consolidated Fund of India is not submitted to the vote of Parliament, but either House of Parliament can discuss it. It is non-votable. The other expenditure is submitted in the form of demands for grants to the House of the People. The House may assent, or refuse assent to any demand, or assent to any demand subject to a reduction of the amount specified therein. It is, votable, but no demand for grant can be made except on the recommendation of the President.

The Annual Financial Statement or the Budget has to pass through five stages : (1) Introduction or presentation; (2) General discussion; (3) Voting of demands; (4) Consideration and passing of the Appropriation Bill, and (5) Consideration and passing of the taxation proposals; the Finance Bill.

(1) *Introduction or Presentation* : The Budget session of Parliament commences in mid-February when the Rail way Minister introduces the Railway Budget and subsequently the Finance Minister introduces the Financial Statement in the House of the People. It is accompanied by the Budget Speech made by the Finance Minister. It is an important event as it unfolds the fiscal and economic policy of the Government for the ensuing year. The copies of the Budget together with the Explanatory Memorandum are printed and circulated among members for their reference. The Budget contains the estimates of receipts and expenditure. The Explanatory Memorandum contains a comparative statement of such receipts and expenditure for the current year and the next year and reasons for any increase or decrease in the amounts. The memorandum also furnishes the information relating to estimates.

(2) *General Discussion* : After the Budget has been presented, money has to be asked for as Demands for Grants. Here the Budget is dealt with in two stages a general discussion, and the demands for specific grants. A general discussion of the Budget as a whole is spread over 3 or 4 days. It is customary for the leader of the Opposition to initiate the discussion. No discussion of details and no cut motions are in order at this stage. It is a general discussion which covers all items of expenditure including those that are 'charged' and are excluded from vote. The discussion relates to the policy of the Government involving a review and criticism of

the administration of the various Departments, the general problems connected with nation's finances and the principles involved in the Budget proposals. Following the British practice, the major part of the time for the Budget discussion is allowed to the Opposition to review the work of the Government for the year and ventilate grievances of the people. The discussion is political rather than financial. No vote is taken during the general discussion. But the Finance Minister has the right to reply at the end of the discussion.

(3) *Discussion and Voting* : With the general discussion the work of the Council of States is complete so far as the Annual Financial Statement is concerned. But the House of the People, after general discussion is over, proceeds to the voting of demands not charged on the Consolidated Fund of India. The voting of demands is the exclusive privilege of the House and the Council has no share in it. The House of the People has the following powers in respect of each demand: (i) to assent to the demand; or (ii) to refuse it; or (iii) to reduce it. The House has no power to increase a demand, or to alter the destination of a grant, or to put any condition as to the appropriation of the grant.

The time for debates on the estimates is determined by the Speaker in consultation with the Leader of the House. Reports of the activities of different Ministries during the preceding year are circulated among the members for their references. When the demand for grant of a Ministry is moved it comes under scrutiny and the debate, which usually extends to not more than two days, rivets on the working of the Ministry and its administrative policy. But the real debate takes place when amendments are proposed either for the reduction of the amount demanded or for the omission or reduction of any item in any grant. The voting on the demands must conclude on the fixed day when closure is applied and all outstanding demands are put to vote and disposed of, no matter whether they have been discussed or not.

(4) *Appropriation Bill* : The next stage is the Annual Appropriation Bill which must be passed into a statute. All the demands voted by the House of the People and the expenditure charged on the Consolidated Fund are put together and incorporated in a Bill called the Annual Appropriation Bill. The allotment of time for the different stages of the Bill is determined by the Speaker and debate on the second reading of the Bill is general. When the Bill is moved for consideration, debate is restricted to those points only which have not been discussed during the debate on estimates. Amendments may be moved for reduction in the expenditure alone. No amendments to the grant as voted by the House previously or altering its destination or varying the amount charged on the Consolidated Fund are admissible.

The Appropriation Bill having passed through all the stages is finally voted upon. If passed by the House of the People, it is certified by the Speaker as a Money Bill and transmitted to the Council of States. The Council must return it to the House with its "recommendations" within fourteen days. It is for the House to accept or reject these "recommendations," if any. The assent of the President to the Appropriation Bill is just a matter of formality. He cannot return a Money Bill for reconsideration.

An Appropriation Act embodies the authority given by the House, with the assent of the President, to Government to spend money as authorized in the Act. Without such an authority the Government cannot incur any expenditure. The Comptroller and Auditor-General of India would hold a payment illegal and unauthorized if it were made without authorization in the Appropriation Act. If the Government subsequently finds that the money granted under any head is insufficient for its need, it again comes to the House for a supplementary grant. The supplementary grants are embodied in one or more Appropriation Bills which must be passed by the House before the end of the financial year.

(5) *The Finance Bill* : The Finance Bill incorporates the financial proposals of the Government for the ensuing year and is presented to Parliament at the same time as the Budget. The procedure followed is that of a Money Bill. The Discussion of the Finance Bill in the second reading is confined to general principles. It is only in the Select Committee that the Bill is considered in detail and amendments are moved. Clause by Clause consideration of the Bill follows after the presentation of the Committee Report. The scope of amendments is limited to proposals for the reduction or abolition of a tax. The financial proposals become operative immediately after presentation of the Budget under the Provincial Collection of Taxes Act, 1931. The Finance Bill must be passed before the end of April.

Since the expenditure sanctioned in the preceding Budget expires on March 31, and the discussion on the Budget for the current year can go on till the end of April or beyond, it becomes necessary to keep the Government functioning pending the final supply. The Constitution, accordingly, provides for grants in advance to be made by Parliament, that is, Vote on Account. The House of the People votes provisionally early in March about a 12th of the estimated expenditure under various grants. The necessary Appropriation Bill for this amount as also a similar amount in respect of the "charged" expenditure is passed. There is no discussion on a Vote on Account as it is an unavoidable formality and a sheer necessity.

Committees of Parliament

The Committee System : The principle of appointing committees is not a modern development. It is as old as Parliamentary system itself. The British Parliament soon after its organisation realised that, as a deliberative body, it could not do its work effectively and efficiently, although the business it transacted at that stage of its career was very light and simple. It, accordingly, started the practice of appointing its committees and delegating to them the more detailed consideration of work. With the growth of the parliamentary work and with a view to ensure its smooth, efficient and expeditious disposal the utility and the number of committees increased tremendously, and the House of Commons today relies more on Committees for expertise scrutiny and consideration of legislation and other matters which Parliament is to decide and determine.

The history of the committee system in India goes back to 1854 when the first legislature was established. The Legislative Council appointed its own committee to consider what should be its standing orders. Since then it became a practice of the Council to appoint from time to time committees to deal with varied matters. The existing Committees, may be divided into : (i) Ad-hoc Committees, and (ii) Non-Ad-hoc Committees. In the former category come Select Committees and Joint Committees. Committees in the latter category may be classified according to their functions. The following classification borrowed from S. S. More's *Practice and Procedure of Indian Parliament* presents a matter of fact analysis ;

(a) Committees to inquire

  (1) Committee of Petitions.

  (2) Committee of Privileges.

(b) Committee to scrutinise

  (1) Committee on Government Assurances.

  (2) Committee on Subordinate Legislation.

(c) Committees of an administrative character relating to the business of the House

(1) Committee on Absence of Members from the sittings of the House.

(2) Business Advisory Committee.

(3) Committee on Private Members' Bills and Resolutions.

(4) Rules Committee.

(d) Committees dealing with provision of facilities to Members

(1) General Purpose Committee.

(2) House Committee.

(3) Library Committee.

(4) Joint Committee on Salaries and Allowances of Members of Parliament.

(e) Financial Committees

(1) Estimates Committees.

(2) Public Accounts Committee.

(3) Committee on Public Undertakings.

The Ad Hoc Committee may be broadly classified under two heads :

(1) An Ad-hoc Committee constituted from time to time, either by the House of the People on a motion adopted in that behalf, or by the Speaker, to inquire into and report on specific subject.

(2) Committees set up to advise the House. Under this classification come Select or Joint Committees on Bills which are appointed on a motion made in the House to consider and report on a specific Bill.

A Committee on Public Undertakings has recently been constituted to investigate into the working of public undertakings.

Select Committees : Select Committees are appointed on individual Bills and for making some investigation, inquiry or compilation. The first Select Committee was appointed in 1954 and since then the succeeding Legislatures have invariably appointed numerous such committees. Select Committees, whether for a Bill or for making other investigation, have proved themselves a convenient instrument for detailed examination of Bills and other problems under inquiry. The Speaker remarked in 1955: "when we meet in the committee we do not represent parties, we function as a whole House and we do what, we think, the best in the interest of the House." The Parliamentary Committees help to save time for the House to discuss important matters and prevent Parliament from getting lost in details and thereby losing its hold on matters of policies and broad principles. Apart from this, the very complexity and technical nature of the modern business makes it necessary, that it should be closely scrutinised in a business-like manner, availing of outside technical or expert advice, whenever necessary. The Speaker, accordingly, aptly suggested that the House should rather appoint large Select Committees and leave the "matter to be thrashed out there than in a bigger House."

Members of a Select Committee are appointed or elected by the House itself or nominated by the Speaker. The willingness of the members desired to serve on the committee is ascertained before a proposal for appointment or nomination is made. The chairman is appointed by the Speaker from among its members, but if the Deputy Speaker happens to be a member of the committee, he shall be appointed chairman. One-third of the total membership constitutes the quorum and majority vote determines the decision of a committee. The chairman is entitled to a casting vote in case of a tie. A committee can appoint its own sub-committee. The meetings of a committee are private and are normally held in the precincts of Parliament House. It may send for persons to give evidence and produce papers and records. The report is presented by the chairman of the committee or a member authorised by the committee. Members dissenting from the majority report may submit minutes of dissent. The Speaker has the power to give directions to the committee with a view to regulating its procedure and the organisation of its work. The committee becomes *functus officio* as soon as it has presented its final report.

Joint Committees : In order to avoid duplication of proceedings a Bill may be referred to a Joint Committee composed of members of both Houses. A Joint Committee also saves time and helps to bring about and develop good understanding, an appreciative spirit and cooperation between the representatives of both the Houses. A motion for the appointment of a joint committee and reference of a Bill to such a committee after being carried out in the originating House, is transmitted to the other House for its concurrence. The member-incharge of a Bill indicates the number and names of the members constituting the committee from the House to which he belongs as also the number of the members from the other House. The proportion of members from the House of the People and the Council of States is two to one.

Particular Committees

The Business Advisory Committee :The Business Advisory Committee of the Lok Sabha consists of the Speaker and not more than fourteen members nominated by him. The Speaker is its ex-officio chairman. As the membership of Committee is limited and there are quite a large number of Opposition groups, it is not possible for the Speaker to nominate members from each and every group. However, in order to make the Committee as broad-based as possible certain prominent unattached members and members of some of the Opposition groups, who do not find representation in the Committee, are invited by the Speaker to attend its sittings. The invited members have neither the right to vote nor are they counted for the purpose of a quorum.

The function of the Business Advisory Committee is to

recommend the time that should be allocated for discussion of the stage or stages of such Government Bills or the business which the Speaker in consultation with the Leader of the House may direct to be referred to the Committee. The Committee can indicate in the proposed time table the different hours at which the various stages of the Bill or the business should be completed.

Private Members' Bills Committee : This Committee consists of not more than fifteen members nominated by the Speaker. The Deputy Speaker is invariably its member and as far as possible every section of opinion of the House is represented thereon. The functions of the Committee are , to examine and classify all Private Members' Bills according to their nature, urgency and importance; to allot time to Private Members' Bill and resolutions; to examine Private Members' Bills seeking to amend the Constitution before their introduction in the House; to examine a Private Members' Bill which is opposed in the House on the ground that the Bill initiates legislation outside the legislative competence of the House and to perform such other functions as may be assigned to it by the Speaker from time to time.

Petitions Committee : Article 350 entitles a citizen to submit representation for the redress of grievance to any officer or authority in the Union or a State. It is also considered an inherent right of a citizen to present a petition to Parliament ventilating public grievances and offering suggestions on matters of public importance. Rules of the Lok Sabha (160-67) provide for such petition to be presented.

A petition must be submitted to the House with the consent of the Speaker and it should concern some matter engaging the attention of the House, or some matter which falls within the cognisance of a court of law. A petition cannot be presented if it involved expenditure from the Consolidated Fund of India, or pertains to financial matters. A petition is usually presented by a Member who has to give advance notice of his intention to summit it to the House. On the day fixed for its presentation, the Speaker calls out the member's name and he presents the petition indicating briefly its subject-matter. The House thereupon is seized of it and the petition is remitted for consideration of the Committee of Petitions.

The Committee on Petitions is nominated by the Speaker and consists of not less than fifteen members in proportion to the strength of the parties or groups so as to make it representative of all shades of opinion in the House. It examines the merits of the petitions and makes recommendations to the House after taking such evidence as it may deem necessary. No minutes of dissent can be appended to the Report of the committee.

Balram Jakhar, former Speaker of the Lok Sabha, exhorted the Chairman of the Committees on Petitions of various legislatures, to gear them selves up by reviewing the existing working procedures and devising new ones, if necessary, to handle increasing cases in the future. Legislatures are not "elitist bodies," he affirmed. They are primarily representative institutions of the people and must protect their interests, freedom and public weal. The Committees on Petitions because of the nature of their functions are placed in a unique position to bring the people closer to the legislatures. Therefore, the procedures, "style of working and attitude of the committees should be such as would encourage more and more citizens to approach them for help". Begum Abida Ahmed, who headed the Lok Sabha's Committee on Petitions said, "Our effort should be to strengthen the Committees to an extent, that the common man may look to them with great expectations for redressal of grievances and fulfilment of aspirations."

Government Assurances Committee : While replying to questions and supplementaries in the House or in the course of discussion on Bills, Resolutions and other Motions, Ministers sometimes give assurances or undertakings either to consider a matter or to take action thereon or to provide to the House full information later. The Speaker appoints for one year a Committee of the House consisting of fifteen members on Government Assurances with a view to scrutinising assurances thus made and to report to the House whether such assurances, undertakings and promises have been fulfilled or not. If implemented, the extent of their implementation and whether such implementation was within the time necessary for this purpose. Statements showing action taken by Government in implementation of the assurances are laid periodically on the Table of the House by the Minister of Parliamentary Affairs. No Minister is nominated to this Committee. The Council of States has no such Committee.

Privileges Committee : Members of Parliament enjoy certain amenities, exemptions and privileges to protect their functional freedom individually and the dignity and authority of Parliament collectively. Where there is any question of an alleged breach of a privilege, the matter may be examined by the House but generally it is referred by the House to its Committee of Privileges for examination, investigation and report.

Some of the immunities, exemptions and privileges so enjoyed by members of Parliament are specified in the Constitution, some are contained in statutes, some in the Rules of Procedure and Conduct of Business of the two Houses, and some till recently were based on precedents and conventions of the House of Commons. The Constitution itself provided that until Parliament by law defined these privileges from time to time, if necessary, they would be those of the House of Commons, and of its Members and Committees, at the commencement of the Constitution. The Constitution (Forty-second Amendment) Act, 1976, amended Article 105 (3) and omitted the reference to the British House of Commons and laid down that the powers, privileges and immunities of each House of Parliament would be those of each House that existed at the commencement of the Forty-Second Amendment and as might be evolved by each House from time to time. This provision had not been brought into force till 1978 when the Constitution (Forty-fourth Amendment) Act, 1978, restored the original Clause 3 of Article 105 providing that the powers, privileges and immunities of each House of Parliament, and of the members and committees shall be such as determined by law and till such law is made, they shall be the same as obtaining immediately before the coming into force of Section 15 of Forty-fourth Amendment.

It is now more than four decades that the Constitution came into force, but the parliamentary privileges have not so far been codified. The citizen has, therefore, to consult what the law of British Parliamentary privileges was as on January 26, 1950, what the privileges of the Indian Legislatures and, correspondingly, his rights vis-a-vis the Legislatures are. This situation operates to the detriment of citizen's Fundamental Rights. "But it would seem", A.G. Noorani remarks, "that the legislators are more concerned about their privileges than the rights of citizens" and there appears to be a consensus "about retaining parliamentary privileges in their existing nebulous state."

The Committee of Privileges was first appointed by the Speaker in April 1950. Initially ten Members were appointed to the Committee and now it consists of fifteen Members nominated by the Speaker at the commencement of the House. It examines every issue referred to it, determines whether the facts reveal a breach of privileges and makes its recommendations to the House. On a motion made to that effect, the report is taken into consideration. The House may agree or disagree with the recommendations of the Committee or may agree with amendments and action may be taken accordingly.

Subordinate Legislative Committee : The Indian Legislatures have been delegating the rule-making power for more than a century now, but parliamentary control over subordinate legislation is a recent innovation. Since 1953, a Committee on Subordinate Legislation has been constituted by the Speaker for one year. In making selection from panel of names submitted by the Leader of the House and by the leaders of other parties and groups, the Speaker gives preference to those who have legal background and experience. The main functions of the Committee are to examine and determine :

(1) whether the Rules, Regulations and Orders are in accordance with the general objects of the Constitution or the Act under the authority of which they are made;

(2) whether they contain matters which should be properly dealt with in an Act;

(3) whether they contain the imposition of any tax;

(4) whether they directly or indirectly bar the jurisdiction of the courts;

(5) whether they give retrospective effect to any of the provisions where the Act or Constitution does not confer such authority;

(6) whether they involve expenditure from the Consolidated Fund or the public accounts;

(7) whether they appear to make any unexpected or unusual use of the powers conferred;

(8) whether there have been justifiable delays in the publication of the Rules or in laying them before Parliament;

(9) whether for any reason they call for any elucidation.

If the Committee is of the opinion that any Order should be annulled wholly or partially, or should be amended in any respect, it reports that opinion, together with the grounds thereof to the House. If the Committee opines that any other matter relating to any Order should be brought to notice, it may report that opinion and matter to the House. Usually, the Committee makes one report to the House during a session. Reports of the Committee are not discussed in the House, but it keeps a constant watch on the implementation of its recommendations.

The Ministers concerned are asked to furnish from time to time a statement of action taken or proposed to be taken by them on the recommendations made by the Committee and on the assurances given by them through correspondence with the Committee. The progress of implementation of the various recommendations is reported to the House by the Committee from time to time.

Absence of Members Committee : Article 101(4) of the Constitution provides that if for a period of sixty days a Member of either House of Parliament is, without permission of the House, absent from all meetings thereof, the House may declare his seat vacant. Till the Budget session of 1954, the Speaker would read to the House applications for leave and then ascertain the wishes of the House thereon. But thereafter a Standing Committee was set up comprising fifteen Members nominated by the Speaker for one year. This committee considers applications of Members for leave for absence from the sitting of the House. It examines the cases of Members who had been absent for a period of sixty days or more without permission. The Committee recommends to the House whether absence without permission should be condoned or not. In one case it has so far recommended that absence without permission of a Member should not be condoned. The Council of States has no such committee.

Rules Committee : Article 118(1) of the Constitution empowers each House of Parliament to make rules for regulating the procedure and conduct of its business. The Rules Committee has been constituted in pursuance of this provision. It is nominated by the Speaker—the Chairman, and consists of fifteen members. The Speaker—the Chairman, is its ex-officio Chairman. The committee so nominated holds office until a new committee is nominated.

The function of the Committee is to consider matters of procedure and conduct of business in the House and to recommend any amendments or additions to the Rules of Procedure and Conduct of Business that may be necessary.

Apart from the members of the Committee some other Members of the House may also be invited to attend particular sittings of the Committee. Till 1954 amendments to the Rules of Procedure were made by the Speaker-the Chairman, but now the recommendations of the Rules Committee are placed before the House and adopted.

Facilities Dealing Committees : Besides these, there are three committees dealing with provision of facilities to Members the General Purposes Committee; the House Committee; and the Library Committee. The function of the General Purposes Committee is to consider and advise on such matters concerning the affairs of the House as may be referred to it by the Speaker. The House Committee deals with matters of accommodation, food and medical aid for members. The functions of the Library Committee are : to consider and advise on such matters concerning the Library as may be referred to it by the Speaker, to consider suggestions for the improvement of the Library, and to assist members in fully utilising the services provided by the Committee.

Estimates Committee : To ensure parliamentary control over grants made to the Government and to supervise and control the actual appropriation, Parliament exercises close scrutiny of public accounts through two of its Committees—the Public Accounts Committee on Estimates was constituted for the first time in 1950, replacing the then Standing Finance Committee of Parliament. Speaker Mavalankar observed in the Lok Sabha :

> "Consequent upon the provisions of Articles 113 to 116, as also independently thereof, it was felt to constitute a Committee on Estimates for better financial control of the House over expenditure by the Executive. The chief function of this Committee will be to examine such of the estimates as may seem fit to it and to suggest economies consistent with the policy underlying the estimates. There

> will be, in addition, usual Committee on Public Accounts. The functions of these Committees will be complementary and, it is expected, they will not only give a picture of the entire financial position but the Committees will be mutually helpful in examining the finances for the future in the light of expenditure in the past."

The Committee on Estimates consists of not more than thirty Members who are elected by the House from among its Members every year according to the system of proportional representation by means of the single transferable vote. The motion for election of members of the Committee is moved by the Leader of the House at the commencement of each House of the People and in subsequent years by the Chairman of the Committee before the term of that Committee is due to expire. In order to maintain continuity in membership of the Committee a convention has been established since 1955-57 that while nominating Members for election parties and groups in the House should keep in view that as far as possible nearly one-third of the Members retire every year and two-thirds of the outgoing Members are returned. A Minister is not elected to the Committee, and if any Member after his election to the Committee is appointed a Minister, he ceases to be a member of the Committee from the date of his appointment.

The Chairman of the Committee is appointed by the Speaker from among the members of the Committee. It is a Committee of the House of the People exclusively and unlike the Public Accounts Committee no member of the Council of States is associated with it.

The function of the Committee is to scrutinize the Budget estimates for the year, to suggest economies in the expenditure, improvement in organisation and other steps for increasing efficiency, to find out whether the money is well laid out and also to suggest the form in which the estimates should be presented to Parliament. Usually the Committee functions through the Sub-Committees, one corresponding to one or more Departments, and their reports are submitted both to the House and to the Government. The Committee does not complete its work with the final passage of the Budget. It continues with its labours throughout the year and exercises scrutiny over one Department or the other as it chooses and deems necessary.

As a convention, the Reports of the Committee on Estimates, like those of the Public Accounts Committee, are not discussed in the House. It is again a convention that the recommendations of a Parliamentary Committee are regarded as directions, and accordingly, the recommendations of the Committee on Estimates are generally accepted by the Government and acted upon. After the Committee's report has been presented to the House, copies thereof are forwarded to the Ministry or Department concerned with a request that replies to recommendations be sent not later than six months from the date of its presentation to the House. On receipt of the statement showing the action taken by the Government, it is examined by the Study Group appointed for this purpose and is placed before the Chairman together with the findings of the Study Group. If there is any point, which in the opinion of the Study Group or the Chairman, requires consideration by the Committee, it is specially referred to it.

On the basis of the comments made by the Committee, or the Study Group, a draft "Action Taken Report" is prepared which is again considered by the Study Group. After the Chairman's approval it is circulated to the members of the committee. The report is finalized by the Chairman on the basis of the comments received from the members and presented to the House.

Commenting on the utility of the Committee on Estimates, Asok Chanda says, "In recent years, however, the Committee's contribution has been more impressive .... While the Committee refrains even now from openly criticizing the policy implicit in the estimates, its examination does often indirectly reflect on the manner in which a particular policy has been evolved or is being implemented. There has also been considerable improvement in the organisation of the Committee and in its technique, which has better equipped it to fulfil its responsibilities. Even though it works within the limitations inherent in a democratic form of government, its contributions are tending to become more and more effective in economizing national expenditure.," Morrison Jones is rather critical of the role of the Estimates Committee.

Its Members, he says, "are supposed to look for possible economies but they have in fact been happy to rule out the faint line between economy and efficiency. Further, they have not hesitated to recommend in the name of efficiency large administrative reforms and even reorientation of policy. Their audacity occasioned strong comment and it may be that they have in the last few years been more modest in the scope of their reports." But "of their growing competence and effectiveness as a control over ministries," he adds, "there can be no doubt. If they find less to be indignant about it, it is in part because their influence is now automatically reckoned with.,

Committee on Public Accounts : The Public Accounts Committee considers the Appropriation Accounts in details and it is the twin brother of the Estimates Committee. Public Accounts Committee were for the first time constituted at the Centre and in the Provinces as early as 1923. But they met under the chairmanship of the Finance Member of the Governor-General's or Governor's Executive Council. Their secretariat consisted of the Finance Department and their role was technicalities. Moreover, the position of the Auditor-General was more governmental than independent and he was in no sense a servant of the Legislature.

In 1950, the Public Accounts Committee was made a real parliamentary committee. The Comptroller and Auditor-

General is an important adjunct of the Committee. His audit reports stand automatically referred to the Committee. When the official witnesses are being examined by the Committee, the Comptroller and Auditor-General sits to the right of the Chairman and assists him as the evidence is being taken. With the permission of the Chairman, he may ask a witness to clarify a point and he may further make a statement on the facts of the case.

The Committee consists of not more than fifteen members who are elected by the House every year from among its Members according to the principle of proportional representation by means of the single transferable vote. A Minister is not elected a member of this Committee, and if a member, after his election to the Committee, is appointed a Minister, he ceases to be a member of the Committee from the date of his appointment. Since 1954, seven members of the Council of States have been associated with the Committee. The Chairman of the Committee is appointed by the Speaker from among the members of the Committee.

The main function of the Public Accounts Committee is to scrutinize the Appropriation Accounts of the Government of India and other accounts laid before the House and the report of the Comptroller and Auditor-General of India and to satisfy itself that moneys shown in the accounts have been legally disbursed, that expenditure conforms to the authority that governs it and that re-appropriation has been according to rules. The Committee has also to examine the statement of accounts showing the income and expenditure of State Corporations, trading and manufacturing schemes and concerns and projects of autonomous and semi-autonomous bodies whose audit is conducted by the Comptroller and Auditor-General.

The Report of the Comptroller and Auditor-General of India furnishes the Public Accounts Committee with most of the material on which it functions. The Committee has, however, the power to scrutinize and report on almost any matter relating to the management of public finance. The report of the Comptroller and Auditor-General is taken up Ministry wise, and the Departmental Secretaries are required to appear as witnesses to elucidate and explain the observations of audit, in order to enable the Committee to reach final conclusions and formulate its recommendations.

The examination of the Committee extends "beyond the formality of the expenditure to its wisdom, faithfulness and economy." Specifically, the examination covers the manner in which approved policy is being implemented, the degree of efficiency and economy with which plans and programmes are being executed and the manner in which discretionary powers are being exercised. The Committee is not concerned with the policy of the method of expenditure. The question whether there is any extravagance or waste in carrying out that policy is within the competence of the Committee. Whenever the Committee decides to examine a matter involving serious financial irregularities, it may appoint a Sub-Committee to go into the matter. A Sub-Committee so appointed, has the powers of the undivided Committee and its report after the Committee's approval, is deemed to be the report of the whole committee.

The utility of the Public Accounts Committee is immense. It is a representative Committee of all shades of opinion and Members of Parliament, who constitute the Committee, recognise the question of public accounts as a national question and, accordingly, its deliberations and findings are devoid of party feelings and partisan approach. It directly contacts the executive officers, the administrators and all those who spend money and, thus, direct elucidation of the disputed matters can be sought from these officials. It may even summon further evidence, oral and documentary. If necessary, evidence may be taken on oath, but in practice that is not done by any Select Committee except in very special cases.

This is a post-mortem examination, all the same, very effective. The Committee has no power to complete any administrative action to be taken on its observations, but that has not detracted from the effectiveness of its recommendations. Recommendations of the Committee are treated with respect by the Government and most of them are accepted and implemented. In case of disagreement between the Government and the Committee with respect to any recommendation the Government must apprise the Committee of the reasons that might have weighed in not accepting or implementing a recommendation.

The views of the government are considered by the Committee and it may, if deemed necessary, present a further report to the House. In the event of difference of opinion between the Government and the Committee remaining unresolved, the matters are referred to the Speaker for his guidance. The House seldom discusses reports of the Committee, but Members may use observations of the Committee in their speeches during the discussion on the Budget, demands for grants, etc. However, if there is a specific issue, over which there is difference of opinion between the Committee or the Government or a Minister, that issue can be brought before the House for discussion on a motion.

The utility of the Public Accounts Committee has been variously interpreted. Asok Chanda says that its power is indirect "and lies nominally in the potential results of its reports and the publicity which it is able to give to the question it investigates and in the moral effect of its criticism. " Morris-Jones puts it in another way. He says, "The fact that their scrutiny is ex post facto is less important than that the government has continuously to act in the knowledge that scrutiny of any item may take place and that waste and impropriety may be widely exposed in the House and the Press. The fact that the Government replies to the Public Accounts Committee are often vague and cool is less important than that behind the reply there has often been embarrassment and some resolve not to let it happen again. "

Five important points were made by the Finance Minister in his address to the Chairmen of the Public Accounts Committees of the Lok Sabha and the State Assemblies in September 1986. First, that the Public Accounts Committees should while relying on the Comptroller and Auditor-General's report, also take into confidence the Finance Ministry or the Finance Departments of State Governments. Second, that the Public Accounts Committees would discharge their functions more effectively if they gave up their pre-occupation with nit-picking issues of non-compliance with rules and regulations, etc., and instead took a broader view, from time to time.

Third, that in view of the resources constraint, which involves having to choose between different projects, the Public Accounts Committees should seek the assistance of the Comptroller and Auditor-General in drawing up a list of projects and programmes that have lost their relevance so that these can be scrapped and the money thus saved diverted to more useful programmes or projects.

Fourth, that the Public Accounts Committees should insist on accounts of the previous year being presented in the winter session at the latest, instead of having to wait for almost two years. Lastly, that the accounting practice of State Governments, specially at the district treasury level, should be strengthened along the lines suggested by the Finance Ministry in 1976.

These suggestions deserve to be taken seriously. The Public Accounts Committees should take up the really serious issues and give up their excessive preoccupation with trivial. The crux of the issue is watch-dog function that the Public Accounts Committees are supposed to perform. While by and large they have discharged this function reasonably well, they have mostly succeeded in highlighting relatively minor financial irregularities. The bigger sins of omission and commission, such as time and cost over-runs, poor choice of technologies, bad project planning and implementation, etc., have escaped their notice. N.C. Ranga, who was Chairman of the Central Public Accounts Committee in 1958-59, said, "It is a notorious fact that politics comes in as one of the elements to bloat demands and expenditures; inefficiency and indifferent management of funds, whether from the Centre or the States, have become endemic feature, that result in heavy wastage of public funds."

Public Undertakings Committee : The demand' for a separate committee on Public Undertakings goes back to 1953. Speaker Mavalankar, in a letter dated December 19,1953, wrote to the Prime Minister that there was a general feeling in favour of setting up a Standing Committee to examine the working of autonomous Corporations. He pointed out that the Estimates Committee and the-Public Accounts Committee were already overburdened with work and would not, therefore, be able to find time to go into the working of the Corporations. But the Prime Minister did not accept the suggestion and the matter lingered on till 1964 when a Committee on Public Undertakings was constituted.

The Committee on Public Undertakings consists of not more than ten members elected by the House of the People from among its members according to the principle of proportional representation by means of the single transferable vote. Five members from the Council of States elected in the same manner, are associated with the Committee. The members of the Council are invited to associate with the Committee on a motion adopted by the House and concurred by the Council. A Minister is not elected a member of the Committee. If a member elected to the Committee is subsequently appointed Minister, he ceases to be a member of the Committee from the date of his appointment. The chairman is appointed by the Speaker from among the members of the Committee.

The functions of the Committee are:

(1) to examine the report and accounts of the such public

undertakings as have been specifically allotted to the Committee for this purpose;

(2) to examine the reports, if any, of the Comptroller and Auditor-General on the Public undertakings;

(3) to examine, in the context of autonomy and efficiency of public under takings, whether the affairs of the public under taking are being managed in accordance with the sound business principles and prudent commercial practices; and

(4) to exercise such other functions vested in the Public Accounts Committee and the Estimates Committee in relation to the public undertakings specified for the Committee as are not covered by (1), (2), and (3) above and as may be allotted to the Committee by the Speaker from time to time.

The Committee shall, however, not examine and investigate any of the following matters:

(a) matters of major Government policy as distinct from business or commercial functions of the Public undertakings;

(b) matters of day-to-day administration; and

(c) matters for the consideration of which machinery has been established by any special statute under which a particular undertaking is established.

The total Government investments in public undertakings in different States amounted to Rs. 25,000 crores on March 31, 1983. The Committee has investigated into and examined all aspects of the working of these undertakings. One innovation introduced by the committee is the "horizontal study," where some aspect of the working of all public undertakings is studied and norms of performance, cost, practices, etc., are set down.

The Committee in its 32nd report voiced concern at the gradual erosion of the decision-making powers of the public sector enterprises. It noted that to ensure an efficient running of the public sector companies the Industrial Policy Resolution, 1956, had clearly stated that the managers should have the largest possible measure of freedom. It is precisely for this reason that the then prevailing practice of having departmental undertakings was jettisoned and public sector firms were set up as corporate entities. Over the years, however, the autonomy that these corporate entities should have enjoyed and exercised, was gradually encroached upon and they came to be run as mere extensions of the ministries. According to the Committee, although on paper the public sector managers enjoy large autonomy, ministries and government departments have virtually usurped their decision-making powers. The Committee has recommended that "necessary ground rules should be laid down to restrict the Government directions only to matters of policy without transgressing into the spheres of detailed administration."

Consultative Committee : Apart form the Committee of the Legislative Assembly, prior to 1950, members of both Houses of the Central Legislature also served on the Standing Advisory Committees attached to various Departments of the Government of India. All these Committees were purely advisory bodies and functioned under the control of the Government and the Minister incharge of the department acted as the Chairman of the Standing Advisory Committee. After the 1950 Constitution became operative, the position of the Central Legislature changed, significantly and these Committees were consequently abolished.

But the Government had been seriously thinking all that time how to associate the members of the Parliament with the working of various Ministries and Departments of the Government and thereby provide them with opportunities for discussion of broad policies of the Government in an informal manner.

In 1954 the Government decided to establish Informal Consultative Committees for the various Ministries. But the

Opposition parties and groups did not take kindly to the Consultative Committee. As a result of discussion between the Government and the Opposition at different levels in 1969, it was decided to delete the word "Informal" from their nomenclature. Mutually agreed "Guidelines" were also formulated to regulate their functioning. The Government, however, did not accept the suggestion of the Opposition for the formation of the Parliamentary Committees in place of Consultative Committees.

Members of both Houses of Parliament are nominated on the Consultative Committees for various Ministries by the Minister of Parliamentary Affairs, on the basis of preference indicated by the members themselves or by the party leaders. Members of the Opposition parties are nominated in proportion to their numerical strength in Parliament. Every Opposition party or group has, thus, its fixed quota for representation on the Consultative Committees and these parties and groups are free to nominate their members on more than one Committee within the quota allotted to them. The unattached members, and members belonging to the ruling party are nominated on the basis of the preferences indicated by them and sent individually to the Department of Parliamentary Affairs.

The Committees are reconstituted every year and a member once assigned a Committee for a Ministry, according to the preference indicated by him, continues to be a member of that Committee unless he himself opts for another Committee. The Minister concerned presides over the meetings of the Consultative Committee attached to his Ministry. The Committees provide a forum of informal discussions between the members, Ministers and senior officials of the Government on the problems and policies of the Government relating to administration in a manner which is not practicable on the floor of the House. The deliberations of these Committees are informal and no reference to the discussions held in the meetings is made on the floor of the House and it is binding on the Government as well as the members of the Committees.

Members of these Committees are free to discuss any matter which can appropriately be discussed in Parliament. The practice is to invite suggestions and items for discussion from members and thereupon agenda with notes is prepared and circulated among members. The Committees cannot summon witnesses, to send for or demand the production of any files, or to examine any official records.

The Chairman of the Committee may, however, furnish any additional information required by members. A brief record of the discussion in the meeting of a Committee is prepared and circulated among members, except in the case of Ministries of Defence, External Affairs and Department of Atomic Energy:

In matters where there is unanimity, the Government normally accepts the view of the committee subject to the following exceptions :

(i) any view having financial implications;
(ii) any view concerning security, defence, external affairs and atomic energy; and
(iii) any matters falling within the purview of an autonomous corporation.

If the Government finds it difficult to accept the view of the committee, the reasons thereof are explained to the members of the Committee.

But the Consultative Committees, it is widely felt, do not function as committees and still less discharge the functions of consultation except in a purely formal sense. The committee, attached to a Ministry, does not meet by itself without the Minister to discuss or deliberate. It is convened by the Minister. Polemics and partisanship are as present in the committees' deliberations as they are in Parliament itself. The duration of the meeting is decided by the Minister concerned who presides as chairman. The frequency of the meeting varies from two to six per year. Each meeting lasts about a couple of hours unless it is extended to the following day as it happened on January

25, 1978 in the case of the committee attached to the Ministry of External Affairs.

The need for effective Parliamentary Committees is being widely recognised and there was a demand of a cross-section of the Members in the House of the People for increased powers and functions to Parliamentary Consultative Committees. Members generally wanted their status as Standing Committees to be restored so that they might share some of the burdens of Parliament. The Parliamentary Affairs Minister, Ravindra Verma, ruled out the demand and asserted that the Consultative Committees were functioning satisfactorily and the present Government (Janata) had no proposal to increase their powers.

A proposal to do away with the Consultative Committees and replace them with Subjects Committees, as the Public Accounts Committee and the Public Understanding Committee of Parliament, had come up during the late half of 1989. It was considered with some trepidation by the Congress Government of the day headed by Rajiv Gandhi. Even though the move had the backing of the then Speaker of the Lok Sabha Balram Jakhar, it remained a non-starter as the Ministry of Parliamentary Affairs was opposed to it as also various other Ministries and Departments who had expressed strong reservations about such Committees. The Subjects Committees pertaining to agriculture, environments, and science and technology were, however, subsequently set up, though they have so far remained only on paper.

It was reported in September 1991 that the Lok Sabha and Rajya Sabha Secretariats were making a fresh attempt to resurrect the proposal to do away with the Consultative Committees.

But it again created a mild flutter in the Ministry of Parliamentary Affairs. The lobby in the Government was for continuing the system of consultative committees. In their opinion the idea of having subjects committees was sought to be pushed by the Secretariats of the Lok Sabha and Rajya Sabha allegedly to enlarge their sphere of influence. This is, however, neither a valid nor a logical argument to rebut the cogency of proposal. Several veteran Members of Parliament during the recently concluded 1991 Budget session of Parliament underlined the need for setting up subjects committees ensuring thereby a proper scrutiny of the functioning of various Ministries and Departments and accountability fixed in case of any lapse or dereliction. But the Minister of Parliamentary Affairs had obliquely ruled out the setting up of subjects committees on the ground that the country had given itself a "Parliamentary system of functioning".

11

Fundamental Rights

Past Developments

Before the enactment of the 1950 Constitution there was no charter of fundamental rights of a justiciable nature, although the demand for such rights and their constitutional guarantees had its deep roots in the nineteenth century. It was implicit in the formation of the Indian National Congress in 1885, which wanted the same rights and privileges for Indians that the British enjoyed in their own country.

The promoters of the Indian National Congress emphatically demanded an end to discrimination inherent in a colonial regime. Perhaps, the first implicit demand for fundamental rights appeared in the Constitution of India Bill, 1895. This bill, described by Mrs. Annie Besant as the Home Rule Bill, envisaged to guarantee to all citizens freedom of speech and expression, right to personal liberty, inviolability of one's house, right to property, equality before the law, equality to admission to public offices and right to petition for redress of grievances. Immediately after the publication of the Montagu-Chelmsford Report, the Indian National Congress, at its Bombay session in August 1918, demanded that the new constitution of India should contain a "declaration of the rights of the people of India as British citizens," guaranteeing equality before the law, freedom of speech and press, and protection in respect of liberty, life and property.

By the mid-twenties, Congress and Indian leaders had acquired a forceful consciousness of their rights which was influenced by various factors, especially by the experience of World War I, the deep disappointment which the Montagu-Chelmsford Reforms had caused, President Woodrow Wilson's support for self-determination and M.K. Gandhi's arrival in India and his active participation in the politics of the country. The Constitution of the Irish Free State in 1921, which contained a Bill of Rights, had also a profound effect on political thought in India. The Commonwealth of India Bill, drafted by the National Convention under the inspiration of Mrs. Annie Besant in 1925, embodied a declaration of rights more or less similar to the provisions of the Irish Constitution.

Within two years of the publication of the Commonwealth of India Bill came the announcement of the appointment of the Indian Statutory (Simon) Commission. To set a model for the Simon Commission, the Forty-third Annual Session of the Congress at Madras in 1927 resolved that the Working Committee be empowered to set up a Committee "to draft a Swaraj Constitution for India on the basis of a declaration of rights." The Nehru Committee was, accordingly, appointed in 1928, which included in its membership representatives of all the political parties. The Nehru Committee in its report included a comprehensive bill of rights and in recommending their declaration the Committee urged that "Ireland is the only country where conditions obtaining before the Treaty are nearest approach to those we have in India. The first concern of the people of Ireland was, as it is indeed with the people of India today, to secure fundamental rights that had been denied to them". Another reason why India attached importance to the declaration of the fundamental rights, in the opinion of the Committee, was the unfortunate existence of communal differences in India. "Certain safeguards and guarantees," the Committee urged, "are necessary to create and establish a sense of security among those who look upon each other with distrust and suspicion. We could not better secure the full enjoyment of religious and communal rights to all communities than by including them among the basic principles of the constitution." The Committee added, "It is obvious that our first care should be to have our fundamental rights guaranteed in a manner which will not permit their withdrawal under any circumstances."

In 1931, the Indian National Congress passed a Resolution on Fundamental Rights. In order to end the exploitation of the masses, the Resolution emphasised, political freedom must include real economic freedom of the starving millions. It was further declared that any constitution which might be agreed to on behalf of the Indian National Congress should provide, or enable the Swaraj Government to provide, for certain fundamental rights and duties. But the British Government was in no mood to reconcile itself to this primary demand of the Indians. In fact, such a demand was unsuited to the British genius. The Simon Commission had ridiculed the idea of fundamental rights. "Abstract declarations", the Commission observed, "are useless unless there exists the will and the means to make them effective."

All the same, the matter came up for consideration during the Round Table Conferences. At the Second Round Table Conference, M. K. Gandhi, the sole representative of the Indian National Congress, circulated a memorandum, *inter alia*, demanding that the new Constitution should "include a guarantee to the communities concerned for the protection of their cultures, languages, scripts, education, profession and practice of religion and religious endowments." Another memorandum on the subject was put forward jointly by the representatives of the minorities. Ramsay MacDonald, the then Labour Prime Minister, announced that he felt the need of incorporating fundamental rights in the proposed constitution of India for safeguarding the interests of the minorities. Immediately after came the National Government into power with Ramsay MacDonald as Prime Minister, but with a clear majority of the Conservatives in the Government. This made a sharp swing in the official policy. Lord Reading and Sir John Simon were vehement in opposing the inclusion of fundamental rights in the new constitution for India. The Indian representatives at the Conference could not agree amongst themselves on the basic problems of constitutional reforms and, accordingly, the issue of fundamental rights also lapsed.

The Joint Parliamentary Committee on the Government of India Bill, 1934, endorsed the observations of the Simon Commission on the demand for a constitutional guarantee of fundamental rights to subjects of British India. The Committee, however, conceded that there were some legally recognised principles which could be included in the new constitution and, accordingly, the Government of India Act, 1935, conferred certain rights and forms of protection on British subjects in India.

The subject of fundamental rights came up for active consideration in the deliberations of the Conciliation Committee, also known as the Sapru Committee, appointed by the All-Parties Conference *(1944-45)*. The Committee was of the opinion that fundamental rights were not only assurances and guarantees to the minorities but also prescribing a standard of conduct for the legislatures, governments and the courts. The Committee further said that it was for the Constitution-making body to settle the list of fundamental rights and, then, to decide about their division into justiciable and non-justiciable rights and to provide in the case of the former, suitable machinery for their enforcement. A few months more than a year later the Constituent Assembly of India began framing the Fundamental Rights and the Directive Principles of State Policy, the former justiciable and the latter non justiciable. The most striking feature about the treatment of rights in the Sapru Report was the distinction between justiciable and non justiciable rights.

The Debate

The Cabinet Mission Plan conceded the demand for the Constituent Assembly as well as the need for a written guarantee of fundamental rights in the Constitution of India. It recommended the appointment of an Advisory Committee on the Rights of Citizens, Minorities and Tribal and Excluded Areas, containing the interests affected, which would prepare a list of fundamental rights and also to recommend their inclusion in the State or the Union List. By the Objectives Resolution introduced by Jawaharlal Nehru and adopted on January 22, 1947, the Constituent Assembly solemnly pledged itself to draw up for India's future governance a constitution wherein "shall be guaranteed and secured to all the people of India, justice, social. economic and political, equality of status, of opportunity and before the law; freedom of thought, expression, belief, faith, worship, vocation, association and action, subject to law and public morality."

Two days after adopting Objectives Resolution, the Constituent Assembly elected an Advisory Committee for reporting on minorities, fundamental rights and on the tribal and excluded areas. The Advisory Committee consisted of 54 members with Sardar Vallabhbhai Patel as its Chairman. The Committee was constituted on February 12, 1947, with five Sub-Committees one of which was to deal with fundamental rights . The draft report of the Sub-Committee was circulated to its members with the explanatory notes on various clauses prepared by B.N. Rau, Constitutional Adviser to the Constituent Assembly. These were thereafter discussed in the Sub-Committee in the light of the comments offered by the members and the final report was submitted to the Chairman of the Advisory Committee on April 16, 1947. The Advisory Committee accepted the recommendations of the Sub-Committee : (1) for division of rights into justiciable and non-justiciable rights; that is, rights enforceable by appropriate legal process and rights consisting of directive principles of state policy, which though not enforceable in courts, were nevertheless to be regarded as fundamental in the governance of the country; (2) certain rights being guaranteed to all persons and certain others to citizens only; and (3) all such rights being made uniformly applicable to the Union and the units. The Constituent Assembly adopted all these recommendations and the Constitution of 1950 contains two Chapters-Chapter III enumerating the Fundamental Rights and Chapter IV dealing with the Directive Principles of State Policy. The Constitution (Forty-second Amendment) Act, 1976, inserted a new Chapter Part IV A containing fundamental duties which are covered by Article 51A.

The Features

The Constitution sets out a most elaborate declaration of human rights as compared with the Bill of Rights contained in any other existing constitution of importance. The provisions of Chapter III are detailed covering a variety of topics and some are purely the outcome of the peculiar social conditions, prevailing in India, but aiming to build a new social structure on the ruins of old time-worn social order based on inequality, untouchability, status—caste and religious considerations and economic exploitation. The new social order envisaged in the Fundamental Rights is intended to help the growth of new sociological processes forging thereby an integrated homogeneous community free from exploitation of any kind and social disability of any nature.

Whereas some of the rights conferred by the Constitution are limited to citizens such as freedom of speech, assembly and cultural and educational rights, in the case of others, as equality before the law, religious freedom, etc., such a limitation does not exist; these are applicable to citizens and aliens alike. The relevant Articles of the Constitution make use of the two terms 'citizens' and 'persons' and they are indicative of the distinction between citizens and aliens. Even in the absence of such a distinction all the rights could not have been available to citizens and aliens alike, but the matter would have remained undecided until the Supreme Court had determined so.

Some of the provisions of Chapter III of the Constitution are of the nature of prohibitions and place constitutional limitations on the authority of the State, for instance, no authority of the State can deny to any person equality before the law or the equal protection of the laws; discrimination against any citizen; and no titles other than a military or academic distinction can be conferred. From the point of view of an individual, such rights may be termed as negative rights. The remaining provisions of the Chapter on Fundamental Rights, as such, can be said to contain positive rights of the individuals. In spite of this distinction no clear-cut line of division can be drawn between the two. There is, however, one important distinction between them. The provisions which impose constitutional limitation on the authority of the State are binding for all intents and purposes and any action, legislative or executive, which contravenes any of these provisions, would be void altogether. The provisions relating to individual rights, on the other hand, are subject to the regulation of the State within certain prescribed limits and restrictions so imposed cannot be held to be void unless they travel beyond those limits.

The Fundamental Rights place limitations on all kinds of authority that has either the power to make laws or have discretion vested in it. The Fundamental Rights are, accordingly, binding on the Union Government, the State Governments and the local bodies including village Panchayats, and other authorities within the territory of India. Article 12 of the Constitution defines the State, inclusively, to mean the Government and Parliament of India and the Government and Legislature of each of the States and all local or other authorities within the territory of India or under the control of the Government of India. Ambedkar made this point clear in the Constituent Assembly. He explained that the object of the Fundamental Rights was twofold. "First, that every citizen must be in a position to claim those rights. Secondly, they must be binding upon every authority ..... upon every authority which has got either the power to make laws or the power to have discretion vested in it. Therefore, it is quite clear that if the Fundamental Rights are to be real, then they must be binding not only upon the Central Government, they must not only be binding upon the Provincial Government .... they must also be binding upon District Local Boards, Municipalities, even authority which has been created by law and which has got certain power to make laws, to make rules, or make by-laws."

Absolute or unrestricted rights are not possible. This is the position in Britain, although there are no constitutional guarantees of fundamental rights in that country. In the United States there are no direct restrictions imposed by the First Ten Amendments which determine the American Bill of Rights. But under the doctrine of Police Power the Supreme Court has recognised the inherent power of the State to impose such restrictions on Fundamental Rights as may be deemed reasonable to protect the common good. The Constitution of India, on the other hand, imposes direct limitations on Fundamental Rights. Ambedkar, while introducing the Draft Constitution and supporting the restriction clauses, maintained, "what the Draft Constitution had done is that instead of formulating fundamental rights in absolute terms and depending upon our Supreme Court to come to the rescue of Parliament by inventing doctrine of police power, it permits the State directly to impose limitations upon the fundamental rights." Courts in India cannot, therefore, question the propriety of legislation once it has been established that it is within the competence of the legislature to make such a law or in any way to modify its effect on the ground that it seeks to "unduly restrict personal liberty. "

The Constitution of India, thus, did not recognise the supremacy of the judiciary against the Legislature, although the Constitution gave to the judiciary the power to review legislation repugnant to the Fundamental Rights. The position before February 1967 was that Parliament would abrogate or abridge Fundamental Rights by amending the Constitution under the provisions of Article 368 and thereby override the unwholesome decision of the Judiciary simply by securing the requisite special majority, which the Congress Party had commanded in Parliament all those years. In 1961 and 1963, the Supreme Court declared that the Kerala and Madras Land Reform Acts, which provided for a ceiling on land holdings, were bad. In the wake of these declarations the Seventeenth Amendment was enacted in 1964 whereunder 44 laws passed by both the States were included in the Ninth Schedule in order to maintain them valid. A good number of writ petitions challenging the competence of Parliament to enact the Seventeenth Amendment were moved in the Supreme Court.

The Supreme Court by a 6-59 ruling on February 27, 1967 reversed its earlier decisions and declared that Parliament has no power to abridge or take away Fundamental Rights by amending the Constitution under Article 368. Chief Justice Subba Rao, speaking for the majority, declared, "The Constitution has given by its scheme a place of permanence to the fundamental freedoms. In giving to themselves the Constitution, the people have reserved the fundamental freedoms to themselves. Article 13 merely incorporates that reservation.

The importance attached to the fundamental freedoms is so transcendental that a bill enacted by a unanimous vote of all the members of both Houses (of Parliament) is ineffective to derogate from its guaranteed exercise....." The Court rejected the Government's argument that if the power to amend the Constitution was not all-comprehensive, no way would be left to change the structure of the Constitution or to abridge the Fundamental Rights even if the whole county demanded such a change. It was declared that "this visualizes an extremely enforceable and extravagant demand; but even if such a contingency arises, the residuary power of the Parliament may be relied upon to call for a Constituent Assembly for making a new Constitution or radically changing it."

The resultant position was that the amendment of the Fundamental Rights was not forbidden, but the Supreme Court reserved to itself the power of determining in each specific case whether the amendment in question took away or abridged those rights contained in Part III of the Constitution. Thus, the precariously balanced six to five decision established the supremacy of the Judiciary so far as Fundamental Rights were involved. The Supreme Court of India, like its counterpart in the United States, assumed the role of a super legislature because what is taken away by the Justices from Parliament is taken away from the people.

The Constitution (Twenty-fourth Amendment) Act, 1971, was enacted to get over the difficulty created by the *Golak Nath* case. The amendment empowered Parliament to abrogate any of Fundamental Rights including the right, under Article 32, to move the Supreme Court for the enforcement of Fundamental Rights. The validity of this amendment was questioned in the Supreme Court through a series of writ petitions. In *Kesavananda Bharati v. The State of Kerala* the Court reversed the *Golak Nath* case judgement by upholding the validity of the Twenty-fourth Amendment and thereby restored the supremacy of Parliament in regard to legislation on Fundamental Rights, a position that existed prior to 1967. But the Court also ruled that Parliament cannot alter the basic structure or framework of the Constitution. What exactly did the basic structure mean, the Court said nothing about it. The Thirty-fourth Amendment enacted in 1974 put out of the pale of judicial review a bunch of laws designed to alter the structure of the ownership of agricultural land and tenurial relations. The Thirty-ninth Amendment (1975) sought to amend the Ninth Schedule of the Constitution so as to bring within its scope 38 Central and certain State enactments and thereby protecting them from challenge in any court of law on the ground of violation of any of the Fundamental Rights.

Soon in the wake of the Thirty-ninth Amendment came the Fortieth in May, 1976, which provided for addition of 64 Central and State laws in the Ninth Schedule with a view to protecting them from challenge in the courts on constitutional grounds. By including these nine Central Acts and fifty-five State laws in the Ninth Schedule, the new doctrine of the Congress Government that the Directive Principles of State Policy should prevail over Fundamental Rights was reaffirmed in no uncertain terms.

The President of the Indian National Congress appointed the Swaran Singh Committee on Constitutional Reforms early in 1976. The Committee suggested that primacy of the Directive Principles of State Policy must be proclaimed once for all and no law giving effect to Directive Principles should be called in question on the ground of infringement of any of the Fundamental Rights. The Constitution (Forty-second Amendment) Act, 1976, was mainly based on the recommendations of the Swaran Singh Committee Report.

The Janata Party, formed just before the Parliamentary elections held in March 1977, pledged in its manifesto "to rescind the 42nd Amendment." The electorate reposed their confidence in the Janata and the Party assumed office on the 25th March. In the April session of Parliament the Government introduced the Constitution (Forty-third Amendment) Bill seeking to repeal, *inter alia,* Article 31-D. The Bill was passed in the House of the People but before the Council of States could consider it, the Bill was virtually withdrawn. The Janata Government apprehended that the Bill might be overthrown by the Council of States where the Congress Party still commanded a massive majority. However, as a result of consensus between the Prime Minister and leaders of the Opposition parties the Constitution (Forty-third Amendment) Act, 1977, *inter alia,* omitted Article 31-D, saving the laws in respect of anti-national activities, and anti-national associations, and Article 32A, constitutional validity of State laws not to be considered in proceedings under Article 32.

Thereafter, consensus was also reached on the provisions of the Forty-fourth Amendment Bill and it became an Act of

Parliament in 1978. Though a comprehensive Act, the Forty-fourth Amendment did not rescind the provisions of Article 368 Sections 4 and 5; the former debarring the courts to question on any ground the validity of any amendment (including the provisions of Part III) and the latter declaring that there shall be no limitation whatever on the constituent power of Parliament to amend by way of addition, variation or repeal the provisions of "this Constitution under this article."

The supremacy of Parliament, thus, remained unchallenged, though the decision in the *Kesavananda Bharati* case and reaffirmed in *Indira Gandhi v. Raj Narain* still prevailed. The validity of the Forty-second Amendment was questioned through various writs and the Supreme Court in the *Minerva Mills* case struck down in May 1980 Sections 4 and 55 of the Amendment incorporated in Articles 31-C and 368 (4) (5) of the Constitution. The Court held that giving boundless and unchallengeable power to Parliament is violative of the basic structure or essential features of the Constitution and, accordingly, void in terms of the *Kesavananda Bharati* judgement of April 24, 1973.

Another important feature of the Fundamental Rights is that there is a special constitutional provision (Article 32) for their enforcement. The right to move the Supreme Court for the enforcement of Fundamental Rights is itself a guaranteed right under Article 32. A citizen whose rights have been infringed by any public authority in India can move the Supreme Court by appropriate proceedings for the enforcement of his rights and the Court is empowered to issue directions or orders including writs in the nature of *Habeas Corpus*, *mandamus*, prohibition, *quo warranto* and *certiorari*, whichever may be appropriate. The State High Courts have also the power of issuing writs under Article 226 and enforce rights in the same manner within the limits of their respective jurisdictions. Thus, the constitutional remedies after the enforcement of Fundamental Rights are made available to every citizen and within his easy reach. But during the operation of emergency, under Article 352, the President may by order suspend the right to move any court for the enforcement of any rights mentioned in the Presidential order except the rights conferred by Articles 20 and 21—protection in respect of conviction for offences, and protection of life and personal liberty.

Fundamental Rights can also be restricted or suspended. Article 33 provides that Parliament may by law determine to what extent any of the rights conferred by Part III shall, in their application to members of the Armed Forces or the Forces charged with the maintenance of public order, be restricted or abrogated so as to ensure the proper discharge of their duties and maintenance of discipline among them. The special feature of the Indian Constitution is that the provisions of Article 33 apply not only to the Armed Forces but also to the ordinary police and the civil employees in the defence establishment as also the office bearers of their Unions.

Rights relating to freedoms as contained in Article 19 may be suspended during the period when the Proclamation of Emergency is in operation. Article 358 (1) provides that while a Proclamation of Emergency is in operation, "nothing in Article 19 shall restrict the power of the State as defined in Part III to make any law or to take any executive action which the State would but for the provision contained in that Part (Part III-Fundamental Rights) be competent to make or to take." But any law so made, shall to the extent of incompetence, cease to have effect as soon as the Proclamation of Emergency ceases to operate. If the Proclamation of Emergency is in operation only in any part of the territory of India, any such law may be made, or any such action may be taken, under Article 358 (1) in relation to any State or Union Territory in which the Proclamation of Emergency is not in operation, if the security of India or any part thereof is deemed to be threatened by activities in that part of the territory of India in which the Proclamation of Emergency is in operation.

The Janata Party's 1977 election manifesto stated that the right to property would be removed from the Chapter on

Fundamental Rights and made "a legal right enforceable in a court of law." In fulfilment of its election commitment, the Constitution (Forty-fourth Amendment) Act, 1978, abolished the right to property as a Fundamental Right and, accordingly, omitted the subheading "Right of Property" occurring after Article 30 and Article 31 which guaranteed to every person the right not to be deprived of his property except by authority of law. Omission of right to property from Part III of the Constitution does not affect the right of a citizen to acquire, hold or dispose of property. Nor can it be acquired except by the authority of law.

The only difference that its omission from the Chapter on Fundamental Rights makes is that while under the omitted constitutional provision the right to property could be adversely affected by a constitutional amendment in accordance with the prescribed procedure whereas now the right to property can be modified by a law passed by Parliament in accordance with the procedure adopted for ordinary laws. The sanctity hitherto attached to the right to property as an inalienable right, therefore, disappears by its omission from the Chapter on Fundamental Rights.

There are no natural or unenumerated rights under the Indian Constitution. The Supreme Court has definitely held that unless there is an express provision in the Constitution with which the Act of a Legislature conflicts, it cannot be held to be void merely on the ground of its being inconsistent with what the court considers to be the spirit of the Constitution. In other words, a right which has not been enumerated and expressly declared to be a Fundamental Right in Part III of the Constitution is not a Fundamental Right. It does not, however, mean that there are no rights apart from those included in the Fundamental Rights. But all such rights are ordinary rights and not Fundamental Rights and they cannot be enforced in the Supreme Court under Article 32 or in the State High Courts under Article 226. The legal remedies provided under Article 32 are only applicable to Fundamental Rights.

exercise and enjoyment. This is an improvement on the American Constitution which leaves the determination of restrictions and adjustment of conflicting interests of the individual and society to the courts. The Constitution of India defines the scope of limitations and authorises the State to restrict the exercise of freedoms guaranteed by Article 19 within the restricting clauses of the Article. It has been maintained that these limitations are, in fact, a partial justification of the American doctrine of Police Power.

The limitations imposed on the freedom of speech and the right to property were substantially modified by the Constitution (First Amendment) Act, 1951. The scope of the freedom of speech under the original provision was exceptionally wide. There were only four reservations restricting this right, viz., laws relating to libel, slander and defamation; contempt of court; decency or morality; and security of the State. Thus, "public order" was not one of the purposes for which the freedom of speech could be restricted. Similarly, incitement to an offence was not made one of the objects to restrict the freedom of speech. The Supreme Court held in a series of cases that a law restricting the freedom of speech and not relating to defamation or contempt of, court and not involving offences against decency or morality would be ultra vires unless it related to any matter which undermined the security of, or tended to overthrow the State. The 1951 Amendment added three more reservations to existing list contained in Article 19(2). The new reservations were: (1) friendly relations with foreign states; (2) public order; and (3) incitement to an offence. With the inclusion of these three additional reservations the right to freedom of speech was considerably curtailed and the scope of interference appreciably widened, provided the courts could be satisfied about the reasonableness of restrictions. By reasonable restrictions, the Supreme Court meant restrictions which are not excessive in nature and beyond what is required in the interests of the public. The Supreme Court also held that "the determination by the Legislature of what constitutes a reasonable restriction is not final or conclusive; it is subject to supervision by this Court. In the matter of Fundamental Rights the Supreme Court watches and guards the rights guaranteed by the Constitution and in exercising its functions it has the power to set aside the Act of the Legislature if it is in violation of the freedoms guaranteed by the Constitution."

The Constitution (Sixteenth Amendment) Act, 1963, added the" Sovereignty and integrity of India" as one of the grounds in the interests of which Legislatures could impose reasonable restrictions on freedom of speech and expression, assembly, and forming of associations, or unions. Ashok K. Sen, the Law Minister, while moving a motion to refer the Constitution (Sixteenth) Amendment Bill to a Joint Committee of Parliament, said in the House of the People on January 22, 1963 that powers were also being taken to impose restrictions on those individuals or organisations who wanted to make secession from India as political issues for the purposes of fighting elections. This, he maintained, had become necessary as some decisions of the Supreme Court made it clear that Article 19 of the Constitution in its present form was not enough to ban secessionist activity. He further said that it was also being provided that any persons who wanted to stand as a candidate for a seat in the Assembly in a State or in the House of People or a State Council or the Council of States should take an oath, pledging himself to uphold the sovereignty and integrity of India. This would ensure that no candidate would make secession a political issue in the elections. Furthermore after elections, every member would have to take another oath, pledging himself to the same thing, namely, upholding the sovereignty and integrity of India.

Similarly, sub-clauses (b) and (c) of Article 19 (1) confer the freedom to assemble peaceably and to form associations or unions. The freedom to speech is complimentary to the freedom to assemble and the freedom to form associations or unions. The Sixteenth Amendment, however, restricted their scope. Clauses 3 and 4 of Article 19 empower the State to make any law imposing, in the interests of sovereignty and integrity of

India or public order or morality reasonable restrictions on the exercise of these freedoms.

Other rights guaranteed by Article 19 may be briefly stated. The right to move freely is the right of movement unchecked and unrestricted anywhere within the territory of the Indian Union, subject to such restrictions as are imposed by any existing law or such as the State may in future impose in the public interest or to safeguard the interests of any Scheduled Tribes. In times of emergency, such as war, every citizen cannot claim as a matter of right access to places considered of military or strategic importance. Similarly, when an epidemic spreads in one part of the country, people may be prohibited by law from entering or leaving the affected area in the interest of public health. The freedom of movement also does not take away the right which law gave to the Government to extern any person from any part of the country for a particular period in the interests of maintenance of law and order, as also to detain any person for sufficient grounds if the public interest demanded it.

Allied to the right of free movement is the right to reside and settle in any part of the territory of India. This right is limited by reasonable restrictions in the interests of general public or for the protection of the interests of Scheduled Tribes.

Finally, the right to practise any trade or profession is subject to the right of the State to prescribe professional or technical qualifications to enable a citizen to become a lawyer or an engineer. This restriction is natural and necessary. The Constitution (First Amendment) Act, 1951, further empowered the State to reserve to itself the right to carry on any trade, business, industry or service either directly or through State controlled corporations to the complete or partial exclusion of private citizens. The purpose of the amendment was explained by the Law Minister during the course of debate on the Amendment Bill. He said that the State Governments would gradually take to nationalization; hence it was necessary that the Constitution should be amended to provide authority for the same. Article 19(6) was, therefore, amended to avoid the adverse implications of this decision as far as State trading was concerned. The reasonableness of any law permitting nationalization of any trade or business cannot be a subject of judicial review.

It will, therefore, be obvious that under the amended Clause (6) of Article 19 the restrictions on the right of carrying on any trade or profession, etc., fall into three classes: (a) reasonable restrictions imposed under the general power in the interest of the general public; (b) restrictions in the form of professional or technical qualifications; and (c) any law relating to carrying on trade or business or industry or service by the State or corporation owned or controlled by the State. Restrictions imposed in the interests of general public give a very wide scope for interference and can include all matters affecting public welfare, such as, public safety, public health, public morals, etc. Reasonable restrictions include "prohibition", having regard to the exceptional circumstances which involve potent and widespread danger to the community. It may, accordingly, prohibit a citizen from carrying on a particular trade, business or profession. The State may also create a monopoly in relation to any trade which is liable to cause injury to the public, or any trade in commodities essential to the life of the community.

Right of Life and Liberty **:** The rights guaranteed in Articles 20, 21 and 22 relate to the individual's personal liberty and collectively come under the sub-heading "Right to Freedom." These rights strengthen the liberties conferred on citizens under Article 19. Article 20 deals with certain Fundamental Rights of a person accused of a crime and embodies certain important principles of criminal jurisprudence, Clause (1) of the Article embodies the principle that no one should be made to suffer any punishment for an offence under any law not in force at the time of the commission of an offence. Similarly, no person shall be subject to a penalty greater than that which might have been inflicted under the law in force at the time of the commission of the offence. Clause (2) of the same Article embodies the fundamental principle that no one should be placed in jeopardy twice for the same offence. The principle underlying this clause is the same as underlies the "double jeopardy" clause of the American Constitution, though the words used are different. Clause (3) gives effect to the principle that no one should be compelled to give evidence against himself in a criminal case. This clause follows the language of the Fifth Amendment of the Constitution of the United States, though the rule laid down in the Indian Constitution is "narrower than the American rule as expanded by interpretation."

The Constitution (Forty-fourth Amendment) Act, 1978, prohibited the suspension, by Presidential Order, during the operation of the Proclamation of Emergency, the right to move the Supreme Court by appropriate proceedings, including the writ of *habeas corpus*, for the enforcement of rights conferred by Article 20 protection in respect of conviction for offences. Nor has the State the power to make any law or take executive action restricting, abridging or abrogating the rights guaranteed under Article 20.

Article 21 guarantees to every person the most essential of all rights, the right to life and personal liberty, which the Article says cannot be taken away except according to procedure established by law. The Constitution permits the continuance of preventive detention, but only in accordance with the laws providing for it. This Article is not intended to be a constitutional limitation upon the powers of the legislatures. The object is simply to serve as a restraint upon the Executive so that it may not proceed against the life or personal liberty of the individual save under the authority of some law and in conformity with the procedure laid therein. The procedure so laid down must be in conformity with Article 22 of the Constitution.

The phrase "established by law" means enacted by law and the word "law" means State made law. No person can, accordingly, claim that the procedure prescribed by law does not conform to the principles of natural justice. Explaining the implications of the phrase "established by law", justice Das observed that Article 21 defines the ambit of the right to life and personal liberty. It is not an absolute right but is a qualified right "a right circumscribed by the possibility or risk of being lost according to the procedure established by law. It is for Parliament to enact a law changing the procedure and once it is changed that procedure becomes the procedure established by law. When a person is deprived of liberty otherwise than procedure established according to law, it is only then the courts will interfere. It is not for the courts to determine whether the law is reasonable or not.

From 1950 to 1977, the Supreme Court took the view that Article 21 is a protection only against executive action which does not have the warrant of law behind and, therefore, if there was a law, it is good enough. It may prescribe any procedure. So long as it prescribes some procedure, it would meet the requirements of Article 21, But in *Maneka Gandhi's* case, the Supreme Court decided for the first time that the procedure to meet the test of Article 21 must be reasonable, fair and just. Just any procedure will not do. It must satisfy the test of reasonableness. The Court held that the concept of reasonableness runs like a golden thread through the entire fabric of the Constitution. Article 14, which guarantees equality before the law, also postulates reasonableness and non-arbitrariness; Article 19 contemplates reasonableness and so also does Article 21.

During the operation of the Proclamation of Emergency the right to move the Supreme Court by appropriate proceedings for the enforce ment of the right to the protection of life and liberty conferred by Article 21 cannot be suspended. By inserting this provision the Constitution (Forty-fourth Amendment) Act, 1978, nullified the effects of the Supreme Court decision during the Emergency in what came to be known as the *Habeas Corpus* case (A. *D. M. Jabalpur v. S. S. Shukla* 1976 (supp.) SCR, 172). In this case the court ruled that in view of the Presidential Order under Article 359 of the Constitution suspending the enforcement of Fundamental Rights no person had any *locus standi* to move any writ petition for *habeas corpus* or any other writ, or order or direction to challenge the legality of an order of detention on the ground that the Order was not under or in compliance with the *statute* or was illegal or was vitiated by mala fides, factual or legal, or was based on extraneous considerations. Justice H. R. Khanna dissented from the majority opinion of the Court.

Article 22 of the Constitution gives certain constitutional rights to arrested persons and also lays down certain fundamental rules with regard to preventive detention. It may, however, be noted that provisions relating to preventive detention are peculiar inasmuch as the Constitution of India permits resort to preventive detention even in peace time. In other democratic countries preventive detention is usually a method resorted to in emergencies like war. Preventive detention in India for reasons connected with the security of the State, or the maintenance of public order, or maintenance of supplies and services essential for the community, is on the Concurrent List but preventive detention for reasons connected with defence, foreign affairs, or the security of India is within the exclusive competence of Parliament.

The first two clauses of Article 22 deal with detention under the ordinary law and prescribe the procedure when a person is arrested. It ensures (i) right to be informed of the grounds of arrest; (ii) right to consult and to be defended by a legal practitioner of his choice; (iii) right to be produced before a magistrate within twenty-four hours; and (iv) freedom from detention beyond the specified period of twenty-four hours except by order of the magistrate.

The remaining clauses of this Article relate to preventive detention. Detention can be of two types : punitive and preventive. A preventive detention is intended to detain a person, without trial and without any charge of commission of an offence. It is a measure to intercept a person as a matter of precaution before he actually commits an offence. No offence is proved nor any charge is formulated, but there is a strong suspicion or reasonable probability that the individual commits or is likely to commit acts prejudicial to the welfare of the society, the security of the State and the stability of the Government established by law. It is not a criminal conviction which can only be warranted by legal evidence. The person under detention (detenu) is not given immediately on his arrest reasons for such arrest and detention. Neither he has any right to consult a lawyer, nor is he to be produced before a magistrate within twenty-four hours. Provisions of clauses (1) and (2) of Article 22 do not apply to a person arrested or detained under any law providing for preventive detention as also to any person who for the time being is an enemy alien.

Preventive detention legislation contemplates executive action for holding a person in custody for indefinite period without trial. The specific heads of prejudicial activities for which preventive detention can be effected are contained in List 1, Entry 9 and List III, Entry 3, of the Seventh Schedule to the Constitution. The sole justification for arrest is the satisfaction of the competent administrative authority or suspicion of reasonable probability of the detenu committing or likely to commit an act which may either cause harm to society or endanger the security of the State. Such detention is outside the reach of Article 19(1) (d) which guarantees the right to all citizens to move freely throughout the territory of India.

Article 22 clauses (4) to (7), however, provide safeguard against the rigours of preventive detention :

(1) detention cannot last for more than three months, except on the report of the Advisory Board consisting of persons who are, or have been, or are qualified to be appointed as, Judge of the High Court, has reported before the expiration of three months that there is in its opinion sufficient cause for such detention;

(2) the period of detention can in no case exceed beyond the maximum period prescribed by law made by Parliament;

(3) the detaining authority shall, as soon as may be, communicate to the detenu the grounds on which the detention has been made and shall afford him the earliest opportunity of making a representation against the order of his detention.

(4) the communication conveying the grounds of detention shall contain facts, except those that cannot be disclosed for reasons of public interest;

(5) Parliament may by law prescribe the circumstances under which, and the class or classes of cases in which, a person may be detained for a period longer than three months under any law providing for detention without obtaining the opinion of the Advisory Board;

(6) the maximum period for which any person in any class or classes of cases may be detained under any law providing for detention;

(7) the procedure to be followed by an Advisory Board in an inquiry.

Security against Exploitation : Articles 23 and 24 come under the subheading right against exploitation. Article 23 categorically prohibits all traffic in human beings and *begar* and other similar forms of forced labour. Traffic in human beings is evidently a very wide expression and would embrace not only the prohibition of slavery and bonded labour but also traffic in women for immoral or other purposes. Contravention of this prohibition has been made an offence punishable in accordance with law. The Constitution-makers had in mind the widespread evil custom of forced labour without remuneration or just a nominal remuneration verging on pittance prevalent in the country since ages. The. National Survey Organisation, commissioned by the Planning Commission, had estimated the bonded labour in the country at 3.45 lakh. Of this number 2.14 lakh had been identified and

1.75 lakh of them had been rehabilitated. The responsibility of rehabilitating the bonded labour lay with the State Governments, but the Labour Minister told the House of the People (Lok Sabha), on March 23, 1987 that the State Governments were not responsive and, therefore, an exact estimate of the existence of bonded labour and their rehabilitation was not possible to give.

Clause 2 of Article 23, however, provides for the power of the State to impose compulsory service for public purposes. The expression public purposes has nowhere has been, defined, but it must include an object or aim in which the general interest of the community, as opposed to particular inters of individuals, is directly and vitally condemned. The expression "public purpose", as Ambedkar explained to the Constituent Assembly, "includes any object or aim in which the general interest of individuals is directly or vitally involved Compulsory service for public purposes necessarily includes military service as it is a service for a public purpose to maintain the sovereignty and integrity of the country. In Dulal *Samanta v. District Magistrate, Howrah,* the Calcutta High Court held that the "conscription for police or military service is neither *begar* nor traffic in human beings and is, therefore, not hit by Article 23." In *Atma Ram v. State of Bihar* it was held that the provision in the Bihar Finance Act, 1950, making it obligatory on owners of motor vehicles to collect rent and taxes imposed on freights was within the exception of Article 23 (2) which allowed the State to impose compulsory service for public purposes.

Article 24 provides that no child below the age of fourteen years shall be employed to work in any factory or mine or engaged in any other hazardous employment. Here the Indian Constitution goes ahead of the American Constitution wherein there is no express prohibition against the employment of children in any factory or mine or in other hazardous occupations.

Religious Freedom : The Preamble to the Constitution expresses a resolve of the people to constitute India into a

Sovereign Socialist Secular Democratic Republic in order to ensure, among other things, "Liberty of thought, expression, belief, faith and worship." The secular principle thus accepted by the people of India was made fundamental and enshrined in Part III of the Constitution as contained in Articles 25 to 28. These rights have a wide scope and include both the personal and social aspects of religion and are equally enjoyed by all persons living in India, citizens and aliens. The Constitution guarantees to all persons freedom of conscience, and to profess, practise and propagate any religion subject to the prescribed limitations of public order, morality and health and other provisions of Part III. The Constitution, as such, does not only guarantee the freedom of religious faith and belief but it protects also acts done in pursuance of religion and this is made clear by the use of expression "practice of religion." All rituals, ceremonies, observances and modes of worship which are considered as integral part of a religion are permitted to be practised unhindered provided they do not offend any of the prescribed limitations.

But religious freedom and freedom of conscience do not diminish in any manner the regulatory power of the State given to it by the provisions of the Constitution. Religious freedom stands harmoniously with other Fundamental Rights. Religious institutions being on the Concurrent List, the right of freedom to religion does not, accordingly, prevent the State Legislatures to enact any law regulating or restricting any economic, financial, political or other secular activity of a religious body, nor render invalid laws throwing open public religious institutions formerly reserved for a section of the adherents of any one of the Hindu, Sikh, Jain, or Buddhist religions, to all adherents of that religion. Similarly, religious freedom is no bar to social welfare and reformatory legislation, though the Muslim Women (Protection of Rights on Divorce) Act, 1986, is a retrograde and discriminatory measure.

Since the provision of Article 25 is analogous to the first amendment to the United States Constitution and certain articles in other Commonwealth Constitutions, the Supreme Court of India has largely based its reasonings on judgements delivered by apex courts in those countries. In the National Anthem case the Supreme Court decided in August 1986 *(Bijoe Emmanuel v. State of Kerala)* that the expulsion of three school students for not singing the National Anthem was violative of Article 25 of the Constitution. It was held by the Supreme Court in 1958 that Article 25 embodied the principle of tolerance which has throughout been the characteristic feature of the Constitution and emphasised the secular motive of the Republic.

Underlining the same sentiments, the Supreme Court judgement in the instant case stated," Article 25 is an Article of faith in the Constitution, incorporated in recognition of the principle that the real test of a true democracy is the ability of even an insignificant minority to find its identity under the country's constitution. This has to be borne in mind in interpreting Article 25." The judgement also held that the Court cannot go into the reasonableness of a particular religious belief or practice. The question is whether the belief is held genuinely and conscientiously. If it is genuinely held, practices which do not violate public order, morality and health cannot be banned.

The judgement makes a third crucial point to be considered when Fundamental Right to freedom of conscience and religion is invoked. It says that the act complained of as offending the right must be examined to discover whether such act is to protect public order, morality or health and whether it is authorised by law made to regulate or restrict any economic, political or secular activity which may be associated with religious practice or to provide for social welfare and reform.

A large volume of cases decided by the Supreme and High Courts on Article 25 raise the question whether a particular practice is a part of religion or not. A government employee in the State of Uttar Pradesh, for instance, claimed that taking a second wife is part of his religion and a service rule banning it violated Article 25. The Allahabad High Court rejected the plea. The same High Court had held in the case of a Muslim that taking four wives is not part of Islam, though the personal law allows a Muslim male to do so. The Bombay High Court has held that polygamy is not a part of Hindu religion. The Kerala High Court has held that a student cannot claim freedom of conscience to come in improper dress in the college against the college rules. A Hindu lady who refused to produce her photograph for identification purpose claimed the right to freedom of religion, but the Calcutta High Court rejected the defence.

The Supreme Court has held that the Tandava dance in processions or public places by Anand Margis carrying lethal weapons and human skulls was not an essential rite. In a recent case relating to the shifting of Muslim graves in Varanasi, the Court held that there was nothing in Islam which prohibits the shifting of graves.

Even the right to practice religion is not absolute and is subject to public order, morality and health empowering the State to make laws restricting, economic, political or secular activity, though such activity may be associated with religious practise, the Supreme Court has held, The State has the power to legislate for social welfare and reform and any such legislation may extend even to some interference with the practice and propagation of religion. For instance, on the vexing question of religious processions, which often end in bloody riots, the Supreme Court has repeatedly granted powers to the authorities to control or even ban such activities. In the Varanasi graves case, it reiterated in 1984 that "the exercise of fundamental rights is not absolute and must yield to maintenance of public order."

All religious denominations are guaranteed autonomy, the right to establish institutions, and the right to acquire and deal with property, but only subject to public order, health and morality. No one can be compelled to pay taxes for the propagation or maintenance of any religion and religious instruction is not to be given in schools and colleges wholly maintained out of government revenues. But religious instruction may be imparted in private institutions receiving a grant from public funds or recognised by the State provided no pupil is given religious instruction or made to attend religious worship in a building attached to the institution without his consent, or, if he is a minor, his guardian's consent.

Right for Cultural and Educational Development : Apart from individual's rights and freedoms, the Constitution recognises and guarantees certain non-political rights of the religious, cultural and linguistic minorities, groups or sections of the people. Article 29 guarantees to every minority or section of the people to preserve its language, script and culture notwithstanding the provisions of Article 343 under which the official language of the Union shall be Hindi in Devanagari script. Clause (2) of the same Article provides that no citizen may be denied admission to State and State-aided educational institutions on the grounds only of religion, race, caste or language. Article 30 guarantees to all minorities whether based on religion or language the right to establish and administer their educational institutions and the State shall not discriminate against them in making grants on grounds of religion, race or language.

There is implicit in the right conferred by Article 30(1) the right to impart instruction in their own institutions to the children of their own community in their own language. To deny it is tantamount to depriving it of the right conferred by Article 29(1) which guarantees to conserve language or script of a minority community and the right to establish and administer educational institutions of their choice under Article 30(1). Article 30 came for discussion in Kerala Education Bill, 1957. Since this Bill, which was reserved for the consideration of the President, imposed serious limitations on the right of the minorities in the administration of their institutions aided and recognised by the Kerala Government, the President referred some of the provisions of the Bill to the Supreme Court for its advisory opinion.

The Court expressed the opinion that the minority community "can effectively conserve its language, script or culture by and through educational institutions and, therefore, the right to establish and maintain educational institutions of its own choice is a necessary concomitant to the right to conserve its distinctive language, script or culture and that is what is conferred on all minorities by Article 30(1)........." There is no constitutional right, the Court remarked, to receive State aid. "If the State does grant aid, it cannot impose such conditions (e.g., that the State will acquire the institution or will take over the management if certain things are not done) as will deprive it of its right under Article 30 (1). The State cannot take over the management of schools established by minority communities on the plea that it (State) seeks to do so or introduce free and compulsory education as required by Directive Principles." The object can be fulfilled through the State-owned or State-aided institutions, the Court said :

A special Constitution Bench of the Supreme Court declared on April 26, 1974 that the provisions of the Gujarat University Act, 1949, as amended in 1972, governing the affiliation of minority colleges, transforming them into constituent colleges of the University, regulating the appointment and service conditions of the staff and providing for arbitration of disputes, violated the fundamental right of the minorities to administer educational institutions of their choice. The Supreme Court, thus, reaffirmed the rights enshrined in Articles 29 and 30. "There can be no surrender of constitutional protection of the right of minorities to popular will masquerading as the common pattern of education," Justice Mathew remarked. This ruling by the Court followed two writ petitions filed by the Ahmedabad St. Xavier's College Society and others.

But in its judgement on November 17, 1986, the Supreme Court declared as "discriminatory and void" Section 12 of the Delhi School Education Act which exempts unaided minority institutions from the provisions of the Act (Sections 8 to 11) dealing with the terms and conditions of employees of recognised private schools". The Bench held that "regulatory measures which are designed towards the achievement of the goal of making the minority educational institutions effective instruments for imparting education cannot be considered to impinge upon the right guaranteed by Article 30(1) of the Constitution." The Court ruled that the requirement (prescribed by Section 10) is a permissible regulation aimed at attracting competent staff and consequently at the "excellence of the institution." The provisions of the Act made applicable to unaided minority educational institutions by this judgement related to payment of scales of pay and allowances, medical facilities, pension, gratuity, provident fund and other prescribed benefits, etc., to the employees of recognised private schools at rates not being less than those allowed to the employees of the corresponding schools run by the Government authority.

The Constitution (Forty-fourth Amendment) Act, 1978, inserted a new Clause 30 (1A) after Article 30 which ordained that in making any law providing for the compulsory acquisition of any property of an educational institution established and administered by a minority, the State shall ensure that the amount fixed by or determined by such law for the acquisition of such property "is such as would not restrict or abrogate the right guaranteed in Article 30".

Right of minorities to establish and administer educational institutions. Whereas the amendment conceded to the State the power to acquire property of an educational institution established and administered by a minority, it is obligatory for the State to ensure that the amount fixed for compensation of that property is adequate enough so that it may enable that minority to establish and administer a similar institution at an other location.

Right to Property : The consensus reached between the Government and the Opposition parties on April 20, 1978 on deleting the right to property from Chapter III on Fundamental Rights and giving it a statutory status was reflected in the Constitution (Forty-fourth Amendment) Act, 1978, by inserting a new Chapter IV with the heading Right to Property and incorporating Article 300-A which ordains that "No person shall be deprived of his property save by authority of law." Section 5 of the Amendment omitted the sub-heading "Right to Property" occurring after Article 30. Article 31 A and Article 31 C have been suitably amended as to omit all references to the right to property. Similarly, Section 2 omitted Sub-cl. (f) in Article 19(1) that read "to acquire, hold and dispose of property." This change does not in any way affect the right of a citizen to hold, acquire or dispose of property except that under the omitted provisions the right to property could be adversely affected only by a constitutional amendment and in accordance with the procedure prescribed under Article 368, whereas under Article 300-A the right to property can be modified by a law passed by Parliament in accordance with the procedure adopted for enactment of an ordinary law. But it does affect the sanctity of property as an inalienable basic right.

The Constitution, however, retains Articles 31A and 31 B—saving of laws providing for acquisition of estates, etc., and validation of certain Acts and Regulations. The effects of both these Articles are very wide and were intended to validate the acquisition of zamindaries on the abolition of Permanent Settlement without interference from Courts.

Article 31A provides that no law, past or future, affecting rights of any proprietor or intermediate holder of any estate or taking over the management of property by the State for a limited period either in the public interest or in order to secure the proper management of the property, or the extinction or modification of any rights of managing agents, secretaries or treasurers, managing directors or managers of corporations or any voting rights of shareholders, or extinction or modification of rights under mining leases and other similar agreements regarding any mineral or mineral oil or the permanent termination or cancellation of any such agreement, lease or licence shall be deemed void on the ground that it is inconsistent with, or takes away or abridges any of the rights by Article 14 or Article 19. If any law is made by the legislature of a State, the provisions of Article 31A shall not apply unless it had been reserved for the consideration of the President and received his assent.

The Constitution (Seventeenth Amendment) Act, 1964, added another provision to Article 31A. It provided that where any law makes any provision for the acquisition by the State of any estate and where any land comprised therein is held by a person under his personal cultivation, it shall not be lawful for the State to acquire any portion of such land as is within ceiling limit applicable to him for the time being or any building or structure standing thereon unless the law relating to the acquisition of such land or structure, provides for payment of compensation at a rate which shall not be less than the market value of such a property. Article 31B was inserted to save the Acts, and Regulations specified in the Ninth Schedule of the Constitution notwithstanding any decision of a court or tribunal that any of these Acts, Regulations or provisions is void on the ground that it takes away or abridges or is inconsistent with any of the Fundamental Rights as contained in Part III of the Constitution. This Article, however, reserves the power of the competent Legislature to repeal or amend any of the Acts or Regulations included in the Ninth Schedule.

Article 31C inserted by the Twenty-fifth Amendment Act, provided that no law passed to give effect to the Directive Principles of State Policy in Article 39 Clauses (b) and (c) would be deemed to be void on the ground that it was inconsistent with, took away or abridged any of the Rights conferred by Articles 14, and 19, and no law containing a declaration that it was for giving effect to such policy would be called in question in any court that it does not give effect to such policy. When such a law was made by the State Legislature, the provisions of Article 31C would not apply unless such law having been reserved for the consideration of the President has received his assent.

In *Keshavananda Bharati* case the Supreme Court allowed the Directive Principles of State Policy as contained in Article 39 Clauses (b) and (c) to override the Fundamental Rights. But the Court also held that any law declared by Parliament to give effect to these two Directive Principles would be subject to judicial review in order to determine whether the law did in fact achieve that objective. To nullify this effect of the Supreme Court's ruling, the Constitution (Forty-Second Amendment) Act, 1976, amended Article 31C and established the primacy of the Directive Principles. The Supreme Court struck down in the *Minerva Mills* case Article 31 C as it changed the basic structure of the Constitution in terms of the *Kesavananda Bharati* case.

Right to Get Constitutional Remedies : Article 32 guarantees to every citizen the right to move the Supreme Court by appropriate proceedings for the enforcement of Fundamental Rights. And for that purpose the Supreme Court is given general powers to safeguard the Fundamental Rights as well as the power to issue directions or orders or writs in the nature of *habeas corpus, mandamus,* prohibition, *quo warranto* and *certiorari,* whichever may be appropriate, for the enforcement of any of the Fundamental Rights. A right without a remedy is a meaningless formality. Ambedkar described in the Constituent Assembly that remedies provided in Article 32 are "the heart and soul of the Constitution." Before 1978, enforcement of rights, as mentioned in the Presidential Order, could be suspended, under Article 359, when a Proclamation of Emergency was in operation. The Presidential Order could also suspend the enforcement of Articles 20 and 21. The Forty-fourth Amendment Act amended Article 359 to the extent that enforcement of rights guaranteed under Articles 20 and 21 cannot be suspended even during the operation of Emergency.

Hitherto resort to the suspension of the enforcement of Fundamental Rights had been made in the event of actual aggression. But lately it has been used for economic offences too on the ground that such offences constituted as serious a threat to the security of the country as an external aggression or internal disturbance and deserved to be dealt with on the same basis. Enforcement of Fundamental Rights for economic purpose was suspended by the Presidential Order on November 16, 1974 in the case of persons detained under the Maintenance of the Internal Security Act, 1971 as amended by the Ordinance of September 18, 1974, and subsequently on December 23, 1974 under the Conservation of Foreign Exchange and Prevention of Smuggling Activities Act, 1974.

The Constitution (Forty-second Amendment) Act, 1976, debarred the Supreme Court, under the newly inserted Article 32A, from considering the constitutional validity of any State law in any proceedings under Article 32 unless the constitutional validity of any Central law was also an issue in such proceedings. Article 32A was, however, omitted by the Constitution (Forty-fourth) Act, 1978.

Fundamental Right's and Armed Forces : One of the points that came at an early stage for consideration was the extent to which Fundamental Rights would apply to the members of the armed forces. By virtue of their nature of service and position, they had necessarily to be subject to a conduct and discipline not entirely consistent with the exercise of fundamental rights as they would apply to an ordinary citizen. This fact was realised at the preliminary stages in the discussions of the Sub-Committee on Fundamental Rights. K. M. Munshi had provided in his draft that Union legislature by law be entitled to determine to what extent any of the fundamental rights should be restricted or abrogated for the members of the armed forces or forces charged with the maintenance of the public order to ensure the fulfilment of their duties and the maintenance of discipline. Munshi's reservation was accepted and adopted by the Advisory Committee and finally adopted by the Constituent Assembly with a minor verbal change suggested by Ambedkar.

Article 33 of the Constitution provides that Parliament may by law determine to what extent any of the rights conferred by Chapter III on Fundamental Rights shall, in their application to the members of the Armed Forces; or the members of the Forces charged with the maintenance of the public order; or persons employed in any bureau or other organisations established by the State for purposes of intelligence or counter-intelligence; or persons employed in, or in connection with the telecommunication systems set up for the purpose of any Force, bureau or organisation of the members of the Armed Forces or for purposes of intelligence or counter-intelligence be restricted or abrogated so as to ensure the proper discharge of their duties and the maintenance of discipline among them.

Public Servant Indemnity : At the revision stage, the Drafting Committee introduced a new Article 34 providing for indemnity to public servants and others for any action taken by them for maintenance or restoration of order in any area where martial law was in force. Justifying the need for such a provision, the Drafting Committee observed that the fundamental rights as contained in Part III might prevent validation by the legislature for acts done during the period when martial law was in force and also prevent the indemnifying of persons in the service of a Union or a State or other persons in respect of actions taken by them during such period.

In the Constituent Assembly when Article 34 came for consideration a number of amendments were proposed and of these one moved by Shibban Lal Saxena sought deletion of the Article on the ground that it might lead to excesses by officers working in the martial law area in the hope of indemnification by an Act of Parliament. Ambedkar replying to the debate maintained that if Article 34 was not included, the administration of martial law would not be possible.

The Assembly rejected the amendments and adopted Article 34. It provides that Parliament may by law, notwithstanding the provisions in Part III relating to the Fundamental Rights, indemnify any person in the service of the Union or of a State or any other person in respect of any act done by him in connection with the maintenance or restoration of order in any area within the territory of India where martial law was in force or validate any sentence passed, punishment inflicted, forfeiture ordered or other act done under martial law in that area.

Right of Legislation Empowerment in Practice : Article 35 empowers Parliament to make laws with respect to any matter under Clause 3 of Article 16 (requirements as to residence to classes or class of employment or appointment); Clause 3 of Article 32 (empowering any court to exercise jurisdiction with respect to enforcement of Rights); Article 33 (modification of Rights in their application to Armed Forces); and Article 34 (restrictions on Rights while martial law is in force in any area). Parliament has also the power to prescribe by law punishment for those acts which are declared to be offences under Part III in case of their violation. Clause (b) of Article 35 provides that in case of Acts already in existence which provide punishment for breach of fundamental rights, unless and until Parliament makes another provision, such laws would continue in operation.

12

Directive Principles of State Policy

Model for the State

If the Preamble is the key to the understanding of the Constitution or to open the mind of its makers, the Directive Principles of State Policy, as enshrined in Part IV, are its beau ideal. It is here that the Constitution-makers poured their mind by setting forth the humanitarian socialist principles which epitomised the hopes and aspirations of the people and declared them as fundamental in the governance of the country. They are affirmative instructions from the ultimate sovereign to the State authorities, which are the creature of the Constitution established by them, to secure to all citizens justice-social, economic and political; liberty of thought, expression, belief, faith and worship; equality of status and opportunity; and to promote among them all fraternity assuring the dignity of the individual and the unity and integrity of the nation.

It is the duty of all the authorities of the state to direct their activities in such a manner so as to secure the high ideals set forth in the Preamble and copiously analysed and enshrined in Part IV of the Constitution. The Directive Principles of State Policy are an amalgam of diverse subjects embracing the life of the nation and include principles which are general statements of social policy, principles of administrative policy, socio-economic rights, and a statement of the international policy of the country. B.R. Ambedkar told the Constituent Assembly that every Government, Central, State and local "shall be on the anvil, both in the daily affairs and at the end of a certain period when the voters and the electorate will be given an opportunity to assess the work done by the Government...... While we have established political democracy it is also the desire that we should lay down as our ideal economic democracy....... There are various ways in which people believe that economic democracy can be brought about, we have deliberately not introduced in the language that we have used in the Directive Principles something which is fixed or rigid. We have left enough room for the people of different ways of thinking, with regard to the reaching of the ideal of economic democracy.

Our object in framing the Constitution is two-fold : (i) to lay down the form of political democracy, and (ii) lay down that our ideal is economic democracy, and also to prescribe that every Government, whatever is in power, shall strive to bring about economic democracy .... "

The idea of making a constitutional declaration of social and economic policy is the recognition of the ideal of a service State in place of a regulatory State which found expression in the 1931 Karachi resolution of the Indian National Congress. The Karachi resolution held that in order to end the exploitation of the masses, political freedom should include economic freedom. Most of the members of the Constituent Assembly, and especially the select group in the Fundamental Rights Committee, were quite familiar with the political thinking at that time, the practice that the United States of America had of late adopted and the manner in which the Federal and State Governments had begun playing an every increasing role in the nation's social and economic life. They had also closely watched the fact that most of the new Constitutions that came into being after World War I, particularly of Germany and East European countries, had recognised that one of the chief functions of the State must be to foster and secure the social well-being of citizens and the economic prosperity of the nation. The Irish Constitution, too, had greatly impressed the wide range of members of the Constituent Assembly. The long-standing-affinity of the Indian National Congress with the Irish Nationalist Movement made the example of constitutional declaration expressed in the Irish Directive Principles of State Policy especially attractive to the Congress Assembly members, particularly the socialist-wing within its fold. But the most weighty support came from B.N. Rau, the Constitutional Adviser to the Constituent Assembly, Alladi Krishnaswami Ayyar, B.R. Ambedkar and K.T. Shah. Of the four, B.N. Rau was the most influential. He emulated in his *Constitutional Precedents* the Irish example of distinguishing between justiciable and non justiciable rights. His *Precedents*, during the actual drafting of the Directive Principles, supplied the members of the Sub-Committee on Fundamental Rights with at least five of the original twelve provisions and the preamble of the Principles.

Various Kinds

The first two Articles (36 and 37) of the Chapter on Directive Principles of the State Policy are general in character and deal with definitions, legal effects and objectives. The remaining Articles may, for purposes of clarity, be grouped into three distinct categories:

(i) those that aim to shape India into a Welfare State;

(ii) those that aim to shape India into a Gandhian State; and

(iii) those that aim to promote international peace.

(i) Article 38 (1) provides that the State shall promote the welfare of the people by securing and protecting as effectively as it may a social order in which justice, social, economic and political shall inform all the institutions of the national life. Clause (2) inserted by the Forty-fourth Amendment, provides that the State shall, in particular, strive to minimise the inequalities in income, and endeavour to eliminate inequalities in status, facilities and opportunities, not only amongst individuals but also amongst groups of people residing in different areas or engaged in different vocations. Thus, promotion of the welfare of people, both residing in urban and rural areas and engaged in different vocations is the objective which the Constitution sets forth by striving to secure a social order where justice, social, economic and political, shall prevail. Welfare and justice are, accordingly, the twin object of the Constitution. Article 39 then, proceeds to particularise some of the methods by which the object of general welfare, through justice, can be obtained and the basis of the new social order established. This Article finds adequate support from the provisions about a tasteless and classless society. With this end in view the State shall direct its policy in securing:

I. (a) adequate means of livelihood for all citizens, men and women equally;

(b) distribution of wealth so as to subserve the common good;

(c) the operation of the economic system which does not result in the concentration of wealth and means of production to the common detriment;

(d) equal pay for equal work for both men and women;

(e) protection of adult and child labour;

(f) the Forty-second amendment altered the original clause, which read : "protection of child and youth against exploitation and against moral and material abandonment, "to emphasise the constructive role of the State with regard to children. It now provides that the "children are given opportunities and facilities to develop in a healthy manner and in conditions of freedom and dignity and that childhood and youth are protected against exploitation and against moral and material abandonment.

(g) provision of work and education for all people, relief in case of unemployment, old age, sickness and disablement and in other cases of undeserved want;

(h) just and humane conditions of work and maternity relief,

(i) a living wage and decent conditions of work for all workers, agricultural, industrial or otherwise as to ensure to them sufficient leisure and enjoyment of social and cultural opportunities;

(j) to secure the participation of workers in the management of undertakings or other organisations engaged in any industry. (This provision was inserted by the Forty-second Amendment as Article 43A);

(k) free and compulsory education for all children until they reach the age of fourteen years;

(l) raising the level of nutrition and the standard of living and the improvement of public health;

(m) to secure that the operation of the legal system promotes justice, on a basis of equal opportunity and in particular, to provide free legal aid to ensure that opportunities for securing justice are not denied to any citizen by reason of economic or other diabilities. (This provision was inserted by the forty-second Amendment as a new Article 39A); and

(n) to endeavour to secure for the citizens a uniform civil code throughout the country.

II. Some of the Directive Principles are in accordance with and conform to the Gandhian way of life and fulfil the requirements of Gandhi's conception of the State. These Directive Principles enjoin that :

(a) the State shall take steps to organise village panchayats and endow them with such power and authority as may be necessary to enable them to function as units of self-government;

(b) the State shall endeavour to promote cottage industries on an individual or cooperative basis in rural areas;

Both these provisions aim at Sarvodaya or pure socialism as Prof. S.N. Aggarwal called it. Sarvodaya is the Gandhian technique of decentralised economy and composite democracy in the form of self-dependent and self-governing village communities or panchayats.

(c) to promote with special care the educational and economic interests of the weaker sections of the people, and, in particular of the Scheduled Castes and the Scheduled Tribes in order to protect them from social injustice and all forms of exploitation;

(d) to bring about prohibition of consumption, except for medicinal purposes, of intoxicating drinks and of drugs which are injurious to health;

(e) to take steps to organise agricultural and animal husbandry on modern and scientific lines and, in particular take steps for preserving and improving the breeds, and prohibiting the slaughter of cows and calves and other milch and drought cattle;

(f) to protect and improve the environment and safeguard the forests and wild life of the country, (This provision has been inserted by the Forty-second amendment as Article 48A);

(g) to protect, preserve and maintain places of national and historical importance; and

(h) to take steps to separate the judiciary from the executive; and to secure for citizens a uniform civil code throughout the country.

III. In the international field India shall strive:

(a) to promote international peace and security;

(b) to maintain just and honourable relations between nations;

(c) to foster respect for international law and treaty obligations; and

(d) to encourage settlement of international disputes by arbitration.

Basic Duties

Need for its Inclusion : Incorporation of a charter of Fundamental Duties in the Constitution is one of the important features of the Constitution (Forty-second Amendment) Act, 1976. The Swaran Singh Committee on constitutional reforms, appointed by the Congress President, was asked in a resolution of the All-India Congress Committee, passed at its meeting in New Delhi on May 29, 1976 to formulate proposals to fill what was widely considered a historical lacuna to India's charter rights. Within the Congress the sentiment was fairly strong that the Constitution-makers went, in the first flush of Independence, to great lengths to articulate the citizen's fundamental rights in the Constitution but overlooked the need to prescribe the corresponding fundamental duties and obligations.

The political crisis that strained the Indian democratic system in the last sixties and again in 1974 and 1975 was one of the compelling reasons to necessitate the inclusion of what the Constitution-makers had in their wisdom omitted, although there was some suggestion at the time when the Constitution was drafted that his important aspect should not be ignored.

Nor is the issue of enumerating the citizen's fundamental duties to society and State in a Constitution totally without a precedent. Nearly fifty countries, as Vinod Sethi enumerated, have incorporated duties in their constitutions, and Japan is one of them whose basic document was consulted by the makers of the Indian Constitution. The Japanese Constitution spells out explicitly some of the citizen's countervailing duties in the same breath as his Fundamental Rights. "Rights and Duties of the People" are enshrined in Chapter III of the Constitution. The Swaran Singh committee proposed an 8-Point code of "fundamental duties" which, after due process of public consultation, were proposed to be enshrined in the Constitution. The proposed duties were :

(1) To respect and abide by the Constitution and the laws.

(2) To uphold the sovereignty of the Nation and to function in such a way as to sustain and strengthen its unity and integrity.

(3) To respect the democratic institutions enshrined in the Constitution, and not to do anything which may impair their dignity or authority.

(4) To defend the country and to render national service including military service when called upon to do so.

(5) To abjure communalism in any form.

(6) To render assistance and cooperation to the state in the implementation of the Directive Principles of State Policy, and to promote the common good of the people so as to subserve the interest of the social and economic justice.

(7) To abjure violence; to protect and safeguard public property and not to do anything which may cause damage and destruction to such property.

(8) To pay taxes according to law.

Bibliography

Andrew Barry : *Foucault and Political Reason : Liberalism, Neo-liberalism and Rationalities of Government*, MacMillan, London, 1996.

Anne Phillips : *Democracy and Difference*, Oxford, New York, 1993.

Appador : *Documents on Political Thought in Modern India*, Oxford Publishers, 1981.

Bakshi, S. R. : *Kashmir : History and People*, Sarup & Sons, New Delhi, 1997.

——— : *Political Ideology of the Sikhs*, Deep & Deep Publications, New Delhi, 2000.

Bhatia, K. L. : *Federation and Frictions in Centre-State Relations*, Deep & Deep Publications, New Delhi, 2001.

——— S. K. : *Jurisprudence of Amending Process under Indian Constitution*, Deep & Deep Publications, New Delhi, 1989.

Chandra, B. : *Communalism in Modern India*, Vikas Publishing House, New Delhi, 1996.

Das and Chaudhury : *Federal and State Politics in India*, Discovery Publishing House, New Delhi, 1990.

Das, Satya Prakash : *Constitutional and Political Dynamics of India*, Sarup & Sons, New Delhi, 2004.

Gaikwad, S. : *Dynamics of Indo-Soviet Relations : The Era of Indira Gandhi*, Deep & Deep Publications, New Delhi, 1990.

Gupta, Manik Lal : *Constitutional Development of India*, Atlantic Publishers, New Delhi, 1989.

Gupta, R. L. : *Electoral Politics in India*, Discovery Publishing House, New Delhi, 1985.

Gupta, U. N. : *Indian Parliamentary Democracy*, Atlantic Publishers, New Delhi, 2003.

——— : *Foreign Policy in India*, Atlantic Publishers, New Delhi, 2000.

——— : *India and her Neighbours*, Atlantic Publishers, New Delhi, 2000.

——— : *Constitutional History of India*, Atlantic Publishers, New Delhi, 1998.

Kanesahingam, V. and Kemal, A.R. : *Trade Liberalisation in South Asia: Liberalisation and Mechanisms*, Macmillan, New Delhi, 1990

Kaur, M. : *Challenges to Secularism in India*, Deep & Deep Publications, New Delhi, 1999.

Khalidi, Omar : *Indian Muslims Since Independence* , Vikas Publishing House, New Delhi, 1993.

Kumar, Ashutosh : *Political Economy of the State in India*, Atlantic Publishers, New Delhi, 1993.

Kumar, D. : *Impact of Indira Gandhi on Indian Political System*, Deep & Deep Publications, New Delhi, 1993.

Kumar, Raj : *Essays on Indian Freedom Movement*, Discovery Publishing House, New Delhi, 2003.

Mehta, J. B. : *Quest for a Better Democratic Alternative*, Vikas Publishing House, New Delhi, 1995.

Mishra, K.P. and Others : *Southern Asia-Pacific Perceptions and Strategies*, Continental Publishing House, New Delhi, 1983.

Naqvi, Syed Nawab Hyder : *SAARC Link: An Economic Approach*, Oxford, New Delhi, 1991.

Nolla, Eduardo : *Liberty Equality Democracy*, MacMillan, London, 1992.

Parashar : *Nationalism : Its Theory and Principles in India,* Sarup & Sons, New Delhi, 1996.

Parmanand, Parashar : *Kashmir and the Freedom Movement,* Sarup & Sons, New Delhi, 2004.

Pati, S. : *Democratic Movements in India,* Discovery Publishing House, New Delhi, 1987.

Rai, Lajipathi Reddi, and Subbi T. : *India's Foreign Trade: Retrospectives and Prospectives,* Uppal Publishing House, New Delhi, 1990.

Rajput, R. S. : *Dynamics of Democratic Politics in India,* Deep & Deep Publications, New Delhi, 1986.

Rajput, R. S. Meghe, D. R. : *Panchayati Raj in India,* Deep & Deep Publications, New Delhi, 1986.

Sankhdher, M. M. and Gurdeep Kaur : *Politics in India : Ancient India, Development of Political Thought, Modern India,* Deep & Deep Publications, New Delhi, 2005.

Sen Gupta : *SAARC-ASEAN: Prospects and Problems of Inter-regional Cooperation,* South Asian Publishers, New Delhi, 1989.

Sharma M. L. : *Gandhi and Democratic Decentralisation in India,* Deep & Deep Publications, New Delhi, 1987.

Talbot, Phillip : *South Asia in the World Today,* University of Chicago Press, Chicago, 1989.

Varma, S. P. : *Modern Political Theory,* Vikas Publishing House, New Delhi, 1997.

Vohra, Dewan C. : *India's Trade Diplomacy in the Third World,* Vikas Publishing House, New Delhi, 1987.

Yasusuke Murakami : *An Anticlassical Political-Economic Analysis: A Vision for the Next Century,* Stanford, London, 1996.

Index

D

E

Q

R

□□□